The life journey
of the Fourth President
of Republic of Somaliland

Ahmed Mahamed Mahamoud
«Silanyo»

The life journey
of the Fourth President
of Republic of Somaliland

Ahmed Mahamed Mahamoud
«Silanyo»

REDSEA-ONLINE.COM Culture Foundation

Fidiyaha Aqoonta iyo Ereyga Dhigan – Xarunta dhexe

Daarta Oriental Hotel - Hargeysa, Somaliland

Telephone: 00 252 2 525109

email: bookshop@redsea-online.com

Copyright © 2022 by Amina Sheikh Mohamed Jirdeh

Translation, Rhoda Aideed Rage and Farah Hersi, 2022

Author of the Somali edition, Cabdiraxmaan Yuusuf Cartan, 2018

Cover and interior design: Cabdilladiif Geelle

Courtesy by Hiil Press - @MadbacaddaHiil

All rights reserved no part of this book may be reproduced in any form or by any means, electronic or mechanical, including photocopying, recording, or by any information storage and retrieval system, without written permission from the Copyright owner.

Published by Ponte Invisibile (redsea-online), 2022, Pisa

Inquiries to the editor

Via Pietro Giordani 4, 56123 Pisa, Italy

www.ponteinvisibile.com

email: editor@redsea-online.com | editor@ponteinvisibile.com

ISBN 88-88934-73-1

EAN 9788888934730

CHAPTER ONE: Mohamed Mohamoud's Marriage — 24

   Ahmed's Birth — 24

   The Sect of Sheikh Mohamed Dhawaaq — 25

   Sheikh and Amoud Schools — 27

   His Leadership Talent — 28

   Ahmed Explains How He Got The Nickname "Silanyo." — 29

   His Disinterest in Tribalism — 29

   University — 30

   The kind of Education Colonial Administration Used to Provide — 31

   Lessons in Social Etiquette — 31

   Colonial Education: The Kind of People They Wanted To Groom — 31

   University Education in the United Kingdom — 32

   The Request of Ahmed's Mother, Maryam Suleiman — 33

   Studying Economics — 33

   Marriage and Family — 34

CHAPTER TWO: Coming Back Home and Job Hunting — 37

   First Job at the Bank — 38

   Ministry of Planning — 39

   The Cold War and the Race for Political Alliance of the 3rd world — 39

   The assassination of President Abdurashed Ali Sharmarke — 40

   People Welcomed the Revolution of 1969 — 40

   Ahmed Silanyo's Critique of Civilian Governments — 41

   Military Coups Reigned over Africa — 42

   Amina-Weris' Description of the Day of the Coup — 42

   Ahmed was Among the Intellectuals Asked to Advise the Revolution — 43

   How the Word "Qorshayn" was Introduced — 44

   Nationalization of Vital Economic Institutions — 44

   Was Economic Nationalization a Ploy to Regress Northern Regions? — 45

   Should We Join the Arab League? — 46

   Ahmed Silanyo is Distinguished from other Ministers — 47

The Meddling Italian Man and Ahmed Silanyo's Transfer to The Ministry of Commerce	48
A discussion between Ismail Dualeh and Silanyo	49
Fixing Trade Balance	49
How was Ahmed Silanyo at Work? A Colleague at the Ministry of Commerce Explains	50
Ahmed Silanyo was not tribalistic.	50
Transferring 'Asassey: The Biggest Confrontation between Ahmed Silanyo and Siad Barre	51
Envoys of the Supreme Revolutionary Council	51
Envoys of the Isaaq Clan's Senior Officers	52
Siad Bare Intercedes Personally For 'Asassey	52
Defending the Rights of the Northern Regions	53
As things Deteriorated	55
Southern Businesses Want to Patronize Northern Businessmen	55
Burao-Berbera Road	55
Siad Barre Presides a Debate among Cabinet Ministers over the Cement Factory	56
Siad Barre sent Farah Harbi as His Final Emissary.	56
Ahmed Silanyo's Adamant Refusal to Falsify a Delegation's Report	58
Ahmed Silanyo Advises Siad Barre not to Exaggerate the Population Count for Increased Foreign Aid	58
A Governor's Tale	58
Silanyo's Stand When the Regime Harassed the Warsengali Clan	59
Appoint Silanyo as Prime Minister to Placate the Northern Region Turmoil:	59
Beginning of the 1980s and the Intensification of the Northern Revolt	60
Adan-Weyne is to be arrested for Visiting Silanyo at the Hospital	60
CHAPTER THREE: Formation of Somali National Movement and Siad Barre's Continuous Carnage	61
The Only Road Open is an Armed Struggle	62
People's Feeling before the Establishment of SNM	63
Prelude to SNM Formation	64
Ahmed Silanyo Deserts Siad Barre's Administration after Nearly Twenty Years	66
Oh, Siad Barre! Abdullah Shihiri Left You and Your Demise is Imminent'	66
Ahmed Silanyo Meets with the Isaaq Clan in Jeddah in 1982	68
Role Model to Trust	69
Ahmed Hashi Oday: Influential Leader to Emulate	69
Abdirahman Osman Alin: We Supported Him for His Prior Record	69
Abdirahman Abdulqadir's Encounter with Silanyo in London	70
Khader Ali Haaf: Transformational Leader to Follow	70
The Cry of Abdillahi Abdi Faroole, Dhakar, Idris Osman Guray, and Mohamed Jama Nur (Blacki)	71
Somali Embassies in London and Washington Spying on Silanyo's Intentions	72
Somali Ambassador to Washington Pries into Rumors about Silanyo	73

Time to Join Millions of Refugees from Somalia: Ahmed Silanyo Requests for Political Asylum	74
The First SNM Conference (April 1981)	74
Siad Barre's Reaction to the Announcement of The Somali National Movement	75
Ahmed Silanyo's Intent to Unite Opposition Groups	76
The World Woke Up to the Genocide in the Northern Regions	77
Ahmed Silanyo Opened SNM Offices and Reorganized Existing Ones	78
Abdillahi Omaar: His Unwavering Support of SNM	78
Jama Mohamed Ghalib (Jama Yare): His Role in the Struggle	79
2nd SNM Conference (April 1982) Held in Nazareth and the situation in Ethiopia	80
Somali Salvation Democratic Front (SSDF): A strong opposition with limited movement.	80
Facilitated Discussion between SSDF and SNM	81
SNM Delegation Traveled to Libya	81
3rd SNM Conference (July 1983)	83
Revolt against the Leadership of the Sheikhs	83
Central Committee Congress: Nomination of Military Commanders	84
Abdulqadir Kosar Accused of Heresy	85
Gesturing Silanyo	86
SNM Fights for a Cause Not for Money	86
Why Was The 4th SNM Congress in August 1984 Different From Prior Ones?	88
SNM Members Unite under Ahmed Silanyo's Leadership	88
The Conflict That Resulted From the Conference of 1984	89
Michael Mariano's Advice to Ahmed Silanyo	90
How Did Ahmed Silanyo Handle That Sensitive Situation?	90
The War of the Mountains	91
Ahmed Silanyo's Work Plan After He Took over the Leadership	92
Weaving Different Groups Together	92
Selecting Mohamed Hashi for the Finance Minister	93
The Rift from Transferring Mohamed Hashi from Minister of Finance	94
What Had Ahmed Silanyo Brought To SNM?	95
Restoring the Trust of the Host Country Was an Urgent and Top Priority	96
Resisting Unity with SSDF	97
Rejecting Libyan Money Passionately	97
Ahmed Silanyo attained Offices in Ethiopia and Structured Work Ethics	98
Chairman Silanyo Established Transparency within the Movement	99
He Strengthened Relationship with the Ethiopian Government and Elevated SNM Status to a Government in Exile	99
Investigating Keyse's Arrest is a Testimony to his Firm but Cordial Relationship with Ethiopia	100
Chairman Silanyo Allocated Money to Injured Soldiers for the First Time	101
He Expanded War Fronts	102

He Intensified Wars (June 1985 to February 1986)	102
Silanyo Accused of Building a House in London	103
Silanyo's Refusal to Drive a Car Bought By His Clan	104
An Encounter At Egal International Airport: Jama Omaar's Testament to Silanyo's Leadership during the Struggle	104
Mohamed Haji Ibrahim Egal: "There Is a Man Better Than Me"	105
The 5th SNM Conference and the Ensued Conflict (February 1987)	105
Conflict of the Commanders	107
Ahmed Silanyo Accused of Not Making His Cabinet Accountable	107
Conflict of SNM Leadership Brought to the Public	108
The Arrest of the Commanders	108
How Did Silanyo Manage the Arrest of the Commanders?	109
Boobe Yusuf Dualeh's Provocation of Chairman Silanyo	110
Affairs inside Somalia	111
The Essence of the Ultimate Solution of Genocide Proposed By Morgan	111
Siad Barre's Misinformation to the World was countered by Ahmed Silanyo's Heartbreaking Press Release Detailing the Reality of the Statement by Ahmed Mohamed Mohamoud Silanyo, Chairman of Somali National Movement (SNM)	112
Objective of SNM	114
Amidst Siad Barre's Carnage, a Pilot Defied Orders to Kill, and Landed His Jet in Djibouti	121
Mengistu And Siad Barre's Agreement	121
Siad Barre's Resolve to Negotiate with SNM	122
Meeting Between Mengistu and Siad Barre	123
Siad Barre's Proposed Concessions	123
The Meeting between Siad Barre and the Isaaq Clan	123
Mengistu's Telegram to Said Barre	124
Meeting the Public at Hargeisa Football Stadium	125
Awarding the Contract for Handcuffs	126
Man Proposes and God Disposes off: SNM's Planned Vulnerability Turned into Impressive Victory	126
Abshir Walde Approaches Ahmed Silanyo about Uniting SNM and SSDF	126
How SNM Viewed the Agreement between Mengistu and Siad Barre	127
The Feeling of SNM Fighters	128
The Meeting between Mengistu and Ahmed Silanyo	128
Ahmed Silanyo Meet with the Commanders	129
SNM's Resolve to Enter Somalia	130
Silanyo: To Openly Deny the Rush War Was Our Decision	130
The Ethiopian Minister of Security Visited JiJiga	130
The Resolution to Fight	130

The Ismaqiiq (Rush) War Resolution	131
Ahmed Silanyo Signed the Ismaqiiq (rush) War Operation under a Tree	132
The Elders Should Not Join the Soldiers	132
Moving the Regiment to Enter Burao on 27 May 1988	133
The Attack on Adaadley 28 My 1988	134
Declaration of War: External Media War	135
SNM Fighters Isolated the Cities of Northern Regions	136
The Results of the Rush to War Operation	137
Siad Barre: Mengistu, You Have Betrayed Me	138
Tens of Thousands of Civilians Took Up Arms	138
The 6th Congress and the Controversial Central Committee Resolution of 31st March –28 April 1990	139
Condemning the Controversial Resolutions of the 6th Congress	140
The 2nd Extraordinary Central Committee Congress	140
Silanyo Does Not Arrest Anyone	141
Silanyo Hands over SNM Leadership	141
The Results of the 6th Congress	143
Ali Assey: Feeling of Emptiness – Poem	143
The SNM Plan after It Enters the Country	145
BBC Interview with Ahmed Silanyo on Monday, May 30, 1988	145
Constitutional Guurti: Aydaroosh 1988	148
The SNM Guurti Conference in Hargeisa	149
CHAPTER FOUR: Somalia After Siad Barre: Ahmed Silanyo's Paper on Transitional Government	151
Somalia after Siad Barre 18 March 1991: Proposed Structure of Transitional Arrangement	152
Summary of Proposed Structure	154
Autonomous Organs	156
BBC Interview with Ahmed Mohamed Mohamoud January 30, 1991, 1709 GMT	157
Chaotic Time (The Meeting in Burao in 1991)	158
Ahmed Silanyo Came to Burao	159
Silanyo Defends Jama Mohamed Ghalib	160
Ahmed Silanyo Reveals Two Secrets (Silanyo's Secrets)	160
The conflict between Ahmed Silanyo and Abdirahman Ahmed Ali	162
BBC: Is There an Army Fighting on The Road Between Hargeisa And Berbera?	164
Saeed Mohamed Mohamoud	166
Safeguarding the Weapons Depots	166
Pillars of Islamic Faith and Pillars of Government	167
Ahmed Silanyo's Car Was Seized in Berbera	168
Silanyo: 'Position is the Source of Conflict'	168

Silanyo's Advice for The Meeting in Borama	168
Mohamed Haji Ibrahim Egal: Ahmed Silanyo Is More Worthy of President	169
Ahmed Silanyo A Member of Parliament	170
A Delegation Mohamed Haji Ibrahim Egal Sent to Ethiopia	170
Aide Memoire by Ahmed Mohamed Mohamoud Silanyo	171
The Conflict Of 1994: Abdirahman Ahmed Ali called for Federalism	174
Ahmed Silanyo's Role in Calming the Conflict Of 1994-1996 And Restoring Peace	174
The Strong Opposition to Beer Decided To Hold Its Own Clan Conference	176
SNM Was Limping When It Entered the Country	176
Mediating Between Ahmed Silanyo and Suleiman Mohamoud Aden	177
Ninety Stronger Than Iron	178
Mohamed H. I. Egal, Sh. Ibrahim Sh. Yusuf and Ahmed Mohamed Mohamoud Silanyo	178
Establishing Financial Policy	179
President Egal's Attempt to Dissolve the Parliament	180
Demobilizing of the Clan-Based Militia in Togdheer	180
President Mohamed Haji Ibrahim Egal: 'There Are Terrorists in Burao'	181
Mediating President Egal and the Clerics	181
Ahmed Silanyo's Resignation from the Ministry of Planning	182
The Conflict That Resulted From the Multi-Party System	182
The conflict between Clan Elders and President Egal's Government	183
Ahmed Silanyo's Mediation	183
President Mohamed Haji Ibrahim Egal Dies and Dahir Riyale Kahin Becomes the New President	184

CHAPTER FIVE: Building KULMIYE from the Ground — 187

His Name and Reputation Represented His Politics	189
The Bali-Alanleh Ballot Box	190
Disbelief in 2003 Presidential Election Results	190
Ahmed Silanyo's Feelings When the High Court Announced for UDUB	192
Calming Kulmiye's Militant Members	193
Guurti Interference	195
Accepting Election Results	195
A Period of Calm Sorting	196
The Members Kulmiye Eliminated from The List of Parliamentary Candidacy in 2005	196
Kulmiye Prepares for the 2008 Elections	197
If You Lose the Kulmiye Chairmanship Would You Accept?	197
The 2nd Congress of Kulmiye Party	197
The Central Committee Chooses the Candidates for President and Vice President.	198
Let Us Bring Back the Annoyed Members	199

Responsible Opposition	200
Opposition Before Ahmed Silanyo	200
Here is Ahmed Silanyo speaking about the dangers of delayed elections.	201
Did the Current President Take Office by Force?	201
I Am Not Reporting to Anyone	202
Our Party is Democratic	202
Universities are Where Ideas Begin	202
Our Country Does Not Need Problems	203
The Leader Should Be Reliable and Trustworthy	203
Ahmed Silanyo Speaking in Washington	203
What Does Kulmiye Have for The Youth?	204
Ahmed Silanyo Speaking About the Genocide	204
Encouraging Opposition	205
Shotgun Aimed at Ahmed Silanyo	205
Electrifying Election In 2010	206
National Election Commission Announced Election Results	206
The Elation of Dr. Abdishakur Sheikh Ali Jawhar	207
Dahir Riyale Congratulated Ahmed Silanyo	207
President-Elect Silanyo Praises Incumbent President Dahir Riyale	207
Selection of Various Committees and Duties Specified	208
IRIN News of United Nations Office in Somalia and Somaliland Interviewed Ahmed Silanyo	209
CHAPTER SIX: Ahmed Silanyo's Inaugural Speech	**211**
We Are Not Taking Off Our Shoes Until We Fulfill Our Campaign Promises	211
Berbera Thrives with Ahmed Silanyo	213
Somaliland and DP World Signed a Contract	213
Military Base	215
Ahmed Silanyo and Burao-Erigavo Road	215
Silanyo Prepared a Proposal to Build the Erigavo Road in 1978	216
Feelings of People in Sanaag About the Erigavo Road	216
When Determination is Combined with The Will of Allah It materializes	217
Foreign Affairs Policy	219
Ismail Omar Guelleh's Speech	220
Ahmed Silanyo's Speech in Djibouti	220
We Do Not Want Mogadishu: Somaliland Did Not Want to Negotiate with Mogadishu	220
Ahmed Silanyo Knocks at The Doors of Arab Countries	221
Offering Ranks to Commanders: Creating Hierarchical System for The Somaliland Army	222
Extending the Hand of Peace	223

Ahmed Silanyo's Response to The President of Turkey	225
People Create Dictators:	225
Parliamentarian Talyanle: Ahmed Silanyo during Kulmiye Opposition	226
Meles Zenawi: A Miracle Occurred in Somaliland	227
Ahmed Silanyo's Leadership Style	227
Nominating Hersi to the National Election Commission	227
Subsequent Appointment of Hersi to the Chief of Cabinet	228
In Defense of His Cabinet Ministers	229
Defending Mohammad Abdullahi Omar Former Minister of Foreign Affairs	229
Interview With Al Jazeera Television	230
The Economist: Another Country Waiting for Recognition	234

Epilogue: Ahmed Silanyo's feelings after his election victory — 236

Late Rhoda Aideed Rageh was a Somalilander who lived in Hargeisa; she was a freelance writer and translator. She was also a lecturer at Zayed University in the United Arab Emirates in the early 2000s. She earned her bachelor's and master's degrees in English Literature from San Jose State University in California. She also had a postgraduate diploma in Human Resources Practices from Cornell University (Online). Her Training Consultancy: "Loaghe.Com" registered in Hargeisa, providing Human Resources Training and English Language Courses.

TRANSLATOR'S NOTE

This book is translated from "Ahmed Silanyo's" biography written in Somali by Abdirahman Yusuf Artan. It is the life journey of the Fourth President of Somaliland intertwined with the history of Somaliland and Somalia as encountered with his life during Somaliland's independence and the hasty unity with Somalia and after. As a young graduate, he worked for the Somali government for four years before the revolution of 1969. Among several young graduates, he worked enthusiastically with the military administration until he turned against the regime's harsh policies, especially its harsh measures against the Isaaq Clan in the northern regions. He jumped from a cabinet position to the chairmanship of the Somali National Movement liberation struggle until they freed Somaliland from the grip of tyranny in 1989. After the liberation and ensuing clan conflict, he took an integral part in peacemaking. A decade after SNM freed Somaliland, Ahmed Silanyo played a vital role in peace negotiations and peacebuilding. When Somaliland adopted the multi-party system, he founded the Kulmiye Opposition party. He ran for presidential election first in 2003 and conceded a questionable 80 votes. He ran again and became the Fourth President of Somaliland from 2010 until 2017.

This version is a translation of the original. However, the layout is different. I have edited it f of clarity. Since the universal audience differs from the Somali audience, I have tried to make the book more fluid and accessible to all readers.

As a translator, I encountered an intense nationalist as a Somalilander and a Somali. He is a peaceful and profoundly democratic man who believes in the freedoms of the individual and society as inalienable rights.

Farah Ahmed Hersi of Hamad Bin Khalifa University, Qatar, co-authored this work by initially assisting the lead author, Late Rhoda Aideed Raghe (May Allah Rest Her Soul in Peace), in bringing the book's mission to fruition. Some of his specific roles and responsibilities were to restructure the work after the translation, edit several drafts of the work, and, most importantly, complete the task when his colleague tragically passed away in August 2021.

PROLOGUE

"Never in my entire life has my consciousness directed me to advance my interest before the interest of the public" (Ahmed Mohamed Mohamoud Silanyo)

Ahmed was among the first group of students who have formally completed 11th grade –O-Level by the British Education System—including seven years of primary and intermediate education and four years of secondary school. Before that, education for some ended at the intermediate level; some attended non-formal education, and those combined the meeeee level with technical training (trade school). Ahmed's group was the first to complete continuous formal education before they proceeded to university. The first school in Somaliland started in 1943. Ahmed was in the 4th batch to register for school. The first batch included Abdirahman Ahmed Ali and Mohamed Haji Ibrahim Egal, both former presidents of present-day Somaliland.

THE INDEPENDENCE BREEZE

Ahmed's age group evolved at a time of intense African resolve to unravel and remove the colonial yoke from the continent. It was also time European colonizers realized and accepted the wind of change. It was time to let go of African and Asian colonies. Ahmed and his generation gained consciousness when political parties started in the Somaliland Protectorate in 1952. Their nationalism was intense and shaped by 1954 concessions of Hawd and Reserved area (Somaliland's animal graze lands) to Ethiopia. The reaction of the people in the Somaliland Protectorate was somber and widespread. The people of Somaliland protectorate then started a vigorous awareness campaign in all major cities. National United Front (NUF), determined to return the lost reserved area, began in 1955. Young Somalis of Ahmed's age were deeply affected by the sense of loss felt all over the protectorate, and the intent to return the lost territory to the fold lodged deeply in their psyche. They knew they were the first to attend university abroad and were sentient of the role they should be playing. Not only were they committed to participating in building the nation that would soon come to being, but they also saw it as their binding duty to unite all the portioned parts that European colonizers scrambled. Here is how Ahmed Silanyo explains:

"We were young men when Somaliland's imminent independence gained momentum, and we had only one vision - Our thoughts, dreams, and aspirations were to unite all Somalis wherever that partitioning threw them. They should be united under one flag."

Ahmed and his friends were serious nationalists who loved their country. Their lives were brimmed with the desire to participate in the shining future of freedom. They saw their role as pulling their culture out of regressive tribalism. It was their national responsibility and the obligatory onus to build Somali unity.

The people's dreams were crushed soon after independence. The leaders of the newly formed Somali Republic turned out to be visionless. They put their interest ahead of the interest of the public. Corruption, tribalism, and nepotism became rampant practices.

The northern parts of Somalia (now Somaliland) soon realized the void that resulted from the union, and people asked: Where is the Republic? Where is the Flag we hoisted? What happened to our hope?

THE REVOLUTION

The deep disappointment felt by the Somali people encouraged the military to overthrow the elected government and usurp power. It gave birth to the bloodless revolution of 1969 that ensued soon after Somali president Abdirashid Ali Sharmarke was assassinated in Las Anod. Initially, People were enthused with the steps taken by the military administration. Writing the Somali script, among other development projects, was a significant highlight. However, the regime soon lost track and went off course. It has transformed itself into a severe dictatorship exploiting the complex Somali clan system.

When the oppression of the people in the northern parts of Somalia became aggressive and unyielding, those who envisioned the evil that could transpire advised the regime to change its approach toward the northern parts. Siad Barre did not heed the advice of those loyal to him. Instead, he fired them. Those actions buried any hope that Siad Barre might change things for the better. Nobody could convince him to relinquish the many powers he assumed under him. For many, the only option to change things was guerrilla warfare. His motto: "I came to power by the barrel of the gun, and only by the barrel of the gun will I leave power," echoed in everyone's ears. That statement resonated all over northern regions. Siad Barre determined the course of action and the direction the Somali society would soon take. Another one of his principles was, "Neither people nor land will remain after me. I will take down everything with me." His devilish utterance would soon come to life.

The Somali people, notably the Majeerteen and the Isaaq clans, took the only road open to them to arm themselves and removed him by force. They formed their two groups with the same intention, though they never managed to combine their forces into one.

A TIMED GLANCE
AHMED SILANYO'S LEADERSHIP

For more than 50 years, Ahmed Silanyo, like the stars, glowed in the political arena of Somalis. Interestingly, these fifty years are divided into segments of 10 years.

1969-1982: *Ahmed Silanyo was an outspoken minister who never feared to speak his mind in Siad Barre's brutal government.*

1982-1990: *Organizer and leader of the guerilla struggle. He was the Fourth and the longest-reigning chairman of the Somali National Movement. He was also the firm leader of the 1988 kamikaze-style raid. He instructed the decisive Ismaqiiq operation, where SNM soldiers simultaneously raided and captured all the major cities of Somaliland in broad daylight.*

1991-2001: *A political leader renowned for building peace in a fragmented society, who had also participated in rebuilding the country. He became a parliamentarian, then a minister whose only reminder to his people was: "We have overcome the small battle, but the big battle is yet to be won."*

2002-2010 *A model and democratic leader of one of the opposition political parties. His deeply held belief that after 20 years under dictatorship, Somaliland should test and live in a democracy earned him the respect of voters.*

2010-2017: *Ahmed Silanyo became the 4th president of Somaliland who has not only realized the dream of leading an effectual government, but he has also achieved a long-held dream of starting the building of one of the longest roads in Somaliland, Erigavo–Burao road, dubbed "Silanyo Road" and modernization of Berbera port. Under his vision and leadership, the isolated northern parts of Somaliland are now connected, while Berbera port is transformed into an international hub.*

AUTHOR'S NOTE
HOW INFORMATION WAS GATHERED

Information about Silanyo is widely recorded in print, documentaries, and videos on YouTube. There are interviews he gave as the chairman of the Somali National Movement. Interviews to the press after he handed over the Chairmanship and interviews he held during his participation in peace and nation building, during his tenure as a member of Somaliland's Parliament and later, as a minister in Mohamed Haji Ibrahim Most importantly, the Egal administration's many speeches recorded during his opposition campaign when Somaliland stepped into the multi-party-political system helped. He was the founder and leader of the Kulmiye Opposition Party. Information during his tenure in Siad Barre's administration, I got from Ahmed himself as a reflection on spots of time in his recollection. The bulk of information noted in this book I received from Ahmed's friends. Some of his family members and schoolmates also contributed.

Information about the armed struggle was gathered from the soldiers in the battle that had witnessed different events at different times. I received valuable information from his wife, Amina Sheikh Mohamed Jirdeh. Without Amina's vital contribution, this book would not have been possible. While Ahmed provided the highlights of his life and legacy in detail, Amina-Weris also added a lot, which is a testimony to their beautiful relationship. Their life was not that of husband and wife as we traditionally understand, but they were well-educated partners who shared responsibilities with equal weight. Amina gloats; she and her husband shared a good life: the good times and the difficult times. She is very close to her husband, making it possible for her to remember the situations they faced together or apart. It is not feasible for me to name all the many people who have shared information about Ahmed Silanyo's life. My gratitude to Abdirahman Abdulqadir Farah is immense. He had given me much information about Ahmed Silanyo from the time he left Siad Barre's dictatorship in the 1980s and joined the Somali dissident groups outside the country, his relationship with the Ethiopian administration during SNM, and later when he became an opposition leader in Somaliland, particularly the problematic times his opposition party faced in 2003 presidential election. My special thanks to Abdirahman Osman Alin, who has shared important information about Ahmed Silanyo's leadership style during the SNM struggle and his relationship with the Ethiopian government in safeguarding the SNM's sovereignty. Thanks to Mohamed Bashe for his comments about Ahmed Silanyo's Leadership during the SNM struggle, particularly how he weaved together disparate groups of different ideologies. My thanks to Ali Osman Abdulle (Bikalo) and Mohamoud Hashi Abdi for giving me a clear picture of when SNM first freed Somaliland in 1991 and the role Ahmed Silanyo played in rebuilding the country as well as his role in snuffing the internal conflict that erupted soon after; Hassan Moalim contributed some insight into Baligubadle conference and Ahmed Silanyo's participation and also the role of the Somaliland Guurti. Many thanks to the Chairman of the Somaliland Parliament, Bashe Mohamed Farah and Mohamoud Aden Dheri, who have both commented on Ahmed Silanyo's term in Siad Barre's administration; I want to extend my gratitude to the President of Somaliland, Musa Bihi Abdi and the Chairman of the Somaliland Guurti Suleiman Mohamoud Aden, who both know Ahmed Silanyo very well. They shared their knowledge of Ahmed Silanyo without hesitation. Many other individuals shared information about Ahmed Silanyo with me; for their vital contribution, I say thank you from the bottom of my heart.

CHAPTER ONE

BIRTH TO THE END OF UNIVERSITY (1936-1965)

Ahmed's brother, Ali Mohamed Mohamoud, Ali-Digirin, told me their father's name was Mohamed Mohamoud Adan, nicknamed "Bureeqa." He had a sister--"Timiro"--and a brother--"Abdillahi." Their father—Mohamoud--died when the children were young. They grew up orphans and did not have immediate uncles or cousins. His two sons, Mohamed and Abdillahi, left the rural country and moved to town. Mohamed took a boat from Berbera aiming for Aden; instead, he landed on an island called "Bureeqa." [1] He lived among Arab fishermen. His family lost contact for a while until some Somalis sited him in Bureeqa and reported to his family. The family took him from Bureeqa to Tawahi. [2] Since he was found in Bureeqa, people identified him as the "young man from Bureeqa. That is how he has become Mohamed-Bureeqa. Mohamed later worked in the Navy in Berbera. After saving some money, he bought some livestock and returned to the rural area, where he settled down and married. Mohamed's brother, Abdillahi, later joined the navy and boarded a ship. One day, Abdillahi asked a distant relative named Abdillahi Ali Utubi to draft him an English letter. The man answered: "English can be learned; why don't you learn it yourself?" That statement motivated Abdillahi to start learning English. After he returned from the navy, Abdillahi became a civil servant in many parts of the protectorate like Berbera, Borama, Burao, and Syla'. He later became a judge. Mohamed and Abdillahi were young orphans not supported by anyone who worked hard on their own. Since Abdillahi worked in the government, he helped his brother. In the old Somali tradition, when people from the rural parts visit relatives in the city, they do not come empty-handed, but they bring gifts like ghee, meat, and edible seeds while, at the same time, relatives in the town help their brethren in the rural.

---

(1) Bureeqa in the beginning was not part of Aden but it came part of it later on
(2) Tawahi was among small islands Aden was composed of

Mohamed Mohamoud's Marriage

Mohamed Mohamoud married Maryam Suleiman Farah (Sanweyne).[1] She was an intelligent woman known for her warm welcome to her relatives and in-laws. Both husband and wife were kind, hospitable people. Maryam gave birth to six children. Two girls, Fadumo and Khadra, and four boys: Ali, Ahmed, Jama, and Saeed. As relayed by Ali-Digirin, their family was not wealthy but close-knit. Their parents infused them with respect for each other and others. Their parents were generous and gave what they could to others. Illustrating the generosity of his parents, Ali remembers the following. *There was a time when my father had a ewe that had just given birth when guests visited him for two consecutive nights. He slaughtered the mother the first night and the tiny baby for the guests that followed the second night.*

Ahmed's Birth

Ahmed, the second child of the family, Ali being the first, was born in the village of "Dheryeley, which is part of the Togdheer region in Somaliland. He was born in the 1930s. (Ahmed Silanyo's official record shows 1936). As Ali heard from his mother Maryam, she went into labor after midnight without a drop of water in the house. Soon after Maryam went into labor at about 4:00 am, her husband left in search of water. He embarked on a long journey towards the Ainabo borehole, a distance of 14 days on foot. The closest boreholes to Dharyeley were Burao or Ainabo. Maryam gave birth at about 9:00 am. Since there was not a drop of water in the house, the midwives scrubbed sand to clean blood from their hands. Ali's mother told him that when her baby came out, she washed him with camel milk, dried him, and poured ghee all over him. The rain came six days later. [2]

As Ali-Digirin recalls, they had camels and other livestock when they lived in the rural. Before that, they lived in Berbera, where Mohamed's young children attended Madrasa, owned by a renowned Yamani teacher called Ahmedi. It was located in the Daroole area of Berbera. Ali remembers his teacher Ahmedi also made straw beds. Children in the madrasa used to make their ink to write

---

(1) She was the granddaughter of "the son of Sanweyne," a poet and and wise man among the Somalis. He was well known for his mediation.
(2) Many people may find this strange but the life in the rural is difficult. This story provides a true image of life in the rural.

their lessons. Later they moved back to the rural. Shortly after, Abdillahi sent a message to his brother to send him one of his sons so he could enroll in school. Since Mohamed could not send Ali because he was the oldest and help for the family, while Jama and Saeed were too young to leave the nest, it was Ahmed's luck to live with his uncle and study in Berbera. [1] His uncle enrolled him in a Quranic school to learn Arabic and Qur'an. Ahmed turned out to be an intelligent child. He completed the Holy Qur'an by heart in a short period. He learned to read and write Arabic and showed excellent learning potential. Uncle Abdillahi brought another child of his wife, Fadumo Jama's relative to the house. Osman Sayli', Fadumo's young nephew, and Ahmed grew up in the same household until they finished high school and left for university abroad. Both later became prominent in different governments in the Somali Republic.[2]

The Sect of Sheikh Mohamed Dhawaaq

Ahmed lived in a rural with his family. Once every year, a Sheikh called "Sheikh Mohamed Dhawaaq" used to visit Djibouti. He was a relative of Ahmed's father and ran a masjid in Djibouti. Whenever that Sheikh visited the settlement, he treated ill nomads with Qur'an. People used to wait for his arrival. They give him livestock in exchange for his services. He used to leave with gratitude while people also were happy with his service. His yearly visits were always welcome.

On one of his visits, the Sheikh became a guest of Mohmed-Bureeqa's family. Young Ahmed was among the family household who could recite the Qur'an by heart and read and write Arabic. Ahmed loved to be close to the Sheikh because he was the only one who knew the Qur'an he was reciting. He willingly brought everything the Sheikh asked. Soon the Sheikh realized he was different from other boys and asked him: *"Can you read the Qur'an."* When Ahmed answered yes, the Sheikh asked him to recite. He read flawlessly. The Sheikh said happily, *"Masha Allah, can you write Arabic?"* Ahmed answered: yes, I can. The Sheikh gave him a piece of paper and a pen and asked him to write his name. When Ahmed wrote his name, the Sheikh was pleased and immediately conceived the idea of taking this clever young boy as his aide. There were young men, Sheikh's son among them, who traveled with him and collected livestock for him, but none

---

(1) In those days educating girls was unheard of

(2) The two young men who grew up together in the same household became prominent government officials in Somalia

of them was good in writing. Ahmed became an aid to the Sheikh. He scribed on the amulets whatever the Sheikh dictated that was intended to heal the ill. Ahmed worked with the Sheikh while he remained in the village, and the Sheikh decided to take him to Djibouti. At the time of his departure, the Sheikh asked Ahmed's father to let his son go to Djibouti with him. Ahmed's father accepted the offer. He traveled with the Sheikh and his entourage. They came to Burao and sold the animals. The Sheikh bought Ahmed his Islamic Khamis, hat, and a cover for his Kitab. Ahmed was pleased with his new attire, and he and the sect boarded a lorry to Djibouti.

It was midday when the lorry came to the customs in Sayla' where vehicles on their way to Djibouti were searched. Abdillahi Mohamoud and Ismail Nahar, who worked in the customs office, approached the vehicle and asked the passengers to leave the vehicle. After Abdillahi greeted the Sheikh, he spotted his young nephew among the Sheikh's entourage. He asked his nephew: "Where are you heading?" Before Ahmed answered, Sheikh Mohamed Dhawaaq informed him he was going to Djibouti to work with him in the masjid, and Ahmed's father agreed. Abdillahi told the Sheikh: "No, he is not going to Djibouti. I was thinking of getting him back from the rural. Thanks for bringing him. I am taking him to school." Ignoring the Sheikh's plea to let him take the child, Abdillahi took Ahmed aside. The Sheikh left disappointed.

The year Abdillahi brought Ahmed to the Education Council and accepted him for the first grade was the 1946/7 school year. The other senior government officials working in Sayla' at the time were Ismail Nahar, Haji Dualeh Abdalla, Shire Girig, and Abdirahman Salah.

Inspectors Mohamoud Ahmed Ali and Badham went around all over the districts of the protectorate to select new students for the school year, and they were in Sayla' at the time. Ahmed arrived when they had completed their selection, and students had already left for Sheikh.

On that fateful day, Mohamoud Ahmed Ali and Mr.Badham were still in Sayla'. Also, in Sayla' at the time were elders who advised on education matters called (Education Council). Nasir Nahar was among them. Abdillahi brought Ahmed to the council and asked them to enroll the young boy. They accepted, and Ahmed Silanyo was enrolled in Sayla' for first-grade education. By the time Ahmed arrived, the inspectors, Mohamoud Ahmed Ali and Badham, had collected the students needed for Sheikh and were ready to leave town. Mohamoud and Badham still gave their assurances to Abdillahi by telling him, "don't worry, we will take the kid with us." Ismail Nahar requested them to take him to his brother's house in Hargeisa for the night. Ahmed boarded a small pickup with Mohamoud Ahmed Ali and Badham. He secured a small change his uncle gave him in the back pocket and hopped at the back of the pickup. At the back of the pickup was a giant fish tank full of seawater and a few lobsters the British district commissioner in Sayla' sent to his colleague in Hargeisa and other British colleagues in Sheikh. That was the first time Ahmed saw a fish like that. As he sat at the back, fascinated with the strange fish, *he was told, "Young man, your job is to keep filling the fish tank. It should never be empty."* Ahmed was supposed to draw seawater from another tank and add it to the fish tank. When they reached Hargeisa, the inspectors were dropped off at the HQ, and the driver dropped Ahmed at Naser Nahar's house for the night. He spent the night with Naser Naher's relatives. When he woke up in the morning, he ran to town and bought a few footballs and pockets full of sweets before the inspectors took him to Sheikh. By the time they reached Sheikh early in the evening, students had queued up for dinner. Mohamoud Ahmed Ali took him and informed school staff he was a new child enrolled in Sayla'. The kids from Sayla' gathered around, thinking he was one of them, then started inquiring: who is this unknown from Sayla'? Ahmed told them he was not born in Sayla' but only enrolled in Sayla': Ahmed stood in the dinner line. When he reached a small window where students picked up food. Barre Oday, the cook, looked at him and asked: "who is this boy?" The students quickly introduced: "He is a new boy from Sayla', give him dinner," then instructed him in chorus: spread your hands! Spread your hands!" Because there were no plates to collect food, students opened their palms wide to gather their food. Ahmed opened his hands to receive the dinner. It was two pieces of pancakes. When he received them, the cook poured ghee over them, and the kids shouted again: "slurp it! Slurp it!" They instructed Ahmed to lick the ghee running down his hands. Ahmed was taken to his sleeping quarters called "Lion House." Soon he became famous, and everybody liked him because of his small footballs.

Sheikh and Amoud Schools

The students who knew Arabic and the Qur'an at the time of enrollment were better than others. Ahmed knew both, and because of that, he was a better student. At the inception, he demonstrated two qualities: Education excellence and innate leadership.

Education Excellence: The reward for academic excellence was a tuition waiver for the first three students. Since Ahmed always remained the first or second student in the class, he never paid school fees and enjoyed tuition waivers. He and another student called Adam Amin fought for first place. Education Excellence was his talent until he reached university and after. Ahmed spent his primary, intermediate, and first form of secondary school in Sheikh. He was transferred to Amoud at the beginning of form II and studied in Amoud for the rest of his high school.

His Leadership Talent

He showed leadership talent early in school. He was chosen to be head of prefect and student leader. Usually, only students in the high school serve as student head prefect, but Ahmed became a head prefect while he was still in the intermediate. He served as the leader of the Lion house, where he lived in Sheikh. Ahmed was not a traditional student focused only on his studies but participated in many extra-curricular activities. He always had some responsibility beyond his studies because he impressed others to trust him with responsibility. He was also a student involved in school social activities, good in football and hockey, as well as debates, an exhibition of cultural expos, and even theatre and drama. He was a multi-talented young man.

There was a time in Amoud when the football team was preparing to go to Aden for a friendly match; Ahmed was in Form three at the time and was not the best team member. There were better players. Yet, Ahmed was chosen as the captain of the team. When discontent students complained they were better players than him, school administrators explained that the captain of the team should be one with leadership qualities. Therefore, Ahmed showed these qualities and was going to lead the team from Amoud.

He was good at debates and participated in discussions, theatre, and drama. Once when the school displayed the Shakespearean "Hamlet" in English, Ahmed played the role of Hamlet. In all school plays, he took the role of the lead actor. As Osman Sayli', who grew up in the same household and was in the same school, explains: *from the first grade to secondary school, Ahmed never lost first place in his class. He was exceptional. I used to fight for second, third, or even fourth establishment, but he steadfastly held the first place.* Osman also explains how he got the nickname Sayli'. Abdillahi Mohamoud was transferred to Burao, where Osman Sayli' started primary school. When schoolmates asked where he came from, he answered Sayla,' so they named him Sayli.'

Osman Sayli' reiterates that Ahmed was a well-rounded student. In intermediate school, he participated in plays acting in Arabic and remained head prefect in Amoud and Sheikh.

Ahmed Explains How He Got The Nickname "Silanyo."

"When I was 15 years old, I was tall and thin. I was not exceptional in football, but I remained on the team. A colleague in football named Ahmed Ali Dhaban gave me the name Silanyo. One day we were playing football, and I ran away with the ball, and in desperation, he shouted: "catch that, Silanyo," it simply means "slender." Since that time, the name became part of me." Silanyo is the name of a tiny house lizard.

His Disinterest in Tribalism

Another unique quality Ahmed showed early in his life: his disinterest in tribal affiliation. Osman Sayli' remembers that when they were in Amoud and Ahmed was the head prefect, two groups from two different clans clashed; one group was from Ahmed's clan. He did not know about it and only found out about the fight later. We never invited him to the tribal meetings we held in school, and he never bothered to attend them. He was oblivious to tribal affiliation. His best friends were Abdillahi Saeed Abby, and Boodhe. He was a responsible young man loved by his teachers, said Richard Darlington (gacamadheere)

Amina-Weris explains how Ahmed fondly remembers his schoolmaster Mr. Badham. She says, *at the end of the school term, the school used to invite parents and elders from the town. One day, at the end of the term, all the elders, like Mohamoud Hussein Jirde, who was the judge of the town and Sheikh Adan, who taught at the school, sat among the invited when Mr. Badham announced the names of the first students in the class and called Ahmed's name in his accent unable to articulate the Arabic letter (x). Sheikh Adan felt outraged by the mispronunciation and murmured: 'this is our prophet's name!'*

University

Ahmed was an exemplary student, good in all academic subjects, especially science subjects; however, the colonial administration did not encourage students to learn subjects like medicine, engineering, geology, and veterinary that were much needed in the country. They offered scholarships in social science subjects like history, economics, and law. Since Ahmed Silanyo was a bright student, they encouraged him to study Architecture. He left for university to study that subject but changed his subject to economics when he reached the university. Students who insisted on studying science subjects were forced to become science teachers.

Before leaving for university in England, students asked themselves what academic subjects to study. What would be helpful for an independent nation called Somaliland that would soon need everything? They decided on economics and law. Ahmed was good especially in science and math and had a talent for drawing. Therefore, his advisers advised him to study architecture.

He refused to listen to their advice and told them he wanted to be a leader and believed economics and political science would be good subjects to study. This is how Ahmed remembers:

"We believed political science and economics were fundamental to leadership. It was that belief that has encouraged me to study economics."

He completed high school in 1956 and left for university in 1957. He spent most of his school years in the Sheikh District, the intellectual citadel of British Somaliland. Sheikh schools shaped Ahmed Silanyo's academic growth and development since his formative years, as he first enrolled in elementary school in this town. Sheikh is also a beautiful place in terms of its scenery and must have helped Ahmed's imagination, and global outlook develop. Ahmed has developed closer connections with the town of Sheikh over the years and has always looked forward to visiting, as his wife also hails from this town. Ahmed says: "it was wonderful to return to Sheikh and the environment of my school. I enjoyed returning to the mountains I used to trek."

The kind of Education Colonial Administration Used to Provide

Mr. Richard Darlington (gacmodheere) managed education in Sheikh and Amoud, the way elite schools in England were managed. Instead of focusing on politics, they wanted to prepare readers, civilized and cultured youth who enjoyed English literature and eloquence like the British upper class.[1] Though Ahmed liked politics and economics, their training was far from that. The colonial administration did not want them to focus on politics. They trained them to become technocrats. Abdirahman Abdulqadir explains that era: *The youth leaving schools at the time were not interested in politics like the ones today or those educated in Cairo and Aden who returned politically animated. That is why when they returned from England, there wasn't any of them who joined a political party or focused on politics."*

Lessons in Social Etiquette

Before the students left for England while still in Amoud, Richard Darlington taught them how to assimilate into British culture. He held dinners to teach them the etiquette of eating within that culture, mainly how to eat with a fork and a knife, fish, and drink soup. When the students became confused with the many forks and knives, Mr. Darlington instructed them, "Focus on how the cutlery is lined up. Start with the one furthest from your plate and keep coming close to the plate. Finish with the art. He was preparing a society impersonating the British bourgeois. As Kwame Nkrumah commenting on students attending similar schools in Ghana *noticed: 'they were more British than the British themselves.'*

Colonial Education: The Kind of People They Wanted To Groom

They wanted to bring a small elite to be considered the cream of the crop. Like the British upper-middle class, these students were taught the curriculum of the British conservative. Of course, in Somaliland's classless society, most students come from rural. The colonial administration did not tire of building a small elite that was disconnected from its roots. They were to connect with the taste and thinking of those in London and Paris. Nevertheless, the students did not entirely disconnect from their rural culture. Most of them did not have families in the cities and because of that, the majority of them left for the rural

---

[1] Youth training to become technocrats

during holidays. They helped in the rural family business, which was completely different from the orientation they had in schools. They enjoyed pastoral poetry and folk tales based on the roots of the Somali culture. During their holidays, they immersed themselves in the work of the rural whether livestock herding, grazing animals or taking them to boreholes. Even during clan wars, the able youth participated in the war. They were expected to be warriors rather than remain with the women. For that purpose, the young men could not separate themselves from their culture. Besides, the cities in Somaliland were small and well-connected to the rural. People in the cities, whether merchants or civil servants, were few compared to the ones in the rural. Therefore, although colonial education had implications, the youth did not become fully endorsed into the western culture.

University Education in the United Kingdom

When Ahmed and his group reached England, they met Edna Aden Ismail and her father, who lived there. When they arrived, they were taken to their living quarters in London called 'East African House" located in the heart of London. The East African House is now a five-star hotel.

Aden Ismail, nicknamed, "Aden Dhakhtar," was a nurse working in London. Edna lived with her father and was training to become a nurse. They were cultured people. The first day they met the young scholars, they gave them a long lecture about how to live in England, what to do and what not to do. Aden Ismail advised them to protect the reputation of their culture. He did not want them to fall into misbehavior or for their actions to be misinterpreted as rudeness. He used to tell them, "Do not misrepresent Somaliland. Do not let her down." Ahmed says: *"my colleagues and I learned a lot from that old man."* They were grateful to Aden Dhakhtar. Without him, they could have fallen into many mistakes. He took them around shopping for clothes, books, and other accessories. At that time, additional young Somali army cadets were also training at Royal Military Academy, Sandhurst. Some have graduated from vocational schools, and some returned from Arabia. Those students were Hassan Abdulle (Hassan-Kyd), Awil Ali Dualeh, and Ismail Ali Abokor.

The Request of Ahmed's Mother, Maryam Suleiman

Ahmed tells the story: *"Before I left for Europe, I visited my mother. She lived in Balli-Dhiig at the time. When I told her about my journey to England for further education, the only advice she had for me was not to bring her a foreign wife. The single most important advice she imparted was: 'my son, don't bring me a foreign wife.'"* [1] Ahmed could not fathom how anyone could bring a foreign wife or remain in a foreign land. He never thought about living there. Ahmed only thought about returning to his country--not even once did he think of staying in England after he graduated.

Studying Economics

Ahmed refused the advice of his teachers to study architecture believing political science and economy would lead and develop my country. Ahmed says: *"we all believed that economics, political science, and law were fundamental to the progress of our country; therefore, to become politicians, we had to study law or economics. We don't know where we got that idea from; h*e told his professors he was not learning anything else but economics. However, the colonial educators did not heed his wish. They enrolled him in Architecture.

In the British educational system, before students begin their major, they must pass the Advance diploma (A-Levels). When they reached London, he was taken to North London Polytechnic, where Ahmed started his A Levels, and his major was known to be architecture. During the two years he was preparing for his A-levels, he became involved in the activities around campus and enjoyed the social activities, particularly the debating society. His teachers noticed him immediately. They asked him why he was interested in the narrow subject of architecture when he was good at debating. That is when Ahmed found an opportunity to change his major. He informed his teachers that he wanted to study Economics and Banking. They accepted and sent him to the University of Manchester, one of the most prominent universities in England. He completed his Bachelor's Degree in Economics, graduating with first honors, and his Master's Degree in Banking. From primary to university, Ahmed was an honor student. Of all the students who returned from England around the same time, Ahmed was the only one with a Master's Degree and the first Somali to obtain a Master's Degree in England. He attended his A-Levels between 1958-1960. He studied

---

(1) Ahmed's Mother Maryam Suleiman died in Ballidhiig in 1985

for Bachelor's in Economics from 1960-1963. After graduating with Honors, he proceeded to his Master's Degree in Banking from 1963-1965. Abdirahman Abdulqadir mentions that Ahmed Silanyo was the first Somali to earn a Master's Degree from a British university. Ahmed Haji Dualeh (Ahmed-Kayse) was also the first Somali to earn a Bachelor's Degree from a U.K university.

Marriage and Family

Ahmed and his wife Amina-Weris married in 1968. Amina gloats that she and her husband share a good life. They are two educated and equal partners who support each other. Lul is their first child, followed by Hodan. Then they had three sons, Kulmiye, Ali-Salan and Rashid. Amina speaking about their relationship, says: *We have had a good life together; we enjoy chatting. They got married in 1968 when she completed her BSC in Nursing and Midwifery and started working at the National Health Institute where she was a counterpart for a woman director from Australia.*

Abdirahman Abdulqadir, a good friend of Silanyo's family, speaks about their relationship: Ahmed Silanyo is a *very good family man. He and his wife have an enviable relationship. When we were at the Kulmiye party, we were meeting with a foreign delegation and Ahmed told me to 'continue with the meeting; I am going to the airport.' When I asked him why? He responded that Amina was coming. I told him to send the driver. Then he said No. That is not possible.*

I laughed and asked him: Are you still in love with her? Therefore, Ahmed and Amina's relationship is strong and admirable. Another day we were in London in a heated political debate. There were many people, and those debating fiercely with Ahmed was Omar Dihood when Ahmed looked at his watch and suddenly got up and said, 'Look how they drive us crazy. I almost missed calling Amina. Until now, I did not call my wife. (Amina at the time was in Kuwait). He used to call his wife regularly.

His wife took an integral part in bringing up their children. It is an outstanding achievement how they nurtured their children and raised good decent children. Although their father was away at SNM, they grew up as mature, intelligent, and educated children. It is no small feat.

When Ahmed Silanyo decided to leave the Siad Barre administration, he took his young family to London on 13 March 1982. He left the country two days later. His wife and kids went to London but he went to Saudi Arabia, where the SNM movement was in earnest.

It started ten months ago and already a severe conflict emerged in its leadership, and they had already fired their chairman Ahmed Jimale. Many notable people in Saudi Arabia saw Ahmed as the man to lead the Movement. Therefore, it was impressed upon him to get ready for that role. Ahmed informed them that he had a wife and small children in London, and, at that moment was not available for the movement's leadership.

Amina-Weris explains how she and her husband disagreed with him leading the Movement before they left Somalia, but when he arrived in London, he came a changed man. Bashe Mohamed Farah, who knows Ahmed Silanyo, says: *Ahmed Silanyo is a family man. After work, he goes straight to his house. He is not the type to sit in cafes.*

Ahmed is a considerate man for his wife and family, and the most important aspect of their family life is the relationship between him and his wife.

When Ahmed arrived in London, he established the SNM office and did much good work. When Ahmed went to the 4th SNM Annual Conference, he was not planning to become a candidate though many people pressured him from the Gulf and from Ethiopia, especially from the SNM chairman, Abdulqadir Kosar. Nevertheless, when he left his family in London in 1984 for the 4th SNM Conference, he planned to attend the meeting as a delegate from the London office. Amina says the news of his election to the chairman of SNM was unanticipated and a big surprise. I was disappointed and worried and cried days and nights when I heard the news.

Ahmed started writing letters to his wife to console her. He used to call her at night, and she cried on the phone all night long, asking him if they would ever see him again. Ahmed Silanyo sent a letter to Ibrahim Meygag, who was returning from the conference and traveling through London. In his long letter, he explained rationally why he accepted to lead the movement:

'Amina, *'I have to rise to the challenges, don't be narrow-minded.'* Yes, I understand you are alone in a foreign land with very young children but look at it from the challenges and dangers facing our people. I won't consider myself a man if I don't stand up to the complex challenges ahead of me.

That debate had calmed Amina down, and she decided to fill the role of both father and mother for her children. Amina describing the problematic moments she and her children faced, says: *My son Ali-Salan was the most hyper of my kids; when I scolded him, he used to lock himself inside the toilet and howled for his father: 'I wish my mother would take me to my daddy. Daddy where are you? All the other kids and my friends have their daddies around them. You are not here to take me to football on Saturdays or anywhere else. Where are you, daddy?*

Amina says: one day, I stood outside the toilet and recorded his wail for his dad and sent it to him. Ahmed was heartbroken. He realized the hardship his absence imposed on his children. For a period of seven years, Ahmed only stayed with us for nine months. Therefore, when those opposed to him in SNM confronted him, he used to say, I am leaving you. My son Ali-Salan and my family need me.

Amina also talks about her son Kulmiye: 'He was a smart little boy. When his teacher asked him to write an essay, he used to write political essays and discuss the political dictator in his country. His ideas were beyond his age. The stories he heard from us filled his mind.

CHAPTER TWO
PROFESSIONAL CAREER

FROM HIS FIRST JOB AT THE BANK TO THE TIME
HE DEPARTED SIAD BARRE'S GOVERNMENT (1965-1982)

Coming Back Home and Job Hunting

Somaliland gained its independence while Ahmed and his group were overseas. Somaliland has also united with Southern Somalia. Ahmed returned to Hargeisa, but the capital was in Mogadishu, and the government had job opportunities in Mogadishu. That was the place to go. At that time, travel between the north and south was new. Ahmed never saw Mogadishu before. He took a plane from Hargeisa and landed at Mogadishu airport. He did not know anyone and did not have an address or a place to go. He was ambivalent about the trip but enthusiastic about his future and reminded himself that he was a young and confident scholar full of hope with a bright future ahead of him. He got out of the airport dragging his bag, walking into the unknown but looking into a bright future.

Ahmed explains that experience: *"when I stepped outside the airport, taxi drivers rushed toward me, 'Let me take you! Where do you want to go?' I told them why are you rushing at me? I don't know where I am going or where I am supposed to go until one of the taxi drivers said, 'Savoy! Savoy Hotel is where Somali Qaldans stay' I never heard the word Qaldan as a description of Somalilanders. When I asked him what he meant by Qaldan, he answered many people from Somaliland stay in that hotel. I asked him to take me there. I climbed a few steps before I reached the front desk. As I approached the reception, I saw Farah Warsame sitting in the corner near the reception. He was one of our group from England though he graduated from Reading and he and his group returned a year before us. Farah screamed in surprise. 'Oh my God, it is Ahmed Silanyo! Did you arrive today?'"*

Ahmed Silanyo felt, *it is correct. Hotel Savoy is where my fellow Somalilanders reside; this is their address.* He found them all in Savoy. They used to come for afternoon tea and warmly welcomed, invited, and took him around, and he felt at home. Farah Warsame, Abdillahi Saeed, and Hurre, all his colleagues in Sheikh and England, left the hotel and rented a house together. They hired a maid/cook and lived as housemates.

Abdirazak Haji Hussein was the prime minister of the Somali Republic when Ahmed returned to the country. He valued the people educated in Britain. Farah Warsame, one of Ahmed's friends, told him: "Tomorrow, I will take you to Ufficio Governo," a place where all government offices were clustered. We will tour the ministries headed by Somalilanders one by one. Ahmed did not know many people then. Ahmed Ismail Abdi (Dukhsi), then the Minister of Planning, who knew Ahmed invited him for a chat. Ahmed informed him of his studies in economics and banking, and Dukhsi told him that banking is badly needed at present. He took him to Abdirazak Haji Hussein's office. Abdirazak was an open, animated person and welcomed Ahmed as the man needed in the bank. The senior staff at the Somali National Bank was Italian. There were no Somali officers. Ahmed was keen to work, and he was willing to work anywhere.

First Job at the Bank

He was placed in the Bank. As soon as he started his job in the bank, he faced harsh opposition from his colleagues and stiff competition from Italian-educated colleagues. The job at the bank was entering into a zone closed for certain people, particularly the Italian officers, who resented young Somalilanders taking over their jobs. There was also stiff competition between Italian-educated and English-educated Somalis. Combined with that was the problematic Somali tribalism that affected his friends and colleagues. The tough rivalry at the bank was serialized in a local newspaper edited by advocate Yusuf Dhuhul. Instead of accepting his knowledge of banking as the reason for his hiring, they spread rumors that he came on nepotism. Ahmed was unaware of the war directed at him and the stab at the back. He learned later about the newspaper's defending comments. Ahmed was not after a position; he only wanted to work with his specialty and was unaware of the whirlwind of resentment around him. Eventually, he left the bank when he realized the controversy created by his assignment at the bank.

Ministry of Planning

In 1965 he joined the ministry of planning, where he became director of planning and development and later the director general after Ahmed Botan resigned from his position to take a job in the United Nations.

Many foreign experts in the ministry were to provide technical assistance. Ahmed was seen as the able officer that could direct the knowledge transfer they were there to impart. They enjoyed his energy and education. Ahmed quickly adapted to the government system. He became one of the most active young intellectuals. He often represented Somalia at international conferences. Because of his knowledge and confidence, the people he worked with appreciated his intellectual rigor and always welcomed his ideas. They worked as a team, and in a short period, Ahmed became the engine that turned the wheels of the ministry.

The Cold War and the Race for Political Alliance of the 3rd world

In 1960, when many African countries became independent from Europe, was also a period of simmering cold war. The alliances of NATO, led by America, and WARSAW, led by the now defunct Soviet Union, competed for the influence of the newly independent African nations. Two policies were competing for new alliances and world power. Each offered aid and scholarships to convince those young countries they were better examples to emulate. America offered "Leadership Grant" scholarships open to all developing countries. It started in Asia and later in Africa. It was a grant provided to individuals who might have had the leadership potential, an international appointment for training future leaders. Whoever was awarded the grant toured the world, spent three days in each country, and ended in America. Ahmed Silanyo was awarded the leadership grant America and the United Nations offered. America paid the money. It was a grant for development. Participants toured the American federal government and provincial states organized by the Africa-America Institute and Soviet-Asian Republics. In the end, participants were given orientation on good governance aimed at convincing them of Western government methods, particularly the American governing system as the best model. Half the time students traveled the world, and the other half spent touring the American States. Ahmed recalls: *"My biggest surprise was when they told us we would meet the successful black American middle class and took us to people I believed were white people. The American black caucus in California supposedly invited us, but the people they described as wealthy black Americans were not black at all.* [1] *They were, perhaps, people with a drop of black blood in their genes but otherwise white. I wondered where the black people that invited us were until finally, I learned that they were categorized as black even if there was a drop of blackness in them*

They also took them to the state of Arizona, where the cowboy film industry is located. They dressed him like a cowboy with a big cowboy hat, and stiff jeans like the ones cowboys wore in films and mounted him on a horse where they took his picture with the caption, *"Silanyo wanted dead or alive."*

In addition to the political influence, the trip also showed them the American way of life. The reason was to influence future African leaders to become friends with America. They wanted to create sympathetic impressions of America and its way of life. It was in 1966 when Ahmed went on that trip. He enjoyed the trip. He was appointed as the Director General of the Ministry of Planning after he returned from the trip.

The assassination of President Abdurashed Ali Sharmarke

On October 15, 1969, the president of the Somali Republic, Dr. Abdurashed Ali Sharmarke, on an official tour in the northern parts of the country, was assassinated. One of his bodyguards killed him. The Prime Minister, Mohamed Haji Ibrahim Egal, was in America then. When Egal learned about the president's death, he cut his trip short and returned to the country immediately.

The Somali Youth League (SYL) party, which held the majority of the seats in parliament, held meetings in an attempt to fill the position of president. While the Somali parliament was busy with the candidates for the presidency, among them Ali Mohamed Jirde, from the northern regions of Somalia, and Musa Boqor, a close clansman of the deceased president, there was a different movement taking place in the military barracks.

People Welcomed the Revolution of 1969

It was Tuesday early at 3:00 am on 21 October, five days after the assassination of the president, Siad Barre, and a group of primarily young military officers staged a coup d'état and overthrew the civilian government. Immediately, they

---

(1) As he will learn later, in America, A person is considered black if one of his/her parents is black even if by appearance he/she looks white.

took over the most strategic locations, like the Mogadishu and Hargeisa radio stations. They arrested the prime minister, minister of interior and other key government officials. They ditched the constitution, dissolved the parliament, placed a curfew on movements, and restricted association to only five people. They banned the press. More than 70 political parties were also forbidden. It was election time when the coup took place.

Discontent with the civilian governments turned into People's enthusiastic welcome of the revolution. The civilian governments were inept and corrupt and crushed the population's hope with their lack of vision. The abundance expected from the new independence was wealth for all. When that hope and expectation vanished, disappointment became prevalent. People's cynical characterizations of government were: *cross-eyed, a black hole for aid. The interior minister was named dearth Abdi*. Expressions such as this one described the nature of the government and the diminished hope of abundance:

Without a mini-skirted holding your hand

Or a parliamentarian pushing your agenda

Surely the donkey of abgaal would kill you

A famous Somali poet by the name of Qassim expressed his frustration:

I am not transgressing when I say; I have not had the government I wanted.

Another famous poet: Haji Adan Afqalooc: *One who impersonates the departed white man, will not succeed.*

The hopelessness felt by the people was not limited to the poor public only, the intellectuals were also frustrated with the incompetence of successive civilian governments. Because of that, the military government enjoyed the elation of the people. In hindsight, the incompetence of the civilian governments was not bad compared to what came later.

Ahmed Silanyo's Critique of Civilian Governments

Ahmed speaking about the reaction to the news of the military coup, says:

The people who used to criticize the civilian government openly welcomed the military. Coups were happening all over Africa. Some of the coup members, like Ismail Ali Abokor and Mohamed Ali shire, were my acquaintances. We welcomed them because we were tired of the poor governments and yearned for change. Most of the young intellectuals wanted the change. Many officers from the north were part of the coup, and that was another reason we welcomed it.

Military Coups Reigned over Africa

Most of the newly independent African governments were ineffective and was the reason military coups reigned all over Africa. Though the possibility of military rule in Somalia was what people expected, it was unlikely to hope for military rule from a clan-based society. Nevertheless, people wanted a military coup. When the revolution finally happened, people welcomed it with spontaneous songs and poetry. It took a while to realize who was behind the coup. People did not expect the chief of the military to be part of the coup. He was a remnant of the corruption that had regressed the civilian governments, and no one wanted any individual of the earlier administration again in a different cloak. It was disappointing to learn he led the coup, but people needed change.

Amina-Weris' Description of the Day of the Coup

Amina worked at the National Institute of Health: this is how she found out about the coup.

Few days before the coup, my Australian colleague and I traveled to Hargeisa to administer the final exam to some nurses graduating from the Hargeisa Nursing School. We left Mogadishu while SYL parliamentarians, who held the majority of the seats in parliament huddled in meetings in an attempt to choose a candidate for the president. My brother, Ali Mohamed Jirde, was a candidate. Also in the candidacy was Musa Boqor. On the morning of 21 October, we turned on the radio Hargeisa while we were getting ready. There was no signal. The station was dead silent. We were guests of Halima Ahmed Dualeh, and we asked her what had happened to the Hargeisa radio station. Then we tried Mogadishu radio station. Again, there was no signal. We went to work and heard the news of the coup in Mogadishu. There were rumors that my husband, Ahmed Silanyo, and other colleagues were arrested on the first day of the coup. There was a plane from Mogadishu on the second day. I went to the airport worried about my husband and brother. At the time, younger women wore mini dresses. I went to the airport wearing my mini dress looking for any news. When the plane landed, a familiar face from the health ministry called Awil dabayare stepped out of the plane. I was happy to see him and quickly asked about the news of my loved ones. I did not know Awil Dabayare supported Musa Boqor while my husband Ahmed supported my brother Ali Jirde. Awil informed me that my husband was doing well, and he was among a group of young intellectuals the government selected to advise the revolution. I was relieved.

Ahmed was Among the Intellectuals Asked to Advise the Revolution

After the revolution took over the strategic locations, the next step was to collect all the young intellectuals and place them in Police Academy (Scuola di Polizia). They were asked to come up with how the government should be working. That step was seen as the government consulting the public. It was seen as the government listening to its intellectuals. Ahmed was part of the group. Ahmed says: *Dr. Hassan Ali Mire was the head of the group. Every day we sat, and brainstormed ideas and then gave our thoughts to him. Mohamed Farah Aideed came and took the advice back to the military barracks every evening. The SRC has not yet taken shape at the time.*

Some of the advice we gave included: a) The military never become part of the government; only educated individuals should run the government; b) The military to oversee and only interfere if the government system becomes corrupt; and c) Powers of the civilian and military not to be placed in the hands of one figurehead. Eventually, they selected a council of 25 men called the Supreme Revolutionary Council from the coup members.

After a while, eleven out of the 44 advisers received red envelopes appointing them to ministerial positions. For a time, their advice to separate the powers of the military and civilian administration worked. There were two councils: the civilian administration and the military Supreme Revolutionary Council SRC. A lot was done during that period. As the minister of planning, they asked Ahmed to come up with ideas. The Somali script was yet to be written. He prepared a "Crash Program" combined with a "Self Help Scheme." Those two development programs moved people into action. Revolutionary slogans like: *"Spectators, this is your country"* moved the people to participate. Ahmed and his Planning colleagues were the brains behind the significant milestones of three and five-year development plans. Though some people criticized the self-help scheme and the crash program, ideas created by Ahmed Silanyo and his colleagues in the ministry of planning as overly ambitious, and they were pessimistic about them, it was Siad Barre who welcomed and encouraged them, and that was all one needed to make it work. Ideas of the revolution's major strides were not coming from Siad Barre but from young intellectuals who were given the freedom to be creative. Ahmed explains how most of the development ideas, ike the "crash program," were his. *"I wrote the words with my hands when they asked us where we begin. I did not want the 'self-help scheme' to be limited to agriculture only. I created the crash program as a comprehensive development agenda."*

How the Word "Qorshayn" was Introduced

Ahmed Silanyo speaking at the 40th anniversary of when the Somali script was written, says: *it was in 1972 when the government announced the writing of Somali script. I was part of that government. I was the minister of planning. I remember the committee in charge of the script named my ministry the ministry of Jaan-gooyo. I rejected the name. It was not the appropriate name for planning. I was lucky to have had a rural background that clarified things for me. I remember my childhood when the rural family moved and landed in a new place; they always had a plan for where everything would be located. Camels have been placed a slight distance from the living quarters, where the direction of the house was supposed to face. So I suggested the word qorshayn be the appropriate description for planning. Jaan-Gooyo means exacting or matching two things up and is not a proper name for planning.*

Nationalization of Vital Economic Institutions

The SRC believed they would not hang on to power without nationalizing vital economic institutions. The economic institutions of the south were in the hands of Italians, whether they were small industries, big plantations, banks, or insurance companies; therefore, the nationalization of economic institutions directly affected them.

Ahmed was appointed to lead the nationalization committee. The Italian owners of the critical economic institutions made every effort to stop that process with heavy lobbying. They even tried to entice the committee with money. Of course, they could not face Ahmed with their offer, but they used people who knew him. First, they used the influence of Hassan Ali Mire, the head of the Coca-Cola Company, where Ali Jirde was also a major shareholder. Every night, Hassan Ali Mire visited Ahmed Silanyo, reminding him he was a young man with a family; therefore, he should look at his interest. Ahmed asked him to clarify his message. He asked bluntly: *Are you asking me to take a bribe? Do the Italians believe they can buy us out? I swear to Allah that I will issue them 'persona-non-grata' and kick them out of the country if any of them approaches me with such ideas.*

They did not give up but again sent him another older man called Qablan who used to be the minister of planning in the overthrown civilian government, and Ahmed Silanyo's colleague in the ministry of planning. Ahmed told the older man: *Uncle, I have much respect for you, you are my senior and I am not going to be rude to you like I was with Hassan Ali Mire, but please do not come to me with such suggestions ever again. Tell the Italians to stop this.*

When all else failed with the Italians, they did not give up. They sent yet another friend. Ismail Haybe was a childhood friend, and a schoolmate and their two wives, Kinsi Abduldqadir and Amina-Weris, grew up together. He came as the envoy of the Italian tycoons. He asked Ahmed: *Are you crazy turning your back to half a million dollars? You will throw poverty out the door!* Ahmed asked Ismail: *My friend, did you forget our intentions of ending corruption and putting things in order. We have just begun living. So why do we need half a million or even a million? Are you worried about the future and whether or not you will live a decent life?* Ismail in disbelief turned to Amina-Weris and said: *Talk to your crazy husband.*

The Italians could not get a way to approach Ahmed, who was the head of the committee. They have influenced the rest but were unable to tackle him. It was at the beginning of the revolution and Siad Barre gave Ahmed full authority for the nationalization process. When the process was completed on 21 October, the revolution handed out awards and Ahmed Silanyo was the only civilian to receive a recognition award for anti-corruption.

Was Economic Nationalization a Ploy to Regress Northern Regions?

Some People interpreted the nationalization of the private sector as a war against the north. They saw it as an indirect economic war and a way the military administration wanted to slow down the growth of the northern economy while, on the other hand building the economy of the south. It was meant to pull together two regions of vast economic disparity. According to Abdirahman Talyanle, the two areas were far apart in economic development, education and commerce. In the South, commerce was in the hands of Italians, Arabs, and Pakistanis; while in the north, commerce was in the hands of Somalilanders. They imported their products, exported their livestock, and signed their commercial agreements. Mohamed-Rashid Ali Ismail signed contracts with the Soviet Union, Haji Jama Mohamed Ismail (Miyatayn), and Haji Abdillahi Ibrahim (Abu Site) signed with Japan in 1962/6. Northern businessmen exported livestock to Aden and used shipping lines called "Baakhashab Lines. Saudi Arabia used to take our livestock and hides from Aden. Northern merchants opened the first direct commercial line between Berbera and Jeddah. Mohamed-Rashid invited the Baakhashab Lines to establish a direct Berbera Jeddah route instead of going through Aden. LCs not opened for Arabs or British were opened only for Somalilanders in the mid-1950s. When the revolution arrived, the two parts of the country were far apart economically and commercially; therefore, the idea was to put limitations on the north while spurring growth in the south.

When Somaliland Protectorate became independent in 1960, many well-educated men left government jobs and established private businesses. They were those who were signing deals with foreign countries. Men like Abdillahi Omaar, Jirde Hussein, Mohamed Talyanle, Ahmed Haji Abdillahi "Hashiish," Haji Abdillahi Ibrahim (Abu Site), Haji Jama Mohamed Ismail "Miyatayn," and Mohamed-Rashid were signing commercial agreements with foreign countries. None of that was encouraged by the British administration. In 1969, they had made good money and were ready to establish small industries when the birth of the revolution stopped them in their tracks. Some had already started the chalk and Pasta factories when Siad Barre nationalized everything and stripped them of their wealth. [1]

Should We Join the Arab League?

Whether Somalia should join the Arab League was Ahmed's idea. Many people believe it was Omar Arteh's idea because he was the foreign minister. This is how the idea came about. Ahmed Silanyo and other ministers touring a city called Wammo came across an island beyond Kismayo. The place was ideal for international investment. Ahmed, who had been thinking about ways to improve the country's economy, thought of encouraging Arab investment by joining the Arab League. When he returned to Mogadishu, Ahmed Silanyo prepared a report asking questions: Why should we join the Arab League? Why should we call ourselves Arabs? Answering his questions, he wrote: *to be an Arab does not mean skin color only, but it is the culture, religion, and geo-political location that compel us to support the Arabs. The value we share is more important than the culture we share with the African people.*

Ahmed's argument has had its weight, and his explanation convinced Siad Barre. He respected Ahmed and welcomed the idea entirely. Early in the military administration, Siad Barre appeared to have been respectful of knowledge. He was smart enough to learn what he did not know from those who did. He put knowledge before everything else, but the curse of tribalism derailed him later. Ahmed Silanyo affirms: *Frankly speaking, the revolution started well. Even when all ended in chaos, Siad Barre still respected him. He saw him as a man who spoke out of his knowledge and background. He was adamant about his beliefs.*

---

[1] It was a ploy to retard the northern progress of long objectivity, but many people did not understand it at the time.

Siad Barre supported Ahmed. He was his speechwriter. There wasn't a trip abroad Siad Barre took without Ahmed Silanyo. Ahmed, on the other hand, collaborated, frankly. Later, when things got worse, Ahmed criticized Siad Barre for issues like the Franco Valuta, livestock export, and development projects; life became very hard.

Ahmed Silanyo is Distinguished from other Ministers

Saeed Ali Giir was one of the young military officers from the north who took part in the 1961 coup d'état. In 1970, Saeed was head of information and translation in the president's office. Saeed, who knows Ahmed Silanyo very well, answers the question: What kind of minister was Ahmed Silanyo? *Weekly meetings used to be attended by the 25 SRC members and the government ministers, both civilian and military. At the time, there were some military ministers. That is where Ahmed Silanyo distinguished himself from other ministers: for example, a minister came with a project. The military administration was rash in acting on issues. Ahmed used to raise his hand and say in English. No, don't act on it unless a feasibility study is done. Don't just sign. Another example was: When the idea of school uniforms for the students in the entire country was introduced, and the Bal'ad factory was supposed to be where the uniform was produced, Ahmed jumped to his feet and announced, 'impossible to just say the words without a feasibility study.' We need to know whether the factory can cover all our materials required. That has to be studied before we decide. We need a feasibility study.*

Siad Barre called Ahmed "Mr. Feasibility Study." Anytime a new project was introduced, Siad Barre would look at Ahmed and say: 'what do you think, Mr. Feasibility Study?' Saeed Ali Giir remembers that two men shouldered the heaviest workload whenever Siad Barre left the country for duty. One was Ahmed Silanyo; the other was Osman Sayli, the director general of the ministry of foreign affairs. They wrote Siad Barre's speeches for his travels to the African Union and the Arab League because they were hard-working, eloquent, and politically informed. They took part in all his trips. Silanyo particularly hardly missed one of Siad Barre's trips abroad.

Saeed Ali Giir reiterates that Ahmed Silanyo was the brain behind the revolution's productive period. He added a lot to the ministries he ran, namely the ministries of planning and commerce. Notably, when he was the minister of planning, he put magnificent effort into building and equipping the self-help scheme.' It was the biggest project in building the country using people's energy. Although Siad Barre did not hear any advice, Ahmed Silanyo used to speak his mind and frankly gave his opinion. Saeed Ali Giir also mentioned that Siad Barre liked people to tell him the truth, but people feared him. Ahmed Silanyo stated his belief in the meeting regardless of who was there.

Whatever international newspapers wrote about Somalia used to be sent to the office of Information and translation headed by Saeed Ali Giir. English was left as it was, but Arabic ones were translated into Somali and distributed to the five political bureau members. One day, Siad Barre asked him to let him see it before distributing it. Then, he started giving orders on who should get copies and who should not. Other internal newspapers were meant only for crucial military personnel. Those newspapers were like tabloids meant to convey gossip. Ahmed Silanyo was not supposed to see them, but Saeed says he used to give him copies in secret. One day, Abdirahman Jama Barre, who at the time was the minister of foreign affairs and Siad Barre's brother, saw Saeed giving something to Silanyo, and he did not like that; when Saeed went to his office later to provide him with the newspaper, Abdirahman threw it at his face, showing his discontent with what he saw earlier.

Ahmed Silanyo was an eloquent, forthright, and intelligent young man early in the revolution, so Siad Barre brought him close. He was the longest reigning minister in Said Barre's administration, although everything turned into tribalism later.

The Meddling Italian Man and Ahmed Silanyo's Transfer to The Ministry of Commerce

While Ahmed was the minister of planning, there was a complaint about one Italian man who was one of the experts in the ministry. He interfered in the country's affairs a lot, but he had close ties to some of the highest officials in the revolution. When the complaint reached Ahmed Silanyo, he wrote an official letter to the Italian Embassy requesting the man to be replaced. He cited that he was interfering in the country's internal affairs and was unhappy with his work. Many high-ranking officials confronted that request, and the argument about the Italian man reached Siad Barre. When Siad Barre asked Ahmed to withdraw his request to the Italian Embassy, Ahmed refused and told him that the man was meddling with our internal affairs. He rejected Siad Barre's plea to withdraw his request. Ahmed told him bluntly, *no, as minister of planning, I asked the Italian Embassy to take him away from the ministry; I will not say otherwise. You, as the president, should write it and reverse my request.* Finally, Siad Barre let Ahmed have his way but transferred him from planning to the ministry of commerce. *That transfer was a warning,* says Ahmed's wife, Amina-Weris.

A discussion between Ismail Dualeh and Silanyo

Silanyo informs Ismail Dualeh's son Abdulaziz Ismail Dualeh: *Let me tell you about a story I had never told anyone. Your father was one of the people who used to encourage us in our youth. When the revolution started, the ministers in the civilian government were all jailed. I was the minister of commerce when your father was released from jail. One day, I was told Ismail Dualeh was waiting for me. I let him in. He told me he had just left the prison and did not save any money before going to jail. He came to ask me for help. I told him I would contact him however way it goes. When I left the office, I received a phone call from Siad Barre. He told me there was one from his clan who wanted a permit for some elephant tusks he had tried to export. 'He is driving me crazy.' I remember you mentioned that you issue permits periodically; please get him off my back and issue him a permit. I immediately conceived an idea. I remembered the older man, Ismail Dualeh, and how he needed my help when I did not have anything; I told Siad Barre: Comrade President, recently I issued a license to an older man, send me your clansman; I will ask him to buy the license from that older man. When the president agreed, I sent a message to Ismail Dualeh and told them I would issue him a license, and sell it to Siad Barre's clansman, who is eager to get a license. Ismail left me happy with 20,000 Somali Shillings out of that deal. That is how Allah helped me satisfy the older man.*

Fixing Trade Balance

When Ahmed was the minister of commerce, he pulled the country out of difficult situations. He created the balance of trade to balance exports and imports. In a healthy trade, exports should exceed imports. Abdirahman Talyanle, who worked in the ministry of commerce, told Ahmed that usually what we export is not equal to or close to what we import. Our hard currency is spent on food, medicine, and gasoline. The balance of trade at the time was near. The dollar was stable. The Somali shilling was equal to the foreign currency. Silanyo did extensive market research. At the time, he was ready to promote and develop salt, which could bring in a much foreign currency.

How was Ahmed Silanyo at Work?
A Colleague at the Ministry of Commerce Explains

Abdirahman Mohamed Talyanle, who worked with Ahmed Silanyo at the ministry of commerce, explains the kind of man he was: *He came to work at 7:00 in the morning, his door was always open, he did not have any bodyguards. He was a worker who did not have friends and colleagues who sat in his office drinking coffee. Anyone who wanted Silanyo in the office found him immediately, whether staff or the public. Whatever the inquiry, he either did it right away or informed me it was impossible. People did not return several times to the office to meet him. There was never any crowd in his office waiting for him. When people asked for money, he paid from his salary.*

He was a good leader who treated people impartially. He was hardworking, and good at his job. He worked for a military government that used to meet on Thursdays. He used to prepare his agenda before he went to the meeting though he used to say: 'I know they will not agree.' He was a firm negotiator who used to negotiate internationally on behalf of the government. Though Siad Barre did not like to study issues before concluding, Silanyo was an economist who always argued for feasibility studies before they decided, until he was named 'Mr. Feasibility Study.' Ahmed was neither a tribal man nor a corrupt man.

Ahmed Silanyo was not tribalistic.

Abdirahman Abdulqadir: *Ahmed Silanyo was a highly effective technocrat. He was a unique character in that he would not entertain tribal lineage; he was not a greedy man or a corrupt man.* He explained an incident between him and Abdi Hosh when petrol became scarce in the country. Abdi Hosh had the contract. Instead, Jirde Hussein managed to negotiate with a ship in the seas close to Somali waters and was able to bring petrol in three days. Silanyo gave a contract to Jirde Hussein because it was urgent, and the country could not wait. Abdi Hosh, a man from Siad Barre's lineage and an arrogant one, became angry and threw angry comments at Ahmed Silanyo, threatening him with revenge. Silanyo calmly waited for the moment Abdi Hosh would come to kill him. He never faced Silanyo. He was a man of integrity and did what was right for the country. He was an economist who insisted on studying issues before rash decisions were made.

Bashe Mohamed Farah describes Abdi Hosh as a vulgar man of extreme arrogance who would not shy away from insulting ministers who did not do what he wanted as a businessman. On one occasion, he slapped Mohamed

Sheikh Osman, the finance minister. He would go to vice president Mohamed Ali Samater's house and deride him in his own house calling him "tumaalkii faraha gaagaabnaa"--Insulting his tribe and lineage.

Transferring 'Asassey:
The Biggest Confrontation between Ahmed Silanyo and Siad Barre

Ahmed was transferred to the ministry of internal commerce. When he took office, he traveled through the entire country for research. After he finished his tour, he made a significant reshuffle of the ministry staff. 'Asassey (Cascassey), Siad Barre's half-brother, was the head of ENC in Kismayo. Ali Jama ran the Berbera ENC where all the imports for northern regions entered ----Ahmed Suleiman Dafleh watched over him, and both men were out of anybody's reach. Because Ahmed Suleiman Dafleh was not only one of the most powerful ministers but he was Siad Barre's son-in-law. Cascassey was Siad Barre's half-brother, and he watched over him. Ahmed Silanyo dared to touch them both. He transferred Cascassey to Baidoa and Ali Jama to Hudur. Cascassey refused the transfer and returned to Kismayo, and Ahmed Silanyo declined to keep him in Kismayo. Bashe Mohamed Farah remembers one night they were with Ahmed Silanyo when Cascassey came to him and said: *Are you insisting I should go to Baidoa? Yes, answered Ahmed. While I am in this ministry, you will remain in Baidoa. I know I will be transferred soon. When I leave, ask the new minister to take you back to Kismayo. Cascassey answered. Ok, Ok, but he did not go to Baidoa. Ten days after, Ahmed was transferred from the ministry of commerce, and Gen. Liqliqato replaced him. The first letter he drafted was the one reversing Ahmed Silanyo's transfer of Cascassay.*

Envoys of the Supreme Revolutionary Council

When Siad Barre heard about Cascassey's story, he sent the SRC members from the northern regions to speak to Silanyo. He asked them to tell Silanyo to stop transferring Cascassey. Ahmed Hassan Musa, Ismail Ali Abokor, Mohamed Ali Shire, and Ahmed Mohamoud Farah came to Ahmed Silanyo. He relayed that Siad Barre respected him and wanted him to stop that transfer. Ahmed insisted on the transfer, explaining that he was doing what was right. He was always adamant about what he considered correct and fair regardless of clan affiliation, whether Siad Barre's clan or another clan. In the case of Cascassey, even Vice President Mohamed Ali Samater approached Ahmed, reminding him:

don't you know the man? He is the president's brother. Ahmed responded: *I don't care about who he is. I am his boss in the ministry where he works. I am the one accountable for his actions here and the hereafter. If the president fires me tomorrow, I will not change my decision. He is going to Baidoa.*

Envoys of the Isaaq Clan's Senior Officers

The other envoys sent to stop Cascassey's transfer were the officers of the Isaaq clan working in the Lower Juba area. When the story of Cascassey's transfer became known, seventeen senior Isaaq officers, from the regional governor, an officer of the uniformed staff, and regional coordinators working in Kismayo signed a petition, asking Ahmed Silanyo to leave Cascassey in Kismayo. Mohamoud Adan Dheri, who worked at the sugar factory, brought the petition to Ahmed. The contents of the petition were the following: *Please do not transfer Cascassey because he protects us. He stops those who discriminate against us for our clan. He releases him from jail whenever they arrest one of us in the lower juba area. When Mohamoud Adan Dheri and Ahmed greeted each other, he handed him the petition. As he opened the envelope, he saw the list of names of people he knew well. Ahmed Asked: What has brought all these signatories together? Mohamoud answered, read you will know it. The petitioners plead with you to leave Cascassey in Kismayo for us. Mohamoud Adan Dheri told him: Do you know our problem when we are far away from the capital? We are mistreated. We face arbitrary false arrests. They treat us in any way they want.* Ahmed knew how they were treated. He listened quietly, picked up the phone, called Osman Jama (kallun), and asked him to meet him immediately. He asked him: *Please come by my office before you go to work. Come straight to my office.* Osman passed by Silanyo's office and greeted Mohamoud Aden Dheri: *How was the sugar factory? He asked."* Silanyo said: *Leave the factory alone and read this petition.* Osman read the list of names and the plea they submitted, saying: *Forget it! We could not reason with him. We tried.* Ahmed Silanyo tore the petition into pieces and threw it in the garbage. *Let Siad Barre fire me tomorrow. Cascassey is not going to remain in Kismayo. His transfer is final. So, let it be.*

Siad Bare Intercedes Personally For 'Asassey

When all the envoys failed, Siad Barre finally addressed Ahmed. He said: *I think you know my feelings about your decision to transfer Cascassey from Kismayo. I am asking you to let him stay.* Ahmed responded: *Mr. President, it won't be possible to transfer 52 directors and regional coordinators and leave only Cascassey as an exception.* Siad Barre *continued: Minister Ahmed: The work for ENC is small compared to the big job he has for me in the region. Ahmed answered: Ok, fine, Mr. President. In that case, I will assign the ENC responsibility to someone else and let him do your work in the region.* Siad Barre got very angry about Ahmed's adamant response to his discussion and told Ahmed: *Stop this. Don't let us fight over this. Ahmed told Siad Barre: Mr. President, this is a matter of principle. I went all over the country on foot and did extensive research. Reports were prepared. It is my true feeling. The transfer came from that research. I won't be able to explain why I should keep him in Kismayo. Your brother is one of 52 directors and regional coordinators who were part of that transfer, but remember, I did not take him far away. I placed him in Baidoa. When I transferred 52 of my employees, I couldn't keep your brother. Fire me from my job. I am not accepting your instructions. Siad Barre: Ok, go.* After that incident, Ahmed Silanyo was transferred from the ministry of commerce and was left without direct responsibility. [1] Ahmed and many other intellectuals who were the backbone of the revolution were placed in the party headquarters and Ahmed Silanyo was placed in the Economic Committee. Other men who were weeded out of the government were Kimiko, Weirah, Mohamed Adan Sheikh, Abdulaziz Nur Hersi, Silanyo, and Omar Arteh Ghalib. They were the men who were the revolution's happy face in Siad Barre's honeymoon period.

In 1977, Siad Barre again assigned Ahmed Silanyo, the minister of internal and external commerce combined into one. He held that position until 1980. Siad Barre was proud of Silanyo and used to admire him for his vision, service, and creativity. Ahmed was a hard-working intellectual who did his work and knew it, and had confidence in himself and his ability.

Defending the Rights of the Northern Regions

The military administration worked well at first, but later it became retarded. It has become increasingly tribal and regionally oriented. The northern region was collectively isolated from its right to development. Since Ahmed Silanyo was at the forefront of growth in the country, he treated them all fairly, and he wanted this fairness from everyone who worked with him. However, when he realized the military administration was isolating the north, Ahmed Silanyo was the first minister to confront the administration. He started defending the rights of the north. He approached issues of the north boldly. Many men who saw precisely what Ahmed Silanyo witnessed could not articulate their arguments as directly as Ahmed Silanyo.

---

(1) He was left without direct responsibility but was not arrested or fired

Osman Sayli' speaking of that, explains: *When we were in Mogadishu, He fought for the rights of the northern regions. In all the positions he held, he gave the north its right. That has created friction between him and Siad Barre. He was the only minister who rejected what was not just or right without fear of repercussion.* One of the many disagreements between Ahmed and Siad Barre included the cement factory. Siad Barre wanted the cement factory to be built in Mogadishu! And the raw material was to be transported from Berbera. Ahmed Silanyo and Omar Arteh Ghalib were the two men who rejected the thought, and they won. Another incident was the Berbera Port Extension. Money earmarked for its extension was to be transferred to Merka and the road between Burao and Berbera. The World Bank projects for Togwajaleh and the northwestern regions were also the ones Ahmed Silanyo fought very hard for. Ahmed Silanyo was an intellectual who fought for the north as a principle. He never wasted his time on tribal issues. His fight for the north was region-wide, not trivial and clannish.

In the end, when the working relationship between them became terse and tense, Siad Barre did not approach him directly but used envoys to convince Ahmed what he wanted. He did not want to hear Ahmed Silanyo's negative answers now, which could result in his firing. Therefore, instead of hearing the "no" directly from him, he preferred someone else to hear it.

Ahmed Silanyo speaking of his tense relationship with Siad Barre in later years, explains: *Those who were there knew it, but the young generation does not know why my relationship with Siad Barre deteriorated. It began with the cement factory in Berbera, where the raw material was to be taken out of Berbera and transported to support a factory in Mogadishu. I asked him: Are you planning to transport Berbera's hard rocks to build Mogadishu? Siad Barre argued that most of the population lived in Mogadishu, and the consumption was more significant in the south, so the rocks must be moved to the south. I was the man who fought very hard for that not to happen.* [1] *The Berbera port extension was another project whose money was to be used to build a port in the south.*

The time Ahmed Silanyo led the ministry of commerce was the period when the most complex arguments occurred between him and Siad Barre. At that time, Ahmed Silanyo worked hard to lift the burden of commerce in the north. The livestock exporters who suffered most welcomed what Ahmed Silanyo was trying to do for the north.

---

(1) Video about Ahmed Silanyo's life

As things Deteriorated

When Ahmed was the minister of commerce, he allowed the Franco-Valuta[1] system to support the north. The system permitted livestock exporters and workers in the Gulf to use their hard currency to buy essential goods with their money instead of remitting through the bank. Ahmed allowed the system though Siad Barre was against the idea. When Siad Barre stopped the Franco Valuta, the livestock exporters complained to Ahmed. Ahmed organized them and brought them to Mogadishu, so they could discuss their problem while at the same time allowing them to continue with the Franco Valuta. For anyone else, Siad Barre would have accused him of a coup d'état, but with Ahmed, he minimized the confrontation. However, what the businesspeople wanted and Ahmed supported did not happen. Siad Barre discontinued the freedom of businesses and concluded that ENC would bring all goods and the businesses had to buy from it. Ahmed Silanyo tried to lift the burden of his people in any way he could.

Southern Businesses Want to Patronize Northern Businessmen

When Siad Barre stopped the Franco Valuta, some southern businessmen came to Ahmed Silanyo and said: *We can see Siad Barre stopped the Franco Valuta in the north. Allow us because we can get Siad Barre's permission and help the northern businesses.* They also offered Ahmed Silanyo millions of dollars to expedite that request. Outraged by the suggestion, Ahmed told them: *Do you want to be patrons for the northern businesses?* Yes, they said. Ahmed told them: *that would never happen. A Somali businessperson won't become a patron for another Somali businessman in his own country!* Ahmed rejected their request for patronage and their offer of money.

Burao-Berbera Road

Ahmed Hassan Musa, the minister of public works, wrote a proposal to build the Burao-Berbera Road to the UAE. Sheikh Zayed Al Nahyan accepted the proposal. Ahmed Silanyo asked Ahmed Hassan Musa to request UAE to handle

---

(1) Franco Valuta was a system allowing livestock exporters and Gulf workers to buy their hard currency with essential commodities they needed to sell it inside the country instead of sending it through the bank

the contract because if that project's money were brought to Somalia, Siad Barre would misuse it. Sheikh Zayed did that and awarded the contract to an Italian construction company. Siad Barre found out about the project well underway. Before that project, travel between Burao, Berbera, and Sheikh's narrow strip was challenging. It was a dangerous road that claimed so many lives. Burao-Berbera Road and the expansion of the Sheikh strip were serious development for northern regions. A modern road between these two cities was built. The dangerous narrow strip in Sheikh was expanded, and the credit belongs to the men who fought hard for the northern regions to receive their portion of the development.

Siad Barre Presides a Debate among Cabinet Ministers over the Cement Factory

Confrontations between Ahmed Silanyo and Siad Barre were many. Where the cement factory was going to be built was one of them. Ahmed Silanyo negotiated with a French company to make the cement factory in Berbera simply because the cement rocks are abundant around Berbera. Transporting it would have been easy for export because the port was also very close. Some wanted the factory in Mogadishu, where they argued that most of the population lived. Others agreed that since Berbera has the raw material and the port is close for exporting overseas and easy access for local consumption; it should be built in Berbera. Siad Barre took the discussion and suggested it should be built in Mogadishu because it is the capital city. Everything the factory produces will be consumed here in Mogadishu. Ahmed Silanyo got up and said sarcastically, *Mr. President, I agree a cement factory be built in Mogadishu. I also agree with you, Mr. President, that all the cement mountains from the north will be transported to Mogadishu too!* That sarcastic remark annoyed Siad Bare, and he adjourned the meeting.

Siad Barre sent Farah Harbi as His Final Emissary.

The tense relationship between Ahmed Silanyo and Siad Barre brought Siad to complain to Farah Harbi, a man of Ahmed Silanyo's ancestry, who was among the businesspeople from the north affected by the Franco Valuta. He, too, was an outspoken man who was arrested many times. Siad Barre described Ahmed Silanyo as a nationalist, hardworking man who did not hide his opinion but had been patient with him. He told Farah Harbi he would arrest him if he did not change his attitude. Amina-Weris remembering the meeting between Farah Harbi and Ahmed Silanyo, explains: In *the backyard of our house was a swing for the kids. One evening while she and Ahmed were sitting in the swing and it was getting dark walked through the door with a man she could not recognize. Ahmed immediately recognized him as Farah Harbi. He was a man who was thrown in jail many times and was immensely harassed, so he was careful. There was much fear, and things were not good. Farah asked Ahmed to come out. Ahmed got up and went to the door. They left the house. Ahmed did not come back for a while. He got into Farah Harbi's car to talk. When Ahmed did not come back for a while, she started worrying. It was a time of intense frustration, and the famous statement was, so and so, was arrested. Ahmed came back, and she asked him where he had gone. He told her he had gone for a ride with Farah Harbi. That was the only way people could talk. Ahmed and Amina walked around the house while Ahmed told her Farah Harbi informed him that Siad Barre had complained to him. He sent Farah Harbi to control him, or he was going to arrest him. So, Farah Harbi's request was to stop irritating the president. He told Ahmed: 'I don't want him to put you in jail because you are more beneficial for us outside prison. Siad Barre is a thoughtless brute. He does not care about anyone or anything. Farah Harbi narrated his story to Ahmed that, he too, was jailed several times in his youth because of his actions during independence. Ahmed told him, you have every right to speak with me after Siad Barre called you. Our society is tribal-oriented, and Siad Bare is right to complain to you. Still, the generation of my age and the following younger generations of your children are the ones who have now taken responsibility. I heard about your struggles before and I hear them from you directly. Therefore, it is our time to continue the struggle. I will not ask you to confront Siad Barre now, but I will do that instead. It is our turn to go to prison. You have been jailed for your beliefs and are alive and out of jail. We can be arrested or even killed, but it is our cause, not yours. You have done your share. It would be unfortunate if I fail in my fight to stop the cruel treatment of my people, but I won't stop. Every day our elders and intellectuals in Hargeisa and Burao are arrested and harassed. I won't stop fighting that. I understand you don't want us to go through what you went through but don't worry, if we don't find courage from what your generation went through, how could the generation behind me find the courage to fight for their rights? Finally, Ahmed convinced Farah and also advised him: Leave Mogadishu and go back to Hargeisa so that you might not look like a failure with Siad Barre's emissary.*

Ahmed Silanyo's Adamant Refusal to Falsify a Delegation's Report

Once Ahmed was part of a delegation overseas. The trip was not successful. They met with a cold reception in the countries they visited. When they returned, Ahmed was to write the report. He wrote a report detailing exactly how they were treated. His colleagues could not believe his honesty and asked Ahmed to falsify the information. Ahmed refused and asked them to do it themselves. He told them he could only write the truth about what happened and nothing else. His colleagues took over and falsified the report.

Ahmed Silanyo Advises Siad Barre not to Exaggerate the Population Count for Increased Foreign Aid

One day in the cabinet meeting, Siad Barre suggested the government officially exaggerate the world Somali population as 12 million. Ahmed Silanyo immediately advised the president against it: *we should not do that; it will cause much harm*. Siad Barre argued why not explained: *Foreign aid is based on the population count and we could get more assistance if we say that*. Ahmed advised him, that *it would not increase our foreign aid because we would have to provide evidence from school enrollments and hospital births and admissions so the idea would hurt more than help us*.

Although Ahmed was an effective economist and focused more on economic issues in a calm and calculating manner, later on, he discussed tribal evils when the revolution lost track and used tribalism as a weapon. He warned the country would dissipate if the government did not change its attitude toward tribalism.

A Governor's Tale

When Ahmed Silanyo was the minister of commerce, Siad Barre rejected the commercial plan he submitted and accepted a plan proposed by Abdirahman Jama Barre, his cousin and the minister of foreign affairs. One day a governor came to his office and asked him to discuss his plan. Ahmed Silanyo told him bluntly: Go *ask Afweyne, using Siad Barre's nickname--that was never uttered in public. The governor expresses his shock: 'I ran out of Silanyo's office praying to Allah no one heard the statement and told others, my head ached for a few days, wondering all the time when will Siad Barre's forces throw me in jail. I had never heard it mentioned inside a government office.*

Silanyo's Stand When the Regime Harassed the Warsengali Clan

Mohamoud Saeed Ga'ammey, a man from the warsengeli clan who used to be one of Siad Barre's cabinet ministers, a colleague of Ahmed Silanyo and later the minister of environment for Somaliland speaks about an incident during that time. He says: *When Ahmed Silanyo was the minister of commerce, the revolution's sword was on the tribe of Warsengeli. On those days, it was General Qorsheel from that clan, and Siad Barre's vice president was arrested. His clan members were harassed. Three men from that clan named Ali Madar, Ali Hassan, and Tawal worked in the ministry of commerce. Ahmed Silanyo transferred all three to commercial councilors overseas so they could escape from Siad Barre's harassment. Mohamoud saw that step as courageous not everyone could take. Times were tough and nobody could act that boldly. Mohamoud confirms that Ahmed Silanyo was intellectually distinguished from other ministers in fairness, impartiality, leadership, and building relationships.*

Appoint Silanyo as Prime Minister to Placate the Northern Region Turmoil: Advised a few Southern Intellectuals

Many Somali people saw the grim future of the country if Siad Barre did not change his governing method. At the beginning of the 1980s, there was a big uproar in the north that Siad Barre's administration wanted to appease by force, economic sanctions, imprisonment, and execution. The suggestion of the intellectuals to create a powerful executive prime minister from the northern regions, fell on deaf ears. They specifically asked for Ahmed Silanyo. While this debate was going on, Siad Barre announced the revival of the revolution. The intellectuals asked him. *Mr. President, if the revolution is reinvigorating appointing a prime minister should be done quickly.* He wondered whom he should appoint. They decided not to mention names, but they gave him the criteria for selection. Here is how they described: *He should be an intellectual who had worked with the revolution. He should have a clear understanding of how it works and its philosophy; he should be someone western countries can respect, a man who is outspoken and can articulate his arguments well, a man who can be appreciated by north and south Somalia alike.* He asked them to name whoever was in their minds. They refused to name any names because he was a jealous man and was likely to misinterpret that idea. When Siad Barre asked again, Mohamed Samater Ga'alliye announced that Mr. President is Silanyo. Siad Barre told them to go away. You want to overthrow the revolution, he said. He fired all of them.

Beginning of the 1980s and the Intensification of the Northern Revolt

In the 1980, the uprising of the northern regions intensified. Many people advised the regime to change the direction the country was heading and lessen the burden put on the people of the regions of the north, especially the Isaaq clan. Those advising Siad Barre to control the Isaaq clan with an iron fist gained his support.

The Somali people of the north and south identified themselves with the languages of English and Italian. Ahmed Silanyo and Ibrahim Meygag Samater represented English-speaking, while Mohamed Aden Sheikh and Mohamed Yusuf Weirah represented Italian speaking. Though they were friends, their argument always advocated that since most Somalis speak Italian and live in the south, they should be leading the nation, while the northern region should follow and obey. That debate was one of the things that had, in the end, exasperated the north uprising. Nevertheless, the Italian-speaking intellectuals were not happy with the inhumane treatment of the north. As Amina-Weris relays, some ministers like Ga'alliye, Weirah and, Mohamed Aden Sheikh from the south visited Ahmed. They expressed their discontent with the regime's harsh treatment of the north, suggesting they should work together to stop. The advice they gave to alleviate the suffering was to appoint a prime minister from the Isaaq clan and Ahmed Silanyo to be the one. The regime did not accept any of the advice offered by the intellectuals and continued on the path to destruction. In the end, the fiery steps taken by the military administration caused not only the north to collapse but also the entire country to crumble.

Adan-Weyne is to be arrested for Visiting Silanyo at the Hospital

Mohamoud Saeed explains: *In 1982, Ahmed Silanyo concluded soberly to leave the country and join the Somali National Movement. Ahmed was admitted to a hospital in London when he left the country. A friend of Ahmed named Adan-Weyne, from the same clan as Mohamoud Saeed, visited him in the hospital. Then the Somali Embassy in London sent a message to the national security services for Adan-Weyne to be arrested upon returning to Somalia because he associated himself with Ahmed Silanyo. The man came back to Somalia with an arrest warrant waiting for him at the airport. When Mohamoud Saeed heard about it, he requested Siad Barre to hold off his arrest until he spoke with Adan-Weyne. Siad Barre agreed. He was taken to the president and explained that they were friends but not politically affiliated. That is how he escaped his crime of association with Ahmed Silanyo.*

CHAPTER THREE
SOMALI NATIONAL MOVEMENT (SNM)

FROM FEELING TO AN ALL-OUT WAR (1981-1991)

Formation of Somali National Movement and Siad Barre's Continuous Carnage

After the SNM was formed in 1981, Siad Barre stepped into continuous cruel measures in the north. To implement his scorched earth policy towards the north, he appointed Gen. Mohamed Hashi "Gani" as the commander of the 26th regiment placed in the north. That was in 1981. Gani soon became the cruel commander with the final say in everything. He immediately imposed a curfew on the population to justify the summary executions and robbery of people's property. The northern people nicknamed Diiriye (heater) to express how quickly, boldly and brutally he acted on his mandate and how his measures became a rude awakening for the northern people. They quickly understood the hatred Siad Barre's government had for them, which would have taken them longer to comprehend if Gani had not come with his callous manifestations and had he not intensified the regime's violence into a boiling point.

In December 1981 and the beginning of January, the young northern intellectual group, UFFO (in Somali, the breeze before the rain), was arrested. Their judgment of death and life imprisonment handed down instantly created the first violent confrontation. On January 27, 1982, Gani shot Col. Abdillahi Haji Saeed, the Dharkeyn- Geenyo regiment commander without accusing him of anything or putting him on trial. He and another officer were killed. Even though the Isaaq clan was organizing, incidents like the violent death of Abdillahi Haji Saeed sent shockwaves across the military officers from the Isaaq clan. It was a ferocious message that had intensified the war they were organizing. On the 2nd of February, five days after the brutal killing of Abdillahi Haji Saeed and the other officer, the first four military officers, Adan Sheikh Mohamed (Shiine), Ahmed Dahir Nur (Dhagah), Mohamed Kahin Ahmed and Aden Suleiman Farah crossed the border into Ethiopia to anchor the armed struggle. Shortly afterward, the battalion commanded by Mohamed-Ali joined the opposition and SNM used his battalion's barracks as the temporary headquarters for SNM. Within February, the SNM group in London moved to Ethiopia and opened its center there.

From 21-23 February, a massive demonstration organized by teachers, students and the general public shook the nation. Demonstrators outraged by the judgment threw stones at the repressive military officers. Forty-three people, primarily students, lost their lives on that day. That incident caused the first massive anti-government protests in 13 years. The famous poet Mohamed Ibrahim Warsame "Hadrawi," living in Mogadishu at the time created his eminent poem "Hargeisa has awakened," a dissenter's message detailing the regime's cruelty and encouraging the fearless youth. Mohamed Ibrahim Warsame Hadrawi, Mohamed Hashi Dhama' "Gaariye" (college professors and poets), and many youths crossed the border in May of 1982.

The Only Road Open is an Armed Struggle

People had realized the only path open was that of an armed struggle. Ahmed Mohamed Mohamoud Silanyo says: *On that day when the youth were faced with guns and tanks, was the day we asked ourselves the question, "Was there an alternative to war? Should we remain patient anymore? The answers were no, which was the reality check for anyone thinking otherwise.*

On March 15, 1982, Ahmed Silanyo left the country and became the most valuable minister in Siad Barre's administration who left the country. In June 1982, some military officers, ministers, and senior staff were arrested. These were:

Ismail Ali Abokor

Omar Arteh Ghalib

Mohamed Aden Sheikh

Omar Haji Masalle

Mohamed Yusuf Weirah

Osman Mohamed Jelle

Warsame Ali Farah (he died in Jail when he was denied access to medical treatment).

The Harsh Treatment of the North Intensified and Isaaq Elders Sent A Letter to Siad Barre. Siad Barre treated the Isaaq clan in the north with brutal force. It was naked aggression and terrorism in the government cloak. Killing, lynching, raping women, and robbery of personal possessions started as standard practice. On March 30, 1983, 21 Isaaq elders warned Siad Barre of his behavior. They submitted a note to Siad Barre detailing the misuse of power. They reminded him about their struggle for independence, how the Somali Unity came about and inquired about the whereabouts of more than 3 million dollars worth of commercial assets his administration seized. They requested the following, which fell into a vacuum:

a) Leadership to be equal for all

b) Justice and fairness for all

c) Management to be distributed equally

d) Wealth to be shared equally. Siad Barre ignored all of that.

People's Feeling before the Establishment of SNM

Ahmed Silanyo, in an interview, speaks about when SNM started and when he joined SNM: *No one can say when SNM first started. Struggles like this are a stream of consciousness since the beginning of time. They are flowing of interconnected thoughts through which each incident gives birth to another. We will begin in 1960 when we became independent and hastily united with Somalia. Because we desired to create greater Somali unity, we gave up our independence without proper negotiations or conditions. Our love for greater Somalia blinded us and blurred the reality of what it means to submit unconditionally. Though some of our leaders suggested waiting for a while until we recovered from the euphoria, others were overly enthusiastic as the population and wanted the immediate union. We soon realized that the reality was not as we thought, and different feelings of discontent started. The feeling of something going awry was not limited to politicians; our military tried a coup to secede from the union soon after. The feeling simmered and caused our population to say "NO" to the first constitution in 1961. None of that was an active rebellion but a stream of feelings that pinched our consciousness of earlier jubilation.*

The revolution did a lot for the people and country at first, but it lost track, resorted to a clannish mentality and treated the north like an enemy. That feeling again ran through the nerves of the northern people, whether inside or outside the country. It might have been evident to the people of the north but ever since we realized the misstep of the revolution, we had been nurturing that feeling. Though it was not named SNM, it was a deep undercurrent rumbling, a sense of supporting the north and its rights. We were honest about doing our work, but we were also in an internal conflict with the government. The committees I headed fighting for northern projects were part of our internal struggle. That feeling of discontent soaked and permeated. Therefore, SNM was not a movement of a few people's vision. It was a widespread feeling uniting us, locally, internationally, and among government workers. When the SNM movement was announced in 1981, those in the country held a meeting to analyze the new development. The strongest feeling came from the people in the Arab countries, especially those in Saudi Arabia and those of us in the country. We were united. There were also small pockets of dissidents in Burao, Hargeisa, and Mogadishu all of them connected.

Some wanted to create a movement called Isxaaqia because the people harassed the most were from that clan. Still, some of us advised against that name because we felt we were fighting for the rights of the entire population of the north and that name could become an obstacle to the goodwill of the cause. So, we chose a name of the wider context.

When the Somali National Movement was finally established on 6 April 1981, Ahmed Jimale Guled was elected the chairman; Ahmed Ismail Abdi (Dukhsi) was the secretary general, and eight other members were also elected. Those of us in the country were busy ensuring that it grew to its potential. The announcement was going to intensify Siad Barre's hatred. Therefore, organizing the military commanders, and establishing Ethiopia as the center for emergencies was prime responsibility for those of us inside the country. Those containing the movement outside the country did not want Ethiopia to be a center. They remembered the long-held hostility between Somalia and Ethiopia. Siad Barre planned to reach a peace agreement with Ethiopia and created a committee to advise him on that. Ahmed Silanyo was on that committee. The committee's purpose was to advise Siad Barre to stop fighting with his neighbors and create a way for the Somalis in those countries to assimilate and get their rights as citizens. It has already been evident that wars only kill. Siad Barre had other ideas.

Prelude to SNM Formation

Siad Barre put his interest before any other. When he realized the SNM movement's growing momentum and the SSDF movement was already stationed in Ethiopia, he wanted to negotiate peace deals with all the countries hostile to Somalia. He formed a committee to advise him on that in 1982. Ahmed Silanyo explaining Siad Barre's intention says: *Of course, he intended to sign a peace deal with Ethiopia and slam the doors shut on SNM and other movements.*

When we returned from the war of 1977/8, Siad Barre formed a committee and asked them to advise on the missing lands of Somalis. Only Ahmed Silanyo and Ali Khalif Galaydh were from the north. The rest were from the south. After the committee discussed the waste of life and resources in the wars and that we gain nothing from them, they advised him *to reach peace agreements with Ethiopia and Kenya so that the Somalis in those areas could have equal sharing of health and education from those countries. Since we gained nothing from engaging in wars, we should focus on how the Somalis in those areas could assimilate and have freedom for their religion and values. At that point, I got a glimpse of what Siad Barre was planning; He wanted to shake hands with Ethiopia to displace SNM. After Ahmed Silanyo informed his internal group of Siad Barre's plans, they discussed them with the group in London. They reached an agreement for the SNM movement to go to Ethiopia immediately. Our London members were hesitant and worried about Somalia's hostile relationship with Ethiopia. Of course, they were unaware of what Siad Barre was cooking up at home. That is when we (the internal group) decided to send military commanders from Mogadishu to Ethiopia to hasten the London group's move. Aden Sheikh Mohamed (Shine), Ahmed Dahir (Dhagah), Mohamed Kahin Ahmed and Aden Suleiman Farah were the first batch of officers we asked to reach Ethiopia before Siad Barre's envoys get there. I was the one bringing in the details of Siad Barre's plans because I was part of his committee and knew everything. When our commanders reached Ethiopia, the London group had no choice but to join them. Therefore, from its inception until its maturity, I was part of the movement and struggle. We agreed to stage war with Siad Barre and strengthen the movement's leadership, but two other issues were still ambiguous: a) the kind of movement, and the location of its HQ were not entirely clear at first. The London group members were still suspicious of Ethiopia.*

Ahmed Silanyo took a clear stand on both issues. First, in Saudi Arabia where people resolved the movement to be one limited to the Isaaq clan, Ahmed Silanyo advised against any reductive ideas of the movement's internal and international potential. He urged them on the benefits of an all-encompassing national movement that could bring all Somalis together regardless of clan. The second issue of whether Ethiopia should be a center for the movement, people were easily convinced when he informed them of Siad Barre's plans for a peace deal with Ethiopia.

Ahmed Silanyo Deserts Siad Barre's Administration after Nearly Twenty Years

At the beginning of 1982, Siad Barre went to America for an official visit. Ahmed was to be part of the delegation. He prepared his speeches and the plan for the visit. He was registered as a vital member of the delegation. By that time, Siad Barre lost all patience. The last moments before departure, Ahmed was informed he was not part of the delegation and was not traveling with Siad Barre to America. It was Siad Barre's decision. Ahmed was the chairman of the national economic commission. When Siad Barre left for America, the Arab League ministers of commerce conference took place in Saudi Arabia. Ahmed Silanyo prepared all the needed documents for that meeting. In Siad Barre's absence, Mohamed Ali Samater acted as the president and he and Ahmed Silanyo were good friends. He convinced Mohamed Ali Samater to let him attend that conference since he was the one who knew all the details and prepared for it. Mohamed Ali Samater agreed and let him go. Ahmed was planning to depart for good. He began to take his family outside the country. Amina-Weris explaining the situation at the time, says: *Harassment of the north intensifying, and northern ministers not able to help caused Ahmed many sleepless nights and deep disappointment. He is a kind man and he has become emotional. It had become an all-involved struggle. Internal group members like Ismail Ali Abokor and Jirde Hussein were financing the struggle. Ahmed Silanyo informed of his intent to depart to only three people. Ali Jirde, Suleiman Mohamoud Aden and Aden Abdi Hussein. He requested a visit visa for his family from the British Embassy and his family left the country on March 13, 1982. After he made sure of his family's departure, he and a heavy delegation left for Saudi Arabia. At the end of the conference, Ahmed prepared his reports and handed them over to his delegation telling them he was going on a short leave. He traveled through Jeddah.*

Oh, Siad Barre! Abdullah Shihiri Left You and Your Demise is Imminent'

Ahmed Silanyo's departure from the Siad Barre administration left a painful void in his administration because he knew of Ahmed Silanyo's ability to unite different people from different clans, different regions, and different ideologies, all of them with respect. He was equaled to the most important man of Sayyid Mohamed Abdulle Hassan who unveiled his intentions and walked away from him in the end.

When he first came to power, Siad Barre revived the legacy of Sayyid Mohamed Abdulle Hassan and his Daraawiish. He spent much money building a beautiful monument, resurrecting his struggle and resurrecting the man in his image. It was a bold assertion of tribal lineage with Mohamed Abdulla Hassan, who considered himself a man of the same caliber. He saw himself as a man who could carry on all the different faces of the Daraawiish wars. Interestingly there are some parallels in the destinies of the two men. First both Siad Barre and Mohamed Abdulla Hassan moved the people with slogans. Key positions were appointed on merit but shortly after, both reverted to dictators who appointed on nepotism and tribal affiliation; both were called Mohamed; both ruled for twenty years; and both led the country they were claiming to rescue into the path of destruction. The struggle of Mohamed Abdulla Hassan started soon after the worst famine in Somaliland called Haramacune. It was a tough time when one-third of the population in the Somaliland protectorate died as a result. [1]

Many men who could see Siad Barre's imitation of Sayyid Mohamed Abdulla Hassan and the similarities of their actions saw the desertion of Ahmed Silanyo reminiscent of that of Abdulla Shihiri. It was time to leave his administration; noting it was not worth staying once Abdulla Shihiri left and became a dissident. Abdulla Shihiri was the foreign minister of the Daraawiish army and an uncle of Ahmed Silanyo. He was in Aden Colony buying weapons for the struggle when Sayyid Mohamed Abdulla Hassan was told he deserted the Daraawiish. Before he checked on the facts, he went straight to the family home in the Daraawiish barracks and killed his young sons, creating a poem on the spot, informing their father: You won't see your sons again my friend the son of Shihiri. From there on Abdulla Shihiri turned against Sayyid's leadership. He was the man who stripped him of his fake cloak and exposed his movement as unjust and un-Islamic. That has caused Sayyid Mohamed Abdulla Hassan to lose the blessing of his Sheikh Mohamed Salah who threw him out of the Salihiya Sect - the religious sect he followed. That was also the beginning of the end of Sayyid Mohamed Abdulla Hassan and his legacy.

---

(1) (Jardin) Many years later, no one can describe the effects of the aftermath of destruction of Somalia led by Siad Barre. It won't be an exaggeration if it is named the demolishing of Somalia

Ahmed Silanyo Meets with the Isaaq Clan in Jeddah in 1982

People welcomed his visit and organized a big hall in Jeddah to be the meeting place. They came from all parts of the kingdom. Generally, people in the Gulf States were well aware of the situation in Somalia and the harassment of the northern regions. Still, they needed his first-hand information since Ahmed Silanyo was in the government and a close witness of what was happening. He explained the new phase of the movement. The branches inside the country, Europe, America and especially the Gulf and the armed struggle centered in Ethiopia were all working together as one struggle. He warned against reductive explanations of the movement as some people expressed it. Many people outside the country described the movement as a clan war against Siad Barre. Since Siad Barre killed and harassed the Isaaq clan, some people saw it as their war. Ahmed explained that although Siad Barre's war is aimed and directed at the Isaaq clan, we should not fall into a tribalism trap and should avoid the movement being seen as a clan war. He explained that many people from other clans and regions were against the Siad Barre administration; therefore, the name of our movement should embrace all those who want to fight injustice for all Somalis and the entire northern regions.

Musa Ismail Dualeh, who was in the meetings, explains: *Ahmed Silanyo was an eloquent speaker; in one speech he convinced us to broaden our horizons and look at the struggle as the Somalis against Siad Barre administration.*

Many people suggested that Ahmed Silanyo to lead the struggle since he was the most vital minister to leave the administration after the UFFO group members were arrested. They saw him as the only one who could lead the movement. Ahmed Silanyo says: *When I left the country late in 1982, the movement was still fragile. The London group appointed Ahmed Jimale as the chairman and then changed him in three months. A meeting was going to be held in Nazareth in Ethiopia. When I was in Saudi Arabia, I met with Ahmed Jimale and Hassan Adan Wadaadiid. Many people who knew about my internal struggle and confrontations with Siad Barre asked me to lead the movement. Although I left Siad Barre's administration, my intention was not to join the SNM leadership immediately. The idea of going to Ethiopia and leading the movement was not in my mind yet.* Here is how Ahmed Silanyo explains the situation: *My response to that request was, no I won't take the reign of the movement; let's support the present leadership. I met with Ahmed Jimale in Jeddah. He was angry about how quickly they changed him, threatening revenge and insisting on staying. I advised Ahmed Jimale thus: 'Dear Ahmed, one day we build, one day we demolish, today we don't need more disagreements. Let it be.'*

Before he left Saudi Arabia, Ahmed Silanyo informed the people, that his children were very young, they were in a foreign land and he was not sure he could take frontline responsibility at that moment in time. But he promised to remain active in the struggle.

Role Model to Trust

All the young Somalis working for the struggle, whether they were in the Gulf, inside the country or on the war front saw Ahmed Silanyo as a role model worth imitating; and that is how Khadar Ali Haaf, who was then in Saudi Arabia described Ahmed Silanyo as an influencing leader. Saudi Arabia was the most important place for the movement, and it was the management center. They had built their movement, but they still lacked a charismatic leader. Ahmed Silanyo informed them that he would join the struggle, but he would not be the leader at that specific moment in time.

Ahmed Hashi Oday: Influential Leader to Emulate

For those inside the country, we liked his courage and how he stood up to the regime at the time. I knew him by name before I saw his face.

He was my role model. I admired him without knowing his face because I used to hear about his fierce fight for the north whether it was the cement factory or any other issue. I used to admire him. The first time I saw him was in 1992 when he came from Burao to mediate a conflict and I was part of the mediation committee from Hargeisa. I wanted Ahmed to talk with his friend Abdirahman Ahmed Ali to stop the hostility. When I noticed Ahmed averting from doing that, I approached him and told him: you were my role model without seeing you. You have been frank with Siad Barre who was able to put you in Jail. I can't understand why you are hesitant to talk with Abdirahman Ahmed Ali whom you have nominated as the chairman. Please be fair and mediate.

Abdirahman Osman Alin: We Supported Him for His Prior Record

When he was nominated for the highest position of SNM leadership in 1984 was the first time I saw him in person. I was a logistics officer in the center regiment. SNM was divided into three regiments so I was the commander of the central. That was the first time I saw him and Ibrahim Meygag in person, but I have heard about them. I was a delegate at the meeting. When we heard Ahmed Silanyo was a candidate, my colleagues and I supported him blindly because we had heard stories about him that he was a strong man whose ministry did not interfere and that he was the only minister who pushed back on Siad Barre.

Abdirahman Abdulqadir's Encounter with Silanyo in London

I saw Silanyo in London and criticized him as Siad Barre's supporter because he was the longest-reigning minister in his administration. He asked me, "how do people see me" when I told him they like him and respect him, he asked again: "how is that possible if I was his supporter." Now in hindsight, I think I was wrong, and my criticism was unfair because I could not imagine the circumstances under which he worked.

Khader Ali Haaf: Transformational Leader to Follow

Ahmed gave a lot to his people and deserved to be a leader. He was a good leader. I was the cashier and kept the most significant money for the movement. Ahmed never asked me for 100 dollars cash. He never asked to pay for his hotel expenses, or a ticket to visit his family. He used to say, "I don't want the public money. I was the man closest to him. We used to maintain the families of some other officers in the movement in Cairo. The last time I saw him, we were in Balligubaleh, when we entered the country; I used to visit him and had breakfast with him. May Allah give him long life and good health; he had a long history with his people and country. He waited patiently for his chance in politics and always conceded for others. The concession in Baligubadleh was incredible. It has never happened a leader of a movement who concedes for others at the imminence of winning the struggle. It had not happened before Somaliland, and Ahmed led his people to that thinking. SNM members agreed on the leader of the country to be chosen by the people. Ahmed believed that the leader would be the man chosen by the people.

At the time of disarming the paramilitaries of SNM and Mohamed Haji Ibrahim Egal was nominated as president in Borama, he said in his speech: 'Standing by me is Ahmed Mohamed Mohamoud Silanyo who is more worthy of leading this country than me.' Ahmed responded to this remark: 'Our agenda was people's choice president to lead the country and the chosen leader now was Mohamed Haji Ibrahim Egal.' One can see Ahmed Silanyo's courage and dignity. Opposing that was at the time of Dahir Riyale Kahin when Ahmed Silanyo conceded the election for 80 votes. He never asked for a recount or anything. He just accepted the outcome for the love of the country. It took him a long time to become a president and although he came to the presidency tired, his administration did a lot. Khader says, *for me Ahmed is still a role model to follow. I have never entered politics, but I was a student of Ahmed. My generation and I learned a lot from him. Somaliland learned a lot from him.*

It was unforgettable how everyone enjoyed his speeches during the struggle. When he was in Diridhaba the people who worked with him were young and the ones who lost their land and needed guidance the most.

The Cry of Abdillahi Abdi Faroole, Dhakar, Idris Osman Guray, and Mohamed Jama Nur (Blacki)

Amina-Weris narrating Ahmed's departure from Somalia and his trip to Jeddah explains: *It had always been Ahmed's intention to support and work with the SNM movement but to take the reigns of responsibility was not his intention. I was young and my children were very young. Still, the group he met in Jeddah picked him to lead the movement because they believed that [he was the right leader]. But, by the time he reached London, he was between decisions. After all, he was aware of the hard times of his people and how they were treated. For a period of six weeks, he remained silent. Shortly after he arrived in London, some prominent supporters of the movement in East Africa sent him an SOS message. Idris Osman Guray, Mohamed Jama Nur (Blacki) and Abdillahi Abdi Faroole (Dhakar) who were the backbone of the movement in East Africa learned about the Somali Ambassador's intention to deport them to Mogadishu. They did not have travelling documents if they were to escape the ambassador's trap. They sent him an SOS message to find them passports. Ahmed contacted Osman Sayli', the Somali ambassador in Turkey and asked for three passports as soon as possible on DHL. Osman responded: That was not possible because there was an unreliable counselor who would not do it. Ahmed then contacted Omar Abdirahman (Ilay), the counselor at the Somali embassy in Sweden. The ambassador was Abdillahi Isse. When asked Omar for three passports urgently, he asked: how urgent? Ahmed responded: I needed them yesterday. Omar promised to send them by the next day DHL if Ahmed sent their names. The passports came by DHL the next morning and Ahmed sent them to Nairobi through DHL the same day. Amina-Weris says: that incident inflamed Ahmed even more. He could not understand the violation of human rights in that brutal manner.*

Ahmed Silanyo Explains the Definition of a "Dictator"

Ahmed Silanyo is naturally an animated person. He communicates well with young and old people of different backgrounds and ideologies. For the Isaaq individuals who did not welcome his arrival accusing him of serving Siad Barre's administration for twelve years, Ahmed Silanyo proved them wrong. They did not know the reality of the struggle because the struggle began at home inside the country. The essence of SNM started at home. Besides, everyone knew his fight for the north and his constant confrontation with Siad Barre. For those who accused Ahmed Silanyo of instead criticizing the regime from London, why didn't he change things from within since he worked with that administration, his argument was: *Do you understand the definition of a "dictator." If you look it up in the dictionary, it simply means 'an individual who does not listen to anyone," and you are asking the wrong question of why I didn't advise him. If he had listened to others there would not have been a problem. Nevertheless, I was the only cabinet minister who stood up to him and argued with him.*

Somali Embassies in London and Washington Spying on Silanyo's Intentions

When Ahmed Silanyo's family came to London, Abdillahi Omaar gave them a helping hand. They rented a small apartment in London near the Somali Embassy. At the time Mohamed Jama (MJ) was the ambassador. When Ahmed arrived, he did not announce his intentions for two months. People started rumors about his desertion from the regime and wondered whether he was going back.

MJ started worrying because he was asked to report Ahmed Silanyo's intentions. He visited Ahmed at his house and asked permission to give his number to Siad Barre. He requested Ahmed to answer the phone when he called. Ahmed agreed to talk to him if he called and allowed him to give him his number. Again, ambassador MJ visited Ahmed at his house and told him Siad Barre had called, and they had a conversation. He promised to give you the position in FAO that you were selected for, so he wants you to go back and claim your position. Ahmed Silanyo responded: *All right!* MJ called Ahmed every night and gave him messages that the older man was asking when he was returning. Ahmed without disclosing his intentions responded: *Tell the older man, that I am on holiday.* One day MJ visited Ahmed and informed him that Siad Barre asked him to visit the embassy so that he could talk to him about the FAO position. It was a ploy to capture him. Ahmed did not go to the embassy and did not fall for the trick, but he informed MJ that he would think about it and that they would discuss it when he returned. Jama Rabileh was later appointed for the FAO position. Amina-Weris remembers that he never told him the truth that he did not want the position. When the ambassador returned again and asked Siad Barre wants to know when Ahmed was returning. Ahmed told him: *Mr. Ambassador, please tell him I have been working for all those years without ever taking leave. I am on vacation for a month or two so let him allow me to enjoy my leave.* During that period, MJ told Ahmed that many ambassadors called him and wanted to know his intentions: Ali H. Hashi, Somali ambassador in New York, and Mohamoud

Haji Nur, Somali ambassador in Washington. The rumor that Ahmed had departed the regime spread like wildfire within the government circles and they were hungry for the truth. Their inquiry infuriated Ahmed. He wondered: *Is it a problem if I leave that regime? They are tribally selected for ambassadorial positions and are all cousins collaborating tribally and yet they don't want anyone to refute them for their injustice and inhumanity! Ahmed told MJ those men never contacted him. They are his friends. If they want to know whether he left the regime or going back after his holiday, let them talk to him.* Ahmed whose original intention was to move slowly in disclosing his aim, moved quickly when Omar Arteh Ghalib, Ismail Ali Abokor and other parliamentarians were arrested. Their arrest should never have been as rash as it happened. After that arrest, Ahmed Silanyo walked into the BBC Somali Service Studio in London and announced his decision to resign from the chairman of the economic commission and that he was not returning to the country.

Somali Ambassador to Washington Pries into Rumors about Silanyo

Mohamoud Haji Nur and Amina-Weris are cousins on the mother's side. He is also Ahmed Suleiman Dafleh's cousin on the father's side. He approached Ahmed through Amina-Weris.[1] Besides, Amina-Weris is a close relative to his wife Asha Haji Mohamed Sirad. After Ahmed announced his decision, Mohamoud Haji Nur asked: *Ahmed, I am still in disbelief. Is it true?* When Ahmed Silanyo asked him to clarify, he continued: *I expected you to go to the rural and sit there outraged but I never believed Ahmed would become a dissident, join SNM and participate in armed struggle to topple the government!* Ahmed Silanyo was furious: *If this was your perception of me, then you know me very little. You have completely misread my character as a stooge for the Daarood clan. If you imagined me as a dumb person who lost all feelings of humanity, then you were very wrong. Your cousin Ahmed Suleiman Dafleh placed you in Washington as an ambassador when my lineage was eliminated, and you said nothing to expose that atrocity. Fifty-two of the best Somali administrators and senior personnel like Ahmed Haji Dualeh (Ahmed Keyse) and Osman Ahmed Hassan were fired from their jobs. Are you talking to me now, and not when Isaaq was made the lone target for elimination and not a single Dhulbahante person uttered a word!*

---

(1) Later when it became clear 'MOD' the people from north who served Siad Barre as ambassadors were 90% from the Dhulbahante tribe. Only two, Yusuf Dheeg and Dhegaweyne were from the Isaaq clan.

You were wrong if you thought I would go back to the rural area and do nothing. I am not going to the rural, but I am joining the armed struggle and will topple your regime. I promise you, from today, the war has begun. Whatever it takes me, I will work hard to dismantle Siad Barre's regime. The ambassador asked Ahmed to cool down, but Ahmed Silanyo had already exploded. He said: *Why would I sit in Ballidhiig? I have never concerned myself with tribal affiliation, but I would never allow another to kill my clan because of that. If I accept that then I have lost all feelings of humanity.*

Time to Join Millions of Refugees from Somalia: Ahmed Silanyo Requests for Political Asylum

As Amina-Weris relays, when Ahmed left Somalia, he had a small amount of benefit in his account. He wrote a cheque to Ali Jirde to collect it. There was no hard currency in the bank. He left with 3000 dollars for the conference he attended. As soon as he landed in London, Ali Jirde sent them some money to cover their costs in August.

Lord Avebury and Winston Spencer Churchill (Winston Churchill's grandson) helped him. Both men met Ahmed in Somalia. They were part of a mission that was ensuring whether, or not, the Russians had a base in Berbera. Ahmed got to know both men very well while they were in Somalia.

Lord Avebury's wife Liz Stewards were head of Amnesty International. The moment Ahmed announced his political refugee status, Lord Avebury called his wife Liz and she helped Ahmed with his political asylum application. The application was sent to the home office and Lord Avebury called Winston Spencer Churchill; within three months, Ahmed and his family got full political asylum. Their youngest son Rashid who was born in Germany was excluded until his birth certificate was brought and he, too, was given. Their maid Faduma who came later with the help of Ali Jirde was granted special leave – ELR to remain in Britain. She argued that working for Silanyo was enough to earn her torture.

The First SNM Conference (April 1981)

From 1980 to 1981 SNM movement grew. It was tripartite. The workers in the Arab world, the intellectuals in the UK and the population of elders, men and women collaborated. On 6 April 1981 SNM was officially declared an armed struggle against Siad Barre's brutal regime. Three nights before the declaration, a group of men from the Hawiye clan contacted and asked SNM to wait for them. They were told that SNM was temporarily not building a strong structure but only an ad hoc committee. "We were planning a big conference in October; let us converge as Isaaq, Hawiye and the Majeerteen clans and confer in October."

Hawiye did not show up for the October conference. SSDF attended but because of distrust resulting from the 1978 coup, the two clans representing SNM and SSDF were unable to collaborate. Therefore, it was inevitable for SNM to move alone. In April 1981, a meeting was held in the International Student House in London and the first SNM leadership was elected. Ahmed Jimale became the chairman of SNM, Ahmed Ismail Abdi (Dukhsi) as the secretary General, Hassan Issa Jama, Dr. Abdisalam Yassin, Mohamed Hashi Elmi, Ismail Mohamoud, and Hassan Aden Wadaadiid as members. Soon after the committee was elected, before they even left London, the committee turned against Ahmed Jimale. They made an official announcement declaring they had deposed the chairman Ahmed Jimale. Chaos ensued and the SNM movement was in confusion for a year and half. The first discussion was about where to place the headquarters of the movement. SNM members in London and the Arabian Peninsula did not welcome the idea of settling in Ethiopia. Still, that argument was closed after the first batch of military commanders crossed the border into Ethiopia. Thus, Ethiopia has become the headquarters for the armed struggle.

Abdirahman Abdulqadir, a young SNM supporter in London at the time, says: *When SNM first started, we could not find any supporters outside the Isaaq clan. By then the Somali society was already fragmented therefore as the Somali proverb indicates, 'if you can't find the moon, use the stars to guide you.' SNM had to walk alone because it could not find support outside its clan.*

Siad Barre's Reaction to the Announcement of The Somali National Movement

After the SNM was formed in 1981, Siad Barre stepped into continuous cruel measures in the north. To implement his policy towards the north and the Isaaq clan, he appointed General Mohamed Hashi Gani, as the commander of the 26th regiment stationed in the north. That was in 1981. General Gani soon became the ruthless commander with the final say of everything. He immediately imposed a curfew on the population to justify the summary executions and robbery of people's property. The northern people nicknamed him 'Diriye' (heater) to express how quickly, boldly and brutally he acted on his mandate and how his measures became a rude awakening for the northerner. They quickly understood the hatred Siad Barre's government had for them, which would have taken them longer to comprehend if Gani had not come with his cruel manifestation and had he not intensified the regime's violence to a boiling point.

In December 1981 and at the beginning of January 1982, a young northern intellectual group, UFFO (meaning in Somali, the breeze before the rain), was arrested. Their death sentences and life imprisonment instantly created the first violent confrontation. On January 27th, 1982, Gani shot Col. Abdillahi Haji Saeed, the commander of the Dharkeyn Geenyo regiment without accusing him of anything or putting his case through the courts. He and another officer were killed. Even though the Isaaq clan has been organizing, incidents like this sent shockwaves across the military officers from the Isaaq clan. It was a ferocious message that had intensified the war they were organizing. On the 2nd of February, five days after the brutal killing of Abdillahi Haji Saeed and the other officer, the first four military officers: Aden Shine, Ahmed Dhagah, Mohamed Kahin and Aden Suleiman crossed the border into Ethiopia to anchor the armed struggle. Shortly afterward, the battalion commanded by Mohamed Ali joined the operation and SNM used his battalion's barracks as the headquarters for SNM. Within February, the SNM group in London moved to Ethiopia and opened its center there.

Ahmed Silanyo's Intent to Unite Opposition Groups

When Ahmed Silanyo arrived in London, he started organizing anyone who opposed Siad Barre regardless of clan affiliation, whether a movement or individual. He intended to unite all Somali opposition. He saw himself as a Somali statesman and wanted to create a united front for all dissenters because he knew many people outside his clan. People respected him for that and many thought he was the only man who could unite all rebels. By the time Ahmed Silanyo came to London there were different batches of opposition groups scattered around the country. Since Siad Barre's rage was directed at the Isaaq clan and Ahmed Silanyo was from that clan, they saw him as a central pillar to hold together all opposing groups and Ahmed himself believed that Siad Barre used the Somali resources to abuse the population therefore the population should fight him as united Somalis.

In mid-1982 heavyweight political leaders who held positions in successive governments in Somalia converged in London. They aimed to request the world, especially those who supported Siad Barre, to pressure him to relinquish the many powers he assumed under him. They published *open letters of discontent*[1], explaining the country's dire situation. They also wrote other documents entitled *Somalia on the brink of internal conflict*. In June 1983, several political leaders met again in Washington DC and met with the American Congress. Another statement the opposition groups wrote was entitled: *Somalia on the Brink of Civil Wars*[2]. They aimed to convince the American government that Siad Barre needed to step down and restore democracy in the country. Among the suggestions was the need for the disgruntled Isaaq clan to take the reign of the country, or at least be given the executive prime minister position. The key was for the Isaaq clan to accept that suggestion and after SNM and SSDF reached an agreement, they were to seek international support together. The Isaaq clan was supposed to nominate a suitable person for the executive prime minister or the president that could be presented to the world. SNM leaders traveling to Washington passed through London on transit to Washington, DC. They refused to comment on the question of the proposed Isaaq leadership. When they abstained from answering, it was misinterpreted as SNM leadership, not in favor of the proposal.

The World Woke Up to the Genocide in the Northern Regions

Although Ahmed Silanyo was working with the Somali opposition, the SNM affairs in the London office busied him. Ahmed Silanyo, explains: *I was in London for a week when it was suggested I should lead the SNM in London. A few seamen and some youth ran the SNM office at the time. Shortly after I traveled through Europe and Arab countries, some offices and committees existed but nothing was permanent. Therefore, I opened all the SNM offices between 1982 and 1983. I got support from supporters in America, Europe and Arab countries. I opened the SNM offices everywhere. For the SNM office in Rome, I nominated Ali Barre from southern Somalia.* After that Ahmed met with the International Parliamentary Union *facilitated by Lord* Avebury and Winston Spencer Churchill. Ahmed addressed the human rights section of the parliamentary union. When they heard about the human rights abuses in Somalia, they arranged for Ahmed to address the general assembly of the European Union. Ahmed addressed them and that has helped the struggle. Ahmed Silanyo earned many friends through that process, and it became the best political move

---

(1) This has peaked when in June 1982 7 political leaders including the vice president, and others were arrested
(2) (Somalia On The Brink Of Civil Wars): Horn Of Africa Volume VI, #3 (1983/84,) P 40-42)

of the newly formed SNM. It has attracted the attention of the international community. It was Abdillahi Omaar and Ali Jirde who facilitated the expenses of those trips. While Ahmed was in the SNM London office, he succeeded in establishing political, diplomatic and social relationships. He had also become a member of Anglo-Somali society and a member of its board of directors. When he left London, Amina-Weris applied for his position and became a member.

Ahmed Silanyo attracted the world's attention to the inhumane treatment of his people. He established relationships with human rights organizations, international media, European agencies, and Islamic and Arab organizations. Ahmed also tried to attract essential personalities from southern Somalia in Britain and North America to join the SNM. He held debates and intellectual discussions in universities.

Ahmed Silanyo Opened SNM Offices and Reorganized Existing Ones

Amina-Weris says: *When Ahmed first became the Chairman of the SNM Office in London* he started working officially and remained in the office from 9:00 am until 5:00 pm as was the regular working hours in England. He did not have a car and used to travel by foot carrying his briefcase. His office was open all day long and work continued as usual. His discussion of the inhumanities in Somalia prompted Minister Lynda Jocker to implement the most generous family reunion policy for separated families.

Abdillahi Omaar: His Unwavering Support of SNM

It is a fact that Abdillahi Omaar was the backbone of the SNM struggle. What makes him the Unknown Soldier and the unacknowledged hero is that though he was the backbone of the SNM struggle nobody knows about it and no one connects him to the struggle. The Mandheera operation had many aspects; in London Abdillahi Omaar played the most significant role in the financial support of that operation. When Ahmed Silanyo was traveling Europe, America and the Arab world to open SNM offices, Abdillahi Omaar paid his expenses and the rent of those offices. He paid for the entire cost of translating the memorandum of 'Ultimate Solution' written by Morgan. Mohamed Sheikh Ahmed, a Supreme Court judge in Mogadishu, and two British lawyers translated that memorandum. Abdillahi Omaar paid every cost of the memo's translation, discussion and dissemination. The world learned about Morgan's decision to eliminate the Isaaq clan only after translating that memorandum. At the time dispersal of information was not as easy as it is now. There was no Internet or social media. Diffusion of information happened in noisy demonstrations against embassies, documents sent through the mail, and everything cost money. That campaign of information propagation was the sole responsibility of Abdillahi Omaar. He did it single-handedly. The next project was the Mandheera Operation. Yahye Sheikh Ibrahim, who could cross the border without being noticed, took that money and delivered it to Hargeisa. The operation started, the Mandheera prison was broken into, and illegally arrested prisoners were set free. Of course, that operation was all-encompassing. It was strong inside the country and its management spread from Gashaamo where Mohamed Kahin was the commander, to the Golis Mountains where Mohamed Hashi Deria (Lihle) and his group were responsible for accomplishing the operation. It was a successful operation that shocked the regressive regime and exposed the strength and no-nonsense determination of SNM.

Jama Mohamed Ghalib (Jama Yare): His Role in the Struggle

When finally the Hawiye clan decided to become an opposition to the regime, its leader was Dr. Ismail Jimale Osobleh. He asked Jama Mohamed Ghalib to connect him with Ahmed Silanyo. Jama then established indirect communication with Amina-Weris and found a code language to understand each other. Jama informed Dr. Osobleh, when you go to Rome call this number. Identify yourself as "IDO" if the person on the other side is Amina-Weris she will say: *IDO how are you?* But if the person on the other side could not understand "IDO," hang up. The code "IDO" stood for the Italian spelling of Ismail D'giumaleh Osoble. Jama Mohamed Ghalib also connected Ismail Jimale Osobleh with Ahmed Silanyo in Ethiopia. Ismail Jimale called Ahmed Silanyo from Italy and relayed their initial conversation: *When I called Ahmed Silanyo from Italy, he was incensed and scolded me: 'you Hawiye clan, are you waiting until Siad Barre eliminated the entire Somali society? Why didn't you fight the gross injustice facing your people?'*

During the SNM struggle, Jama Mohamed Ghalib was an active member of the country who communicated information from within. He played Golf and was a member of the American Club in Mogadishu. He explained: *Sensitive documents that I needed to send overseas, I used to protect them in my locker inside the club because I could not trust my house or office. My international colleagues and diplomatic staff used to hand-carry them for me.* Once he sent a message to a Dutch colleague who used to work with them in the police and asked him to call Amina-Weris and use the code 'IDO' to identify himself as a person from me. Every member of the Isaaq clan inside the country had a code name. Jama Mohamed Ghalib was a vital member of the struggle says Amina-Weris.

2nd SNM Conference (April 1982) Held in Nazareth and the situation in Ethiopia

In February, the SNM Leadership went to Ethiopia after the military commanders crossed the border. In April 1982 the 2nd SNM Conference was held in Nazareth. Hassan Aden Wadaadiid and Sheikh Yusuf Ali Sh. Madar was campaigning for the SNM leadership. Sheikh Yusuf was elected as chairman, Hassan Aden Wadaadiid was elected vice chairman, and Ahmed Ismail Abdi (Dukhsi) was secretary general.

Somali Salvation Democratic Front (SSDF): A strong opposition with limited movement.

In October 1981 three small Somali movements met in Aden, Yemen. Somali Salvation Front, headed by Abdillahi Yusuf Ahmed, Somali Workers Party, led by Saeed Jama Hussein and Jama Salah Ahmed and Democratic Front for the Liberation of Somalia headed by Abdirahman Aideed. As their names suggest, the last two movements were based on communism. The three movements united into one movement named Somali Salvation Democratic Front (SSDF). It had established a central committee of 11 members of which seven were from SSF and four were from the other two.

When SNM went to Ethiopia in February 1982, SSDF was an already established movement in its military capability and international relationship. SNM was in its initial stages. They still did not have weapons, an economy, or established military and were new to the Ethiopian environment.

Facilitated Discussion between SSDF and SNM

President Muammar Al Gaddafi was one of the African leaders who wanted SNM and SSDF to unite. Abdessalam Jalluud came to Ethiopia. He was informed of the disunity between the two movements. He and SSDF knew each other already but he arranged a meeting with SNM and organized the two movements to meet with Muammar Al Gaddafi so that he could facilitate their unity. Mengistu Haile Mariam of Ethiopia did not like that idea and held an emergency meeting informing them that he was leaving for Moscow and East Germany the next day and wanted the two movements to come up with an agenda of uniting so that he could get support for them from those countries. Ethiopian Ministers of information, justice and internal security attended the emergency meeting between them to facilitate. They were placed inside the ministry of information and told to remain there until they unite for Mengistu to take that to Moscow and East Germany.

As Dr. Abdisalam Yassin and Mohamoud Haji Elmi (Dable) explain: *After a long and complex discussion without results, and Mengistu was waiting for them, they finally agreed to translate* their agreement of sharing the radio station which was written this way: *The two movements of SNM and SSDF agreed to unite their broadcasting propaganda campaign against the regressive regime and cooperate in the united radio broadcasting of the two opposition movements, SSDF and SNM.* They handed over that agreement, which was not what Mengistu asked for and the ministers took that to him.

SNM Delegation Traveled to Libya

Muammar Al Gaddafi sent tickets to the SNM delegation. The Libyan ambassador in Ethiopia escorted them to Rome on their way to Tripoli. SSDF delegation was already there. When the SNM delegation headed by Sheikh Yusuf reached there, Gaddafi suggested the two movements unite and should elect Abdillahi Yusuf as the chairman. As Mohamoud Haji Elmi (Dable) relays: *In the room where Gaddafi was meeting the SNM delegation, there was a big picture of Gaddafi and Abdillahi Yusuf holding the green book.*[1] *Of course, Abdillahi Yusuf told Gaddafi he was going to rule the country by that book and would use the philosophy and guidance in the book written by Gaddafi.*

---

(1) The book written by Gaddafi

Gaddafi's interest was for the two movements to negotiate and declare their unity strategy while still in Libya. The declaration the two parties had to announce was already prepared and lacked only the signatures.

The two parties started their discussion with high-ranking Libyan officers in attendance. SNM argued that they could not decide by themselves. The decision has to come from the members of SNM inside and outside the country. The direction the people chose was the one they were going to go. Even though the chairman was with them, he could not reach any decisions without consulting them. After that impasse, the Libyans decided to take the SNM delegation to Gaddafi.

Before the SNM delegation was taken to Gaddafi, Mengistu and his delegation landed in Tripoli on their way to Ethiopia after they returned from their trip to Moscow and Eastern Germany. The minister of internal security visited the SNM delegation in their hotel and passed a message from Mengistu: *If anyone deserves the credit for uniting the two movements, I should be the one. So if you have decided to unite, let the declaration happen in Addis Ababa. It is not suitable for the declaration to be announced in Tripoli and for someone else to take credit. What did Gaddafi offer you? I am the one who gave you the base to organize and open the route to free your country. Is Tripoli the place to free your country? I am advising you to stand against the idea of declaring your unity in Tripoli.*

The SNM delegation welcomed Mengistu's request because they did not want to sign a declaration at all. The next day the SNM delegation was taken to Gaddafi who already knew about their refusal to sign the statement. Gaddafi instructed them to unite and fight Siad Barre as one movement. Mohamoud Haji Elmi (Dable) remembering the moment explains: *As we sat listening to his suggestions, Gaddafi suddenly changed his tone of voice and said, of course you as SNM movement is regressive, and your supporters are reactionaries. Your supporters who send you money are none other than spies who work in the Gulf. He was angry. The delegation members passed a small note to Sh. Yusuf and asked him to defend them.*

Sheikh Yusuf said *"Brotherly leader* (that was how Gaddafi was addressed) *we see you as a supporter of oppressed people and a leader for people fighting for their rights. That is how we see you. We don't believe what the New York Times and the Guardian write about you. They portray you as a terrorist and we don't accept that* image of you. Gaddafi did not say a word. He stood up and told Jalluud. Give Abdillahi Yusuf one million dollars and buy 'these," meaning SNM delegation, tickets to where they came from. (*Interview with Mohamoud Haji Elmi Dable*)

That is how the SNM delegation left Tripoli. The minister of information escorted them to the airport by bus and asked them: *Were you crazy? Didn't you know the man you were facing? You could not say no to him. He was capable of taking you to the desert or handing you over to the Somali ambassador to deport you to Mogadishu. Didn't you hear about what happened to Musa al-Sadr, the Lebanese opposition leader? It takes him nothing to hand you over to the Somali Embassy and hand you to Siad Barre to say here are the dissidents who refused unity. I am advising you to play low profile while you are here. You don't talk to him like that.* The Libyans told them to return to Ethiopia as national security escorted them out of the country.

Another attempt to unite the two movements was held in Addis Ababa, where Ethiopians and Libyans attended. The meeting ended with SNM rejecting anything beyond sharing radio broadcasting. As Dr. Abdisalam Yassin recollects: *SNM wasted much time in those meetings.*

3rd SNM Conference (July 1983)

SNM held its 3rd conference at the town of Harar in July 1983. Sheikh Yusuf, Hassan Aden Wadaadiid and Ahmed Ismail Abdi (Dukhsi) were again elected as chairman, vice chairman, and secretary general. At that conference, discussions were held about completing the movement's constitution that was agreed upon in the beginning. Finally, important points were agreed upon as written below:

1. The SNM constitution will be discussed in the following central committee congress after the 3rd conference.
2. The central committee could request a central committee conference with an absolute majority.
3. Two-thirds majority of the central committee could change the leadership (Boobe)

Revolt against the Leadership of the Sheikhs

When the negotiations of SNM and SSDF failed to produce results, the different ideological groups of SNM (military, the leftist group, poets, the confused, and non-allied) all started arguing among themselves over which way forward for the struggle. A new wave of disappointment and confusion started. Siad Barre's regressive regime seeking for any opportunity to dismantle SNM took fake steps to show he was changing his attitude toward the policy of the northern regions. That has solidified the accusation against SNM leadership. They were to blame for all that went wrong. SNM central committee congress was quickly organized, and the points agreed at the 3rd SNM conference were upheld. The Sheikhs had to go before they completed their elected term—the SNM leadership of the day, including the chairman, vice-chair, and the secretary general, were more inclined towards the Islamic religion, and hence the nickname "The Sheikhs."

Central Committee Congress: Nomination of Military Commanders

In November 1983, SNM's central committee congress was held in which the religious leadership was to relinquish power and the reign of the leadership was handed over to the military. Abdulqadir Kosar was elected chairman, Aden Sheikh Mohamed (Shiine), was vice chairman, and Mohamed Kahin Ahmed, secretary general, while Siad Barre was working to take advantage of the SNM dispute.

Although the military leadership did not last long, Siad Barre's regime put political and military pressure on them. Abdulqadir Kosar introduced a new direction for SNM, focusing on overthrowing Siad Barre. He discounted political squabble, which he thought was not the movement's aim. Awaareh training center opened in 1984, and the 3rd ordinary central committee congress was held there. Some important decisions were made in that congress as written below:

- SNM flag was recognized for the first time.
- Awaareh was made the SNM headquarters
- Military training camp was opened for the first time in Awaareh.
- Nationalizing people's personal Toyota land cruisers was announced. There was a need to mount military hardware on those vehicles. Immediately people gave up 64 land cruisers for that purpose. Those and other important decisions were made during the reign of Abdulqadir Kosar. Mohamed Hashi Diiriye (Lihleh) was the secretary for the SNM freedom fighters.

Mohamed Bashe Haji Hassan explains that SNM military leadership knew SNM freedom fighters could not expect any support from the west. Therefore, the eastern bloc was where SNM fighters could seek help. SNM had a base in Ethiopia country attached to communist countries. Therefore, SNM could seek support from Russia, Cuba, Yemen, and eastern bloc countries. For that purpose,

SNM did not need to open centers in western countries[1]--even though SNM supporters in the west still ran well-functioning overseas branches for the SNM in the UK, USA, Canada and the Scandinavian countries, to name a few. Those branches provided pivotal support to the struggle, educating western societies about the gross human rights violations by Siad Barre's draconian regime. The SNM overseas branches were also instrumental in raising funds for the struggle. The military leadership also decided to expand the war to the southern regions. SNM should take the struggle away from the north and fuel the fire inside southern areas. Another one of their decisions was to seek scholarships from the communist countries friendly with SNM such as Russia, Cuba, Yugoslavia and other eastern countries[2]--for all the displaced students. The suggestions of the military administration headed by Abdulqadir Kosar did not materialize because many groups opposed their thinking. Among the opposition were the religious groups and members of his clan. The suggestions to connect the movement to the eastern bloc and the idea to send students to communist countries for scholarships were translated into propaganda against the leadership. They were portrayed as promoting communism and turning students into atheists and heretics; Abdulqadir Kosar met with fierce opposition-- even the soldiers at the front revolted against the idea.

Abdulqadir Kosar Accused of Heresy

The religious leaders and members from his clan preferring Hassan Adan Wadaadiid instead turned against him and his leadership agenda of three points. The first one: to connect and find support from eastern bloc countries was twisted into spreading communism. The second: to find scholarships for displaced students were twisted into turning the youth into atheists and heretics and the third to expand the fight into the southern regions was twisted into taking the people back into Siad Barre's grip. Those issues created a great deal of confusion, controversy and misunderstanding that pushed the movement to the brink of dissolution. (Mohamed Bashe)

---

(1) At that time Siad Barre provided America with a Military Base in berbera. He allied himself with America, Britain and the rest of the western countries. Military leadership was planning to 120 students to attend eastern bloc universities so that they could prepare the new leadership when the country was freed.

(2) In the beginning Cuba and Yemen provided some weapons to SNM and the Russian government promised to take 120 students every year. The Cuban government extended speciality training of Guerrilla Warfare for the army

In the middle of the chaos, people wondered what to do? Who would replace them were the questions people asked and the real concerns to be solved. Most of the people did not want the religious groups to come back. The military leadership was facing tough opposition. SNM supporters everywhere started worrying about the future of the movement and wondered if SNM was a dying movement before it even started.

Gesturing Silanyo

There was a dire need for leadership. The military leaders found themselves in a difficult situation. They did not want the religious group to reign again and could not find a leader. Therefore, they looked overseas for a leader who could unite the different sides of the movement. During the rule of the military leadership a new debate to separate the political and military management of the movement started. Ibrahim Meygag wrote that the two powers had to be separated since the SNM movement is political and uses *military might to fulfill its duty*. Abdulqadir Kosar and other military officers accepted the suggestion to end the conflict. The idea of separating powers would return management operations to the hands of civilians and the military would find time for its operations. It was agreed that Ahmed Silanyo was the civilian leader that could take the movement from the ditch. He was educated, patient, decisive, and had the courage to lead the struggle. Ahmed Silanyo, busy with meaningful work at the SNM centers in Europe and America, was summoned. Abdulqadir Kosar was among the people who called Ahmed Silanyo. His message to Silanyo was: *I am stepping down. There is no one to lead the movement. We need a visionary leader who can pave the way for the struggle and take the movement out of this challenging situation.* Abdulqadir Kosar and his colleagues agreed they would hand the reigns to Ahmed Silanyo. Amina-Weris says: that *Abdulqadir Kosar called Ahmed every day, and asked him to come and take over so they could find time for their military operations. We need a civilian strategic leader to do our operations inside the country.*

SNM Fights for a Cause Not for Money

Many supporters of SNM feared the political struggle of the SNM leadership could divert the attention from the real reasons for freeing the country in that SNM was established. People from different parts of the world asked Ahmed Silanyo to take the reign of the movement. But he did not answer those requests for a while. However, when the request came from the military leadership like Abdulqadir Kosar, Aden Sheikh Mohamed (Shiine), Mohamed Hashi Diriye (Lihleh), and Mohamed Kahin and supporters from all over the world informed him, either SNM was going to dissolve or he was going to take the reigns. There was no way Ahmed Silanyo could reject that grim collective request coming from SNM supporters worldwide. Ahmed Silanyo understood very well what he was called to do: not a position and power but serious sacrifice. He knew that SNM changed three leadership groups in two years: Ahmed Jimale, Sh. Yusuf and Abdulqadir Kosar. He also was well aware of the personal, factional, tribal and ideological differences of the SNM members. He knew the SNM movement's failure would be a more significant failure for the supporters and the oppressed people they represented. He also knew that sacrifice and warring factions inside the movement were incompatible. For all those reasons, when Ahmed Silanyo was faced with the request that either SNM was going to dissolve or he was going to take the reign of the movement, he also came with his conditions that he was not going to run for the chairmanship. He would accept the request only if it were unanimous and blessed by all. Otherwise, he was not going to accept it.

Ahmed Silanyo told them: *This leadership you are calling me to handle is not a leadership of monetary value. It is a leadership of sacrifice. It is a leadership surrounded by danger. Therefore, to make the decision unanimously is a blessing for the leadership. He told them. He was ready for that kind of leadership. He had the guts to face it and guide it through the process, but the condition had to be that I don't play politics, run for election or fight others for it. If it had become a mandatory duty to lead and my people asked me to do that, I would do it. I would answer the need of my people but that won't include running for an election.*

Ahmed Silanyo explains that situation: *Inside SNM, the leadership changed three times. Ahmed Jimale was chairman for six months. Sh. Yusuf became the chairman twice and did not complete either of his elected terms. He led once for a year and another for a year and a half. Abdulqadir Kosar was the chairman for nine months. All those men were the men supporting me, working with me and requesting that me to lead the movement. When I came to Ethiopia, I informed them that I was not there for an election but responded to their request. That was the atmosphere under which the 4th SNM Conference took place in Jijiga on 4th August 1984.*

Why Was The 4th SNM Congress in August 1984 Different From Prior Ones?

People were happy with Silanyo's arrival. Their welcoming slogan was: *Silanyo came and Siad Barre deposed.* Ibrahim Meygag relays: *I was the chairman of the ordinary congress held in August 1984. In that congress, the SNM constitution and its program were completed. A new central committee was elected. Ahmed Silanyo was appointed as chairman. Ali Mohamed Wardhügle was elected as vice chairman while he was still in Rome. Also in that meeting, it was agreed that the central committee congress would be held every two years instead of once a year and the leadership tenure would be limited to two years.*

It was agreed that it was not wise to introduce a new chairman to Mengistu every year. Therefore, the term of the chairman was going to be two years. SNM preferred a one-year period instead of two years because people feared a chairman that might not step down. (Boobe Yusuf Dualeh)[1]

The 4th SNM congress was also different from prior ones because it was the first-time non-Isaaq opposition participated in the congress, particularly the Hawiye and Dir clans. That was because SNM worked hard to widen the struggle to all Somalis and opened war fronts in the south-central regions.

SNM continuously communicated with other clans. Those in the west worked hard to communicate with non-Isaaq clans to join the struggle. (Ibrahim Meygag)

Ahmed Silanyo says: *I passed through Rome and met Wardhigle. I brought a man named Nikolina Mohamed with me to expand the participation of other clans in the struggle so that we could have war fronts inside the southern regions. Ali Wardhigle was elected vice chairman while he was in Rome when I brought his news to the 4th SNM conference.*

SNM Members Unite under Ahmed Silanyo's Leadership

After massive communication from people asking me to go to Ethiopia, I was compelled to go to Jijiga in 1984 for the 4th annual conference. I did not go there to run for the chairmanship. I was compelled to accept their request to lead because I had done much for the country and the people. My reputation for what I had done was why people chose me to become

---

[1] In 3rd world movements there were leaders who held positions for 30 years; therefore, the idea was, we ran away from a dictator, let's not start another dictator within the movement. While running away from that, they have swung to the other side of (anarchy) and without giving a chance what he leader could have done deposed him before his term was up

the movement's leader. The grim request was to take the reigns of the movement, or it would dissipate. When Ahmed Silanyo was asked about other candidates, he answered: *No. There might have been people interested in the leadership. Still, I delivered my verdict of not running for election and only accepting their request if the decision was unanimous and blessed.* Abdirahman Aw Ali Farah commenting on why Ahmed Silanyo was pushed to lead says: *Ahmed Silanyo had a good reputation for his contribution and struggle with Siad Barre. Though he worked for a selfish dictator, he was a tough cabinet minister and never shied away from giving his opinions frankly. It was known that he did not fear Siad Barre and stuck to his point regardless of whether it pleased Siad Barre.*

MP Abdirahman Osman Alin speaking about why he chose Silanyo over others also says: *When we heard Ahmed Silanyo was a candidate my friends. I blindly supported him because we heard about him when he was a minister in Siad Barre's administration that he was not corrupt, that no one interfered with the work of his ministry, and that he was the only minister who stood up to Siad Barre. We knew a lot about him.*

The Conflict That Resulted From the Conference of 1984

The biggest challenges facing Ahmed Silanyo's leadership--when he was elected chairman two challenging situations emerged:

1. Solving the conflict among the different groups in the movement in which some valued elders who called themselves Gashaamo Base Committee rejected the chairmanship of Ahmed Mohamoud Silanyo; and

2. Returning the lost trust of the host country Ethiopia questioned the ability of SNM fulfilling its mission to free its country.

When Ahmed Silanyo took the chairmanship, the opposition of the religious group against Abdulqadir Kosar turned its full attention to Ahmed Silanyo's administration. In a matter of weeks, they organized an opposition group called Gashaamo Base Committee led by important elders, and educated elite, namely: Hassan Aden Wadaadiid, Dr. Abdisalam Yassin, Yusuf Ali Harun and Aden Mohamed Sirad. The most significant and unexpected confrontation faced Silanyo immediately after his election.

Michael Mariano's Advice to Ahmed Silanyo

Amina-Weris and Sahra Abdulqadir (Abdillahi Omaar's wife) used to visit him in the hospital. Sahra used to take him soup when they visited him in the hospital. He used to ask about Ahmed and talked about the sacrifices Ahmed and Amina-Weris were making for their country. He used to say: that *only a man like Ahmed could handle the struggle and that he admired how she too was raising her children alone in a foreign land.*

On one of their visits, he requested Amina-Weris to pass a message from him to Ahmed Silanyo: *Tell him that I pray for him for doing an important job and a required responsibility but he should never expect Isaaq clan to thank him for a job well done or praise him for what he was doing. He should expect them to pull him down and always focus on the negative side of things. That was going to happen because I knew the Isaaq clan and I had been there. However, there is no one else I can ask him to hand over.* Later when some movement members harassed Ahmed, he used to recollect Michael Mariano's advice and say: *That was what Michael Mariano warned me against.* He witnessed the Isaaq clan's lack of appreciation for his leadership during the struggle for independence. However, Michael Mariano was one of the most valuable individuals during the struggle for independence. They used to say: "*Be aware of Michael and the snake following him.*" Yet Michael Mariano was among the few well-educated individuals leading the struggle for independence. He was a well-known lawyer and a serious intellectual, but his people did not heed his counsel. He was the head of the National United Front (NUF). He advised the people to establish a government before Somaliland united with Somalia, to become a member of the Commonwealth of Nations, and to give the union time. He warned about the dangers of quick union, but his advice fell on deaf ears. Ahmed Silanyo later wrote Amina-Weris: *The advice Michael Mariano sent through you was accurate. I won't get it if I expect thank you and admiration from my people. Therefore, I must keep working and do what my conscience asks me to do. Truly Michael stands as a symbol of our nation whether people recognize it or not.*

How Did Ahmed Silanyo Handle That Sensitive Situation?

Ahmed Silanyo selected a big delegation from all the clans of the movement and followed the opposition group. He spent a month there. Musa Bihi Abdi speaking about that situation and how Ahmed Silanyo faced it, says: *Many opposed the congress in which Ahmed Silanyo was elected. Gashaamo Base Committee was formed after the congress. I supported his resolution to solve that issue even though he was a young man who had not faced a problem of this magnitude before. He had not been in such a squabble before. He just walked away from a ministerial position and sacrificed for the cause of SNM, yet he faced an unappreciative gesture of rejection.*

He made a wise decision, and it is the decision that heightened his leadership image. He was neither disappointed, nor did he lose his temper. He did not send a huge committee to solve the problem but followed the opposition and remained patiently under a tree for close to 30 days until all SNM members agreed on his nomination. He succeeded in solving that problem with his resilience. Mohamed Bashe Haji Hassan confirms the same.

Boobe Yusuf Dualeh, a member of the delegation Ahmed Silanyo took with him reiterates the same: *We remained in Lanqeyrta Doonbrailey for a month while discussions were taking place. Things were moving in the right direction.*

For more than a month Ahmed Silanyo remained in Lanqeryrta and Doonbrailey until his shoes were stolen and did not leave until a unanimous decision was reached, until every father took his son away from the opposition and the opposition leaders were abandoned. Not only that but 21 of the heavily opposing leaders both civilian and military were arrested in Jijiga and put to trial in an SNM court headed by Mohamed Hersi Omane. At the same time, Abdirahman Osman Alin and Saeed Yusuf Abdi Saeed were members.

Abdirahman Osman Alin speaking about that situation explains: They were accused of creating chaos that could dissipate the movement. Later all the accused were released after the attorney general failed to substantiate the accusations.

Of course, elders like Haji Guhaad, Dhugad and others were instrumental in resolving that conflict.

The War of the Mountains

The war of the mountains was a tripartite operation. The western regiment commanded by Martyr Abdillahi Asker and Ahmed Weysa'adde was composed of 150 SNM fighters and was directed at the north of Hargeisa. The center regiments commanded by Ibrahim Hussein (Dhegaweyne) and Mohamed Ali formed 120 SNM fighters led at the Adaadley and Sheikh mountains. The eastern regiment commanded by Mohamed Kahin Ahmed was composed of 140 soldiers and directed at Negeeger and mirriya.

Musa Bihi Abdi explains a challenge worse than all that faced Ahmed Silanyo: *Ahmed Silanyo inherited a weak military capability movement and politically pressured to unite with SSDF. All of the above problems pushed the movement to take a fuming war. The bottom-line reality was to fight inside the country regardless of consequences. The bright side of the war of the mountains was that it had famed SNM as a serious movement. That war was an earthquake to Ethiopia and other doubting countries and the entire world. Serious questions were being asked after the war of the mountains. How could a movement face the strongest army in Africa and not only fight them inside the country but defeat them? That operation had earned SNM the respect of supporting countries and the pride of the people they were fighting for. It has raised the status of SNM. On the other hand, SNM lost valuable lives and dealt with the aftermath.*

Ahmed Silanyo's Work Plan After He Took over the Leadership

When Ahmed Silanyo took over the SNM leadership, he planned for several important things such as:

1. Holding together the different groups of the movement.
2. Strengthening previous leadership's effort of including other clans in the war struggle.
3. Expanding the war front to the south and closer to Siad Barre.
4. Organizing the management of SNM.

Weaving Different Groups Together

As said by Mohamed Bashe, Ahmed Silanyo was elected in a plan higher than those before him and decided to lace together all the different groups within the Movement.

Ibrahim Meygag explains that situation: *Ahmed Silanyo included his executive committee and all the SNM leaders before him to create and maintain unity among the members. Sh. Yusuf Sh. Ali was his political adviser, Abdulqadir Kosar, was his war advisor and Aden Shine was the commander-in-chief. He added positive changes to the movement that solidified democracy within the movement in a way that each leadership cooperated with the one after it instead of disrupting every new leadership with opposition and rejection. That was a valuable change that has become a foundation for Somaliland itself.*

Ahmed Silanyo resolved to dovetail many groups of different viewpoints and ideologies. He understood from the outset that SNM was not a political party but a movement that brought together people of different attitudes, thoughts, and experiences. The only thing that united them was to topple the regressive regime and depose the dictator Mohamed Siad Barre. The biggest challenge facing Ahmed Silanyo was holding together people of different backgrounds and focusing their energy in one place so that the weapon they shot hit the proper target. In his attempt to keep the movement members united, when he was choosing his ministers, he chose Mohamed Hashi Elmi as his minister of Finance, who was the only member who voted against him.

Dr. Abdisalam Yassin, one of the founders of SNM in London, confirmed what Ibrahim Meygag explained: *Mohamed Hashi Elmi was the only one who raised his hand to vote against Silanyo's leadership. Ahmed Silanyo then asked me to work with him and I told him, I was taking the gun and moving with the military inside the country.*

After that Dr. Abdisalam Yassin, Hassan Aden Wadaadiid and Aden Mohamed Sirad asked Ahmed Silanyo that he should hand the ministry of finance to the only man who voted against him so that the movement's meager funds should be in safe hands. Ahmed Silanyo accepted and that is what Ahmed Silanyo is praised for.

Selecting Mohamed Hashi for the Finance Minister

Ahmed Silanyo asked Hassan Aden Wadaadiid's opposition to his leadership and why he chose the only man who voted against him responded: *Hassan Aden Wadaadiid was my teacher. He began my first English lesson for me. I still remember the first English words he wrote on the board: nose, eyes, and mouth. There are no ill feelings between us, but he had political ambition, which is natural. He competed and that is all right but I have no bad feelings for him.*

As for Mohamed Hashi, I had never interacted with him beyond greetings because our paths never crossed. We did not interact with work. We did not go to school at the same time. If anyone could have said Ahmed Silanyo and Mohamed Hashi met in school and there was a chance of animosity, it did not happen. Our life paths never crossed. The reason I handed the finance ministry to him is that from the little I know about him and the comments others say about him is that he is honest. The resources we had were minimal. Workers of mediocre jobs overseas collected everything we had. Our rural people sacrificed their livestock. They provided us with the little they had. They had also sacrificed the young man watching over the animal to become a soldier. They sent the boy and the beast to the cause. From east to west, the Isaaq clan contributed to the SNM movement. It was not a cause for the educated elite or wealthy merchants but a movement fermenting from the bottom up and people sacrificed everything for it. Everyone viewed it as his struggle. I won't abuse its funds for that purpose because I know myself. People also know I will prevent anyone from abusing or misusing it. Therefore, the little I know of Mohamed Hashi, he is to be trusted. Never mind his vote against me but that was why I handed over the finances to him.

The philosophy of advancing public interest before his interest is a testimony to his leadership. During the election, those who directed vile hostility towards him were welcomed in his government. He gave them vital positions in his administration after becoming Somaliland's president. He saw those men as useful for Somaliland, and that cause superseded any personal hostility they might have had for him. In his world, public interest hovers over personal interest.

The Rift from Transferring Mohamed Hashi from Minister of Finance

Mohamed Hashi held the position of finance minister for close to two years before Ahmed Silanyo transferred him. Ahmed Silanyo explaining why he transferred Mohamed Hashi says: *The transfer was not because he misused or abused the money or had anything to do with corruption. The reason was simply that he was not lenient or sympathetic to the soldiers in the front when they came for emergencies. He could not understand their urgent and humane requests. That has made an enraged soldier almost break down my door every night at midnight complaining about him and asking me to intervene. What they came for was a little bit of money. We were poor and the most we could give was 500 dollars. We rarely gave 1000 for war operations.*

When the commanders were undertaking challenging operations like the war of the mountains, we handed 1000 dollars otherwise 500 or less or nothing. Most of the time we used to tell them to collect resources from the rural people in their area, but the one traveling far away was given 500.

I transferred Mohamed Hashi because, for instance, war has just taken place and money for emergencies was needed. He would say: hand me your expense report! Where is the money given to you earlier? He and the soldiers were always in deadlock. The soldier's answer was I don't know what you are talking about. I did not come from an office; I am dealing with dead and injured soldiers. The 500 dollars you give us does not go to food, but to bury the dead and nurse the injured. When a soldier loses a limp we need to run for his life. We hire a public vehicle and pay for the gasoline. Therefore, when Mohamed could not sympathize with the soldiers and commanders on the war front, I was the one whose door was beaten down every night. That was the reason I transferred him from finances.

The movement's businesses were complex. Most of the SNM money came from Jeddah, Saudi Arabia. The population there was predominantly Sa'ad Musa. When Mohamed Hashi was transferred from Finance some of his friends decided they would not finance SNM directly but would send their money to Mohamed Hashi. A debate started when others disagreed and since Ahmed Silanyo was the chairman of SNM and they knew he was not misusing our funds; it was not wise to divert the funds to Mohamed Hashi. While that debate was raging the funds from Jeddah stopped temporarily. They were the backbone of the movement.

When the HT clan heard about the debate and its essence, they organized themselves and sent mass money to the movement. Ahmed Silanyo realized the direction things were heading; he called the members and informed them *it was impossible to follow that method. Habar-Jeclo cannot support a movement. If Sa'ad Musa leaves the struggle, there won't be one. In fact, if any one clan from Isaaq left, the movement would collapse.* After that, the problem was solved, and the money came through Ahmed Silanyo or whoever he nominated for finances.

What Had Ahmed Silanyo Brought To SNM?

After the 4th SNM conference, he started organizing internal management in line with the democratic constitution of SNM. The attempt was to connect all its aspects local and international. Abdirahman Osman Alin explains that attempt: *we inherited from Silanyo three primary management skills. First, he secured SNM's meager finance. When the funds arrived, it was divided up objectively. It was organized in a budgetary manner. Every minister got a budget. Nothing else was released after that until the minister returned an expense report on how the funds were used. Therefore, Ahmed brought order to the money management, saving the movement's economy. I remember when Ahmed ran out of money, he used to ask me to loan him 100birr, and he used to return it. He was that kind of man. The other thing Ahmed Silanyo brought to the movement was that he separated the work into departments and wrote job descriptions for each department, creating time to start and finish. He has also created Attorney General so that all SNM rules are implemented. I witnessed the system he put in place and saw it work.*

Second, He created a system of administration that clarifies every department's work. Any dispute among departments was solved in line with the constitution. Later on, Abdirahman was appointed as the chief auditor. He describes his appointment and discussion with Ahmed Silanyo: When I was appointed as chief auditor, I asked Ahmed Silanyo if there were *many undercurrents in the movement; tribalism was very much alive there, so I warned against any arguments about money issues later on. He agreed with me. We had limited SNM centers, accounting for the armor SNM had. We also accounted for where the food from the Ethiopian government went. We had created an income and expenses account. We used to ask about what savings we had before we spent because some of the money was lost before it reached us. I was even able to investigate Sayyid Ali's and Sayyid Omar's regiments of how much food and goods had reached them.*

Restoring the Trust of the Host Country Was an Urgent and Top Priority

The second challenge that faced Ahmed Silanyo's leadership was distrusting the host country about SNM's ability. It saw the movement as confused and unable to establish itself because From February1982, when they held their first conference in Nazareth to 1984 when they held their 4th conference in Jijiga the movement has changed its leadership four times. Therefore, Ethiopian government viewed SNM as a movement incapable of bringing results therefore, it was not worth investing in its operations. For that reason, Ahmed Silanyo second and immediate challenge was to earn the trust of the Ethiopian government.

Ahmed explains, after the operation of Burao Duurey occurred, the supporting countries met all the movements in Diridhaba and informed them that they had become regressive. They asked them why the movements failed to take the war inside Somalia. They have also given them the grim news that if things did not improve, they would withdraw their support. Aside from their discontent with the movement's image, the other worrying trend of the Ethiopian government was that they saw Ahmed Silanyo, the new chairman as a man close to western ideology and not interested in eastern mentality. In contrast, the former chairman Abdulqadir Kosar was closer to communist philosophy. Ethiopia was a communist country that had close ties to the eastern bloc. They considered SNM as a movement not worthy of their investment because its belief system was far from that of Ethiopia and communism. It seemed to them that SNM was on shaky grounds and would dissolve like SSDF. They had become cautious of the SNM movement and stopped the little support they offered before.

Ahmed Silanyo finding Ethiopian thinking difficult took his first trip to the war front and shared his feelings with the military commanders in Camp Liban. A soldier from Sayyid Ali's regiment recalls that meeting: *Ahmed Silanyo told us frankly that the Ethiopian government is suspicious of me and I am wary of SNM soldiers. Therefore, he requested us to lift that mindful of him so that he could lift the suspicion Ethiopia had of him. He shared his feelings with the commanders in an honest manner.*

That issue of lifting distrust from the Ethiopian government resulted in the vast operations named "the war of the mountains" that took place in October and November of 1984. As recalls Ahmed Weysa'adde: *the Ethiopian suspicion of SNM stirred things. Aden Shiine, the minister of defense, pushed the soldiers and commanders to move quickly and show the Ethiopians our capability. The chairman, the defense minister and many SNM supporters wanted the war to move from the borders into the heart of the country so Siad Barre could feel our people's pain.* Weysa'adde continues: *No one talked or evaluated the losses that could result from a war in the heart of Somalia. It was a wave of emotional response and young men who had never participated in war could not understand the consequences of such operations.*

Resisting Unity with SSDF

Ahmed says: *If I could not achieve anything else, I succeeded in resisting the unity of SNM and SSDF that Ethiopia, Libya and others were pushing from behind. If we united with them, they would have undoubtedly swallowed us up. Because of their wealth and the number of resources they controlled, they could have dismantled us with their money. Our stand was to collaborate but remain separate movements. Although I knew the validity of uniting our forces also understood that if we joined with them, we would have ended up as they did.* Ahmed Silanyo explains that the uniqueness of SNM thus: *the strength of SNM was that there was no foreign intervention in it. Its money did not come from foreign countries. What saves Somaliland's sovereignty is lack of foreign intervention. Its conflict was internal and its conflict resolution was also internally done. Somalia is controlled from outside and that is one of the sources of its fragility. Also what had crumbled SSDF were foreign intervention and the waves of foreign money that had weakened their resolve and created deadly internal conflict. Abdillahi Yusuf shot his brother-in-law, His sister's husband.*

Rejecting Libyan Money Passionately

To seek the kind of money SSDF commanded was the wish of some SNM members. Some people believed that the movement needed money. Abdirahman Ahmed Ali who had good relationship with Arab countries was among the people who held that belief. He and others with the same reasoning believed in order to strengthen the movement we had to seek those funds. *Send me to Libya and I will bring more money than what SSDF had. No Abdirahman that money is a curse. Let it be away from us* was Ahmed Silanyo's decision. He believed the worst and biggest enemy SNM could have had was to welcome Libyan money. Abdirahman Ahmed Ali approached Amina-Weris several times and asked her to speak with her husband. He told her people were dying of hunger and if Ahmed agreed he knew some ambassadors and he could bring back funds to survive. What our workers remit was not enough to sustain us. If he goes to Libya he could bring more than ten million dollars. He said he failed to convince Ahmed Silanyo and asked Amina to convince him.

The idea appealed to Amina-Weris and she too tried to convince Ahmed to accept Abdirahman's suggestions. Ahmed said bluntly, *I don't want that money. Money is corruption. We were better off with the little our hardworking members send us. If we get that money we won't be able to manage our affairs. I could see how money destroyed SSDF. Please tell Abdirahman that he was not going to Libya, and we did not want Libya's money.*

Ahmed Silanyo attained Offices in Ethiopia and Structured Work Ethics

Before Ahmed Silanyo, there were no SNM Offices. When he went to Diridhaba, Ethiopians allocated a big compound to SNM and SSDF. Ahmed requested the Ethiopian government for a permanent office to work. He introduced working hours and a system of administration. He used to come to office early and when he left the office, he used to go straight to his hotel room. He was not one of those who sat in cafés and engage in idle argument. In the beginning, he lived inside the compound but when Abdirahman Aideed and Ikar Mohamed Haji Hussein were assassinated he moved out of the compound for security reasons.

Abdirahman Osman Alin continues to say: *Before Ahmed Silanyo, people never worked in the afternoon. He introduced staff to work in the afternoons and those of us there worked in the morning and afternoon.*

The kind of administration system he introduced included the establishment of communication file through which workers doing the same job communicated. Every worker recorded what he had done and what was to be done so that the other person should start from there. In the afternoon Ahmed used to sit in front of the office until the Maghreb prayer and do his work. People used to meet him in the hotel in the evening only. Before him no one used to come back to work in the afternoon.

Chairman Silanyo Established Transparency within the Movement

Ahmed Silanyo speaking about his administration explains: *I treated everyone the same and I did not misuse or use the SNM funds. I had never used a shilling of its money. The system of administration I introduced for the movement was transparent. Any SNM funds were in the hands of the minister of finance and the chairman had nothing to do with it.*

He Strengthened Relationship with the Ethiopian Government and Elevated SNM Status to a Government in Exile

Before Ahmed Silanyo, SNM issues were tied to junior military commanders, and they were the ones who informed the government about the future of the movement. Ahmed Silanyo fought against that, arguing that SNM represented a country, and it was not fair for its affairs to be dealt with by junior commanders. They needed to interact with Generals and the highest government officials who could make decisions because they were the ones which could affect SNM affairs. That was the last time we met junior staff. He raised the status of SNM to the highest levels of Ethiopian government officials like the minister of interior and Mengistu. The Ethiopians saw Ahmed Silanyo as a man who could bring results worthy of cooperation.

Ahmed Silanyo speaking about the victories his leadership brought to SNM says: *The biggest achievement was our regaining the trust of our host government and its allies and all the other movements. Ethiopia has reached a level where it announced that it was not allowing any other Somali movement except SNM. Our cooperation with Ethiopia reached a stage when Mohamed Farah Aideed came to Ethiopia. They did not allow him until they asked me and I interceded for him.*

Abdirahman Aw Ali Farah discussing Ahmed Silanyo's leadership in SNM says: *Ahmed Silanyo was not a soldier. He was an open-minded political leader who sat with his people. He is naturally a patient man. He can take a lot. Allah swt supported SNM with his leadership which was its most productive time and the time of the most successful war operations.*

Investigating Keyse's Arrest is a Testimony to his Firm but Cordial Relationship with Ethiopia

Keyse Osman explaining an encounter between him and some Ethiopian officers and how Chairman Ahmed Silanyo handled the situation says:

A soldier was injured in the war of the mountains and was wounded in Adaadley. He lost both of his upper jaws and his tongue. Keyse brought him to Addis Ababa. It was difficult to get a travel passport for him.

While we were in the process of getting him a passport, a young man by the name of Nagib who played football in Hargeisa came to get a passport as well. Nagib's mother was Saynab Habashiya, a nurse at Hargeisa group hospital. His father was the coordinator of the ministry of agriculture.

The Visa section of the interior ministry rejected his request for a passport. Then Keyse and Mijir Qati, head of the SNM interest section, went to the interior ministry's visa section to request a visa for Nagib, a resident of Hargeisa. An Ethiopian officer in the visa office asked: who is from Hargeisa? He brought a file of a woman and asked Mijir if he knew her. He said no. Then he showed the picture to Keyse and asked if he knew her. Keyse recognized her as Seynab Habashiya and the mother of Nagib. The officer brought out another file of a man and asked Keyse if he knew the man. Keyse answered yes, he is Osman, the coordinator of the ministry of agriculture office in Hargeisa and Nagib's father. The officer then asked them why they said the young man is from Hargeisa? Keyse answered, maybe they were your spies living with us since you are telling us they were from Ethiopia's secret service, but they were the parents of this young man and he was born in Hargeisa. The officer got upset and ordered Keyse to be arrested.

A week after Keyse was thrown in jail, Silanyo, Osman Dool Quule, and Mohamed Kahin came to Addis Ababa and heard about Keyse's arrest for no known reason. They asked Mengistu and the interior minister about his arrest. The Ethiopians denied he was arrested for them. They ordered Keyse to be released and he was released. Then they told him to shower and follow them to the hotel, but Ahmed Silanyo told him not to shower until he found out why he was arrested. Let's go to Hotel Gannet, he said.

Keyse told them how things happened and why he was arrested after they requested a visa for Nagib, the files they were shown and the conversation between them. As he relayed the story, Silanyo sat quietly listening to the conversation then suddenly got up and said: 'let us go back to the minister of interior's office. They all returned to the minister's office.

Keyse remembers how Silanyo spoke with the minister. He asked:

Mr. Minister when we were with Mengistu and I asked why keyse was arrested you assured us, you did not know. I signed a declaration that Somali boys born in Baalidhaye and Harshin were Ethiopians and would never join the SNM army. How could you threaten our agents and staff when they speak for a boy born in Hargeisa? You told them Nagib's parents were members of your office. The minister denied he showed Keyse any pictures.

When Silanyo's colleagues tried to leave, he told them to stay until Mijir Qati came and verified if they were shown pictures. When Mijir came, Silanyo asked him, 'Were you shown pictures in files?' Mijir tried to whisper into Mohamed Kahin's ear. Ahmed Silanyo ordered him to speak loudly and tell the truth.

Keyse says: At that moment any anger I had dissipated. I was happy to hear Ahmed Silanyo telling the minister of interior: 'let us respect each other. This is how you destroyed SSDF. The boy born in Baalidhaye whose clothes and food come from Burao and who gets nothing from Ethiopia, was according to you, an Ethiopian citizen and we accepted and respected that. You should respect our citizens who were born in Hargeisa and Burao. Finally, the minister begged Ahmed Silanyo not to take the matter to Mengistu.

When they returned to the hotel Gannet, Ahmed reproached Mijir Qati. How can anyone threaten an SNM member who arrived from Hargeisa in your presence? How can anyone tell you his parents were Ethiopians? Whom do you represent here? Them? Or us?

Keyse explains: that Ahmed Silanyo was different when he spoke to clan members from when he talked to the Ethiopians. The injured man got his passport within five days and was transported to London.

Keyse added: When SSDF supporters were sabotaged, killed and imprisoned, they had no one to ask them to stop and that was how SSDF finally collapsed and that was what Ahmed Silanyo fought against. He did not want it to happen to SNM.

Chairman Silanyo Allocated Money to Injured Soldiers for the First Time

We used to give four birrs to every injured soldier in the hospital. When they left the hospital, their funds did not stop and we used to buy them clothes. I was the one who handed that money to the injured. That had never happened before Ahmed Silanyo's leadership.

He Expanded War Fronts

Since Ahmed Silanyo took SNM leadership, the capacity of the movement spread from the furthest point of the west in northwest regions to the furthest point in the south. SNM established itself all over Somalia from Gurayawl to Bur Aaminow where the three borders of Ethiopia, Somalia and Kenya meet. The SNM center in Suufka could see Buulo Hawa and Mandheera. SNM centers were well-established armed centers.

Mohamed Bashe explains that regions of Bay, Bakool, Gedo, Hiran and Galguduud joined SNM consisting of their politicians, their soldiers and commanders. They got their share of power in both the central and executive committees. Ali Wardhiigley, Ali Hagarleey, Gorgor, Sheikh Yarow, and Abdunasir Sheikh Ali were all on the executive committee. Seven to eight ministers from the south from the clans of Dir, Hawiye, and Digoodi.

He Intensified Wars (June 1985 to February 1986)

In February 1983, Siad Barre visited the northern regions to weaken SNM. He ordered to release of government employees, merchants, and the public accused of opposing the government. He lifted the state of emergency. He offered amnesty to anyone who was returning to the country. Those actions put the SNM movement under pressure for a few months. When Ahmed Silanyo was elected as chairman, from June 1985 to February 1986 SNM took 30 offensive operations inside Somalia directed toward the government officials in the north. They killed 476 soldiers and a commander and injured 263 soldiers, a commander and a deputy. They captured 11 vehicles and destroyed 20 vehicles. SNM lost 38 soldiers and two vehicles. Ahmed Silanyo celebrated EID at the corner of southern Somalia. On 26th of June and 1st of July he gave his congratulatory speech at the SNM base in the border city of Suufka. The program's title was: Ahmed Silanyo standing with the soldiers at the war front in Bay and Bakool sends his congratulations to the Somali people for the occasion of 26 June and 1st July. The events of that day were transmitted through Radio Halgan. Ahmed Silanyo's speech was an unbelievable shock to Siad Barre's administration. SNM intensified its armed struggle against Siad Barre's brutal regime. The largest number of people joined SNM after Ahmed Silanyo took over the leadership. The expansion of war fronts in the south worried Siad Barre. And he attempted to change his aggressive policy. On 25th January 1986, Siad Barre traveled to the north. The atmosphere was tense. He offered a general amnesty to ease tensions and promised he would relinquish power for Silanyo.

When he arrived in Hargeisa, he called for a meeting with all the Isaaq elders and told them: *He was ready for negotiations. He asked them to return their sons from the war. He said he was prepared for anything to bring peace and stop the fight. Silanyo left me. He had much admiration for Silanyo. He said he was ready to hand it over to Silanyo if that was what the people wanted.*

The Isaaq elders listened to him carefully. They spoke frankly with him. At that time, the elders could not do anything. Haji Ibrahim Osman (Basbas) spoke on behalf of the elders and told him. You have come too late. All the mature men in the northern regions took the guns for war. Only the very old disabled are left here. Men cannot here solve the problems you have. Siad Barre's failure to bring peace to the country and convince the Isaaq elders prompted him to intensify his atrocities inside and outside Somalia. Siad Barre took campaigns internally and externally. When he failed to persuade the elders, he continued with his aggressive policy and tried to influence foreign supporters to stop helping SNM. He re-established his diplomatic relations with Libya to convince them not to support SNM though SNM never received any support from Libya.

Silanyo Accused of Building a House in London

Kayse Osman relayed a story that circulated inside the movement accusing Ahmed Silanyo of building a house in London. When the SNM members asked Mohamed Hashi if it was true Ahmed Silanyo built a house in London with the movement's money, he answered: *I am the longest reigning finance minister and if I tell you there was never a paper that did not come through my desk that Ahmed Silanyo wrote except one day: we were closing the office at noon. He came to me and said: Mohamed, I don't have 10b in my pocket. This injured young man cannot travel to Herer; if you have 10b in your pocket please give it to him. Then I asked him to write a request. He responded: you are the minister of finance. Tell me how to write it. I dictated what he was going to write in the request. "I am telling you that this young boy does not have a place to sleep, and you can see he is injured and walking with a limp. Please give him 10b. The travel between Addis Ababa and Herer was 6b. 2b was for lunch. That young boy did not have dinner. There was a similar case in the books in which a person like him was given the same amount for travel expenses.* Therefore, Mohamed Hashi told them: *don't expect corruption from Silanyo. Stop that Silanyo misappropriated money because it would have crossed my office if he had done that.*

Silanyo's Refusal to Drive a Car Bought By His Clan

He was the SNM chairman for six years. There was an SNM army and there were armies representing the clans. Different clans had their committees that collected funds from their clans and there were funds that SNM controlled. HT clan felt the chairman was working hard and his car was not good. They should buy him a presidential vehicle. The car was purchased and brought to Camp Barwaaqo. HT told him the roads were not good and his vehicle was not good for travel so here was a new car. Ahmed Silanyo told the HT bluntly: *Listen! I am not chairman of one clan. I am chairman of people. Don't expect me to be driven around with a clan car. I am not taking the keys to a car bought by a clan. I will not sit and move around in that car, so take it back. The HT clan took their vehicle back disappointed.*

An Encounter At Egal International Airport: Jama Omaar's Testament to Silanyo's Leadership during the Struggle

Amina-Weris relays: *When Ahmed Silanyo was the chairman of the kulmiye party, he met Jama Omaar in the VIP at Egal International Airport. Ahmed asked him, dear Jama I like you very much but I want to ask why you didn't join my party and joined UDUB? Jama responded. I swear to Allah there is no one I like more than you and have confidence in but there is one man in your party I don't like and for that reason, I turned away Announcing to the entire people in the VIP, Jama said: there is no man I trust more than I trust Ahmed Silanyo. He does not concern himself with tribalism. He does not care about money. He is patriotic and cares only about nationalism. I bear witness to that wherever I go. Jama talked about a story between him and Ahmed Silanyo during the SNM struggle when Ahmed was the chairman of SNM: I used to collect the SNM funds from Djibouti. There were previous chairmen of SNM. When we collected money, we used to send the money to their accounts. When Ahmed Silanyo took over, I told him we managed funds. Should we send the money to the usual account? He asked me what money? I told him the funds we collected. He told me, don't send me any money. Just support the regiment in the west. I want you to cover their clothes and shoes. There is a frigid cold weather and wind in Banka Geriyaad. Help me with their clothes, food and their shoes. Don't send me a shilling. Just promise me to cover that.*

I was surprised by his request and when I told my colleagues about the chairman's request, they too were surprised and said, the man is loyal. We all agreed to fulfill his request and do exactly as he asked us to do.

As we followed the way he instructed us to, Abdirahman Ahmed Ali took over. Two days later, he called and instructed us to send our money directly to the center.

Monies collected in the Emirates and Saudi Arabia were used in the center. Still, for any other money collected elsewhere, Ahmed Silanyo instructed us to support it with the army closest to that area. He only required an expense account and a report on how the money was spent.

Ahmed Silanyo was the man who stayed in Diridhaba without money and while everyone was asking him for money responded to us after we asked him if we could send him money, 'not to me, spend it on the army.' Ahmed Silanyo's heroism is impartiality, his lack of corruption and his hard work. He taught his people to work ethics.

Mohamed Haji Ibrahim Egal: "There Is a Man Better Than Me"

When Mohamed Haji Ibrahim Egal was released from Jail, Siad Barre appointed him as the chairman of the chamber of commerce. He conversed with some Isaaq clan elders in Djibouti while on a visit: *Once I became a leader for the Isaaq clan; at a time, they did not have much business and were not urbanized but primarily rural. Then my hands were burnt. Isaaq has now become millions scattered all over the world and now most of them are sitting in refugee camps; the leader holding them together, leading them as one unit is a much better man than me. The elders asked him. Who is that man? He responded: Ahmed Silanyo. The Isaaq clan lost everything and are all in camps in the rural. Have you heard of two of them fighting? The man weaving them together peacefully is better than me.*

The 5th SNM Conference and the Ensued Conflict (February 1987)

The 5th SNM Conference was held in Herer in February 1987. The circumstance under which it was organized was tense.

As Boobe Yusuf Dualeh explains: *The fifth conference was a test for SNM because Ali Wardhiigley, vice chairman, did not show up. The Hawiye clan group that was to attend the meeting did not come. The group from the Dir clan that was coming from Baareey was late. Therefore, only the Isaaq clan was available for the conference. It was agreed to put every effort into how the conference would carry on successfully. It was agreed*:

1. *To put aside any conflict*
2. *To elect Ahmed Silanyo again without any arguments*
3. *To let the term of the chairman be three years*

4. *To rekindle the movement spirit and leave behind group affiliation and group conflict.*

The last point did not materialize because conflict started as soon as the meeting ended. The conflict came from the leftist group that believed they had given concessions to Ahmed Silanyo. They demanded a condition that Ahmed Silanyo not to bring back his Executive Committee.

The 4th central committee congress happened in Diridhaba in March 1987. Ahmed Silanyo returned the six members of the executive committee as they were. A vote was called and his decision was rejected.

Ahmed Silanyo asked. Can you explain why you don't want these men to continue? Dayib Gurey from the leftist group answered: you know why we don't want them. Jama Salah intervened and told him. You have broken the congress spirit!

The leftist group suggested that a committee be elected to advise the chairman on the issue and to advise him not to return to the executive committee. A committee of Musa Bihi and Mohamed Ibrahim Warsame Hadrawi among them was selected. Three days later, the committee returned and announced that Ahmed Silanyo did not change a single executive committee member. Things went into an uproar. [1]

Group factions were rife in SNM and were an obstacle to the movement's leadership and fighters. Each of those factions wanted to influence the leadership or have some supporters in the secretariat. Frankly, all the SNM leadership from the beginning, there were rumors that each leader was affiliated with one faction or another. Ahmed Silanyo guarded against that.

Mataan Hoori explains that situation: *Ahmed Silanyo is a wise man. We were broken into two factions. Religious groups and leftists affiliated with SSDF agreed that Somalia should be liberated as one and should take control of the country. Silanyo's problem was that he switched factions each time. When one group opposed him, he joined the other group. He was not loyal to any one group.*

---

(1) Boobe transmitted to the central committee conflict, which continued into the 6th conference in Baligubadle in 1990. That year and the years after were the most controversial years in the SNM history. The 45 members of the central committee broke into two equal factions, one supporting the chairman and the other opposing him.

Conflict of the Commanders

Ahmed Silanyo's leadership challenge was the conflict among the commanders: when one group was appointed, the other group opposed it. As young men in the movement, we gave him advice: to either appoint civilians and don't appoint commanders or discard one group otherwise that conflict was going to continue.

Abdirahman Osman Alin speaking about the situation explains: *We were young men, I think about seven. I remember Saeed Shuun, Nouradine, Saeed Yusuf Abdi, and Mohamed Hashi. We decided to divide ourselves into two groups to meet him alone and give him the same idea and we did just that. Ahmed refused and said I don't want to be remembered as the destructor. Let it be together. I think that is why some people consider Silanyo "indecisive." He should have discarded both conflicting groups or at least one. But he too was running away from blame. I was the last person to speak with him about this but he rejected it.*

Ahmed Silanyo Accused of Not Making His Cabinet Accountable

Mohamed Bashe said: His administration criticized *that Silanyo could not make those he appointed accountable. That was a problem for his administration. It was rumored that he collected only those who agreed with him and never appointed those who disagreed with him. It had become a source of conflict. There were poems about it. The hottest issue was his appointed ministers whom the leftists refused to accept until he discarded identified individuals. Ahmed Silanyo rejected their request unless they gave him reasons for their concern. If the opposition took a more radical stand, there would be no leader that everyone agreed to replace him.*

When the question of who would replace Silanyo was asked, there was no unanimous decision, and no one could stand up to replace him. Therefore, in every meeting, Ahmed said: "take what I bring forth and if you refuse, I will leave." There was no choice but to accept his suggestion.

Chairman Silanyo: *I won't change my executive committee without a reason*

Opposition: *We won't approve them.*

The argument is that Ahmed's elected cabinet was left unaccountable.

Special Note

Ahmed's adamancy about his appointed officials when he was the chairman of SNM was not because he was an arrogant dictator, but because it is a belief system he has. A testimony to that is just looking back at the time he was a minister in Siad Barre's administration and the confrontations he had regarding similar issues like the transfer of Cascassey where he rejected every envoy's intercession including Siad Barre. Silanyo insisted on what he believed was right.

Conflict of SNM Leadership Brought to the Public

The conflict after the last conference affected the work of the war fronts. The epic center of that conflict remained with the SNM soldiers on the western front. The central committee congress disagreement continued for months and spread to the public and soldiers on the war fronts. Mohamed Hashi, Sheikh Yusuf and Hassan Adan wadaadiid who were the most vigorous opposition to Silanyo also left Herer. For any travel, there was a request to be granted. When Sheikh Yusuf and his wife left, they were stopped at Herer. Although immediately released, that angered many people. Rumors circulated that Ahmed Silanyo arrested Sheikh Yusuf.

Since the leadership was in conflict they were competing for the influence of the public.

In January 1988, Ahmed Silanyo visited the regiment of the west in Duryadheer and Dibiile.

The Arrest of the Commanders

There was a conflict between the chairman and the commanders who were transferred. They refused to accommodate the transfer. The commanders wanted to visit Silanyo in Harshin and complain about arresting the movement's first chairman but did not reach him there because he left for Lanqeyrta. Musa Bihi speaking about that explains:

We were driving a car going for a demonstration. We came to Laanqeryta where the Ethiopian army was guarding him. Little did we know that a man wrote a letter warning Silanyo that if he came by here, they would kill him to avenge Sheikh Yusuf's arrest.

Those of us commanders were not aware of that at all. By Allah's name we did not know that Yusuf Abdi Gaboobe wrote the paper.

Yusuf Abdi Gaboobe speaking about the same issue says:

The entire regiment of the west was waiting for him in Harshin but instead he went to Laanqeyrta. We followed him to Laanqeyrta. I handed a letter to his entourage addressed to him. The essence of that letter was that Silanyo, you could not go east from this place. The whole area was mined. Mataan Hoori who was among his entourage heard about the news of the letter and interpreted the letter as if the commanders driving A Mercedes truck were conspiring to kill Silanyo. The Ethiopians received the information. They lost their temper asking how it could be possible to create a roadblock for our country's SNM chairman. Silanyo told the elders there to inform the men in the ditches to run for their lives.

Mataan Hoori explains that: *When we got the news of the mines, I sent a message to Suldan Mohamed Farah. When the Suldan came to us in a military car, I asked him: if these commanders wanted to kill the chairman, why didn't they do it in their villages? I urged him to take them out of place.*

Musa Bihi Abdi: We were unaware of the situation when Suldan Mohamed Farah came to us and told us to return. We were surprised. We returned without knowing why we were ordered to return. We thought that Silanyo must have gone mad. That he has taken the road of Abdillahi Yusuf, but did not know he too was wondering what happened to us and whether we have become insane: 'did the commanders lose their mind and want to kill me?' Neither one of us knew what the other was thinking.

Mohamed Elmi Galan and I were called to Harshin. When we reached there, we were arrested. We were taken to Herer and thrown in jail. Ibrahim Hussein (Dhegaweyne) was also brought to prison with a broken limb. True confusion in SNM ensued. SNM elders came from overseas to mediate. A central committee congress was held in Awaareh where most of the conflict and perplexity was sorted out, and it was agreed that the executive committee/cabinet be shared and the prisoners be released

How Did Silanyo Manage the Arrest of the Commanders?

Ethiopians wanted to arrest the commanders and treat them harshly because they saw them as men who transgressed the laws of Ethiopia. Silanyo had to release the commanders from jail, and it was difficult to easily release anybody from the Ethiopian prisons.

Ahmed went to the Ethiopians and told them they could not beat the prisoners and could not keep them in jail any longer. He was going to solve their problems. They were his young fighters fighting for him, so he requested the Ethiopians leave the matter for him to settle. The Ethiopians refused to accept his request and said they were criminals who had committed a crime in Ethiopia and would take appropriate action.

Ahmed spoke to General Demisa in Herer and told him, he was going to use the movement's disciplinary action to discipline them and did not want the Ethiopian law to interfere with the steps he wanted to chastise them. Their punishment should be left to us. General Demisa respected Ahmed, called the army from Herer, and asked them to leave the matter to Ahmed Silanyo. The commanders were released and that was how the Commanders escaped the Ethiopian prison and the movement survived.

Boobe Yusuf Dualeh's Provocation of Chairman Silanyo

After the conflict of Ahmed's nomination subsided, Boobe, one of those opposed to him, visited Ahmed Silanyo in a hotel called Karaa Mardha.

He asked Silanyo to buy him food and drink. He knew I was opposed to him and angry with me.

Silanyo: 'Do you want me to buy you food from SNM money or my money?' Boobe: 'you don't have any of your own money, but you carry SNM money in both pockets, so buy me food and drink.'

Silanyo getting upset swore: I swear to Allah I won't buy you anything.' Boobe: 'I will pay for my food and drink, but can we still talk?'

Silanyo: if you are paying for your food, of course we can talk.

Boobe: filled his belly with food and drink, stood up, said I am going to pay my bill, went inside, and disappeared into the hotel. On his way out he told Silanyo he had settled his invoice. Goodbye

Silanyo: Goodbye.

Silanyo got up and asked: Bring me the bill, please. When the bill arrived, he realized they charged for two. He asked why. They told him, the man who sat with him asked them to charge him.

Silanyo: I am not paying his invoice. He told me he was going to settle his bill! Musa Gaggale, Silanyo's bodyguard promised they would pay the bill tomorrow.

Boobe: That night he told me he does not mix finances. His wife sends him 200 dollars for his expenses. Therefore, Ahmed was not corrupt, and neither was he clan oriented. However, there were those responsible for finance that some thought were misusing funds and he did nothing about them.

"I Refuse to Go Mad"

Because of the big problems surrounding him, Ahmed wrote a letter to his wife Amina telling her about them. He said: *Dear Amina: there are moments of intense pain that I lock myself inside my room thinking I was going mad. Then I cry out loud telling myself: No, I am not going to go mad. I refuse to go mad.*

He was referring to the horrible situations surrounding him, such as needy people who accused him of killing their sons. Amina-Weris said Ahmed always admired the rural people who sacrificed animals and humans equally. They were people who trusted the struggle of the movement because they were at the mercy of the brutal regime. They were the victims of genocide, whose villages were burnt to the ground and whose wells were poisoned. Not only that, but their livestock was also seized. Those people were honest about the struggle. They generously handed over their boys and beasts.

Ahmed complained about the educated elites who were not on the war front but chewing Qat in Diridhaba and sipping coffee in cafés. However, he overcame all that with patience and the fact that Ahmed was a loner who could not be found in Qat chewing places or popular cafés.

Affairs inside Somalia

Siad Barre transferred General Gani and later appointed General Mohamed Said Morgan, his son-in-law, to replace Gani. In an interview with the BBC Somali Service, Gen Morgan answered what he had done about the problems in the north: *He took over the northern regions in 1986. There was an upheaval, and it was a hostile place. The SNM movement was fighting there. It was a strong movement that had the support of the people. There was a general curfew. Qat was not allowed. People were arrested and their houses were entered by force. He tried to correct those to earn the respect of the people so that SNM could lose support. As the commander says, he ordered the forced entry into the public houses stopped and Qat to be met at the border. The advice I submitted, such as the Qat business to be left alone, to ease the Berbera port services, to lift the sanctions from the businesses through Djibouti and to release political prisoners all fell apart when the head of national security services was assassinated in Hargeisa.*

When Gen. Morgan failed with his late and symbolic gestures to ease the tension, he started more severe brutality than his predecessor. He wrote a plan for the 'ultimate solution' for Siad Barre and the minister of interior Ahmed Saleban Dafleh, who was also Siad Barre's son-in-law like Gen. Morgan, '

The Essence of the Ultimate Solution of Genocide Proposed By Morgan

When the intensification of the war raged beyond their control, his administration regressed into its violent policy toward the Isaaq clan in every aspect. Gen. Morgan wrote the 'ultimate solution' categorized as top secret. The 'Ultimate Solution' discussed the elimination of the Isaaq clan. He addressed it to Mohamed Siad Barre and the minister of interior. The steps suggested were:

The people from the tribe written above support the SNM movement directly and indirectly and cannot be trusted. Therefore, I am suggesting that we take the steps written below:

1. *To destroy the assets of the people supporting SNM;*

2. *To reorganize the local government council of Hargeisa, Burao and Berbera which are predominantly Isaaq;*

3. *To adulterate the number of students in the northern regions with students from the refugee camps;*

4. *To declare the environment between the border and where SNM Camps are located, "uninhabitable." which means, the water holes to be destroyed, villages to be burnt down; and*

5. *To exile out of the north any army officers and government employees sympathetic to SNM.*

Siad Barre's Misinformation to the World was countered by Ahmed Silanyo's Heartbreaking Press Release Detailing the Reality of the Statement by Ahmed Mohamed Mohamoud Silanyo, Chairman of Somali National Movement (SNM)

Ladies and Gentlemen of the Press,

I wish to welcome you to this conference, which has been called for two reasons. Our first aim is to inform you of the actual situation about to the ongoing national liberation struggle – for it is not a civil war in the conventional sense that is being fought throughout Somalia. The conflict is particularly bitter in the northern parts of the Somali Democratic Republic, but is not confined to any region or ethnic group. We wish to urge you on behalf of all the long-suffering people of Somalia to seek out the truth about the struggle and its causes and publish without fear or favor. We call on you not to support but rather to frustrate the news blackout which the dictator, General Mohamed Siad Barre, seeks to impose on this issue, and to expose the suffering he and his cronies are inflicting daily on the Somali nation and its neighbors.

Our second aim stems from this; you will have noted that the Somali regime is about to mount a large-scale public relations exercise designed to obfuscate the real issues, to hoodwink the world's governments, and to secure such military and economic assistance it adjudges necessary to continue the persecution of our people. Not only Siad Barre, but several leading members of the junta assisted by members of the rump of ministers and diplomats still abetting his oppressive regime, are about to travel with their begging bowls to western Europe, to the Americas and the Arab World. Back home the voiceless Somali masses are watching with grave anxiety as to whether or not their subterfuges will be successful: whether or not they will enable the regime to trample further on the God-given but already mightily abused, human rights of the Somali people. We trust not.

What has happened to Somalia, our strategically important country that controls the coastline, sea and air routes of the horn of northeastern Africa? Ever since 1969, but particularly in the last few years, there has been a steady erosion of liberty, democratic values, human right, fiscal responsibility and the rule of law. Legitimate freedoms have been suppressed and meantime dictatorship by an evil military oligarchy consisting of a few of Siad's clan members, in-laws and hangers-on has steadily destroyed our country's political, education, social and moral fabric.

As a direct result never before has the Somali nation been as politically and economically deprived as it is today. Repression and rampant inflation have been accompanied literally by starvation. A wealthy handful plunders the national economy daily, and clan favoritism and corruption have never been rifer. Excessive centralization of decision-making has been introduced to facilitate this diversion of national resources. Indeed, due to rampant misrule, the overall morality and moral fiber of the Somali nation are more gravely threatened today than ever before. No people - Least of the Somalis, who have strong democratic instincts and tradition and where every aspect of their lifestyle and culture rededicates them daily to the values of truth, fairness and freedom - would accept such a situation forever. Unnoticed on the broader world, and unreported by the international media, there has been continuous fighting in different parts of Somalia, not just the north, for more than ten years. Thus, the Somali National Movement came to be formed in 1981. As a national liberation movement we do not claim to have been the first in the field. We respect the many patriotic Somalis who went before us. But we, like them, have been driven to take up arms in defense of the masses since all legal avenues of redress have been stifled.

Objective of SNM

Our activities escalated over the years until a long-planned major offensive was launched on 27 May 1988. On that day, freedom fighters from the Somali National Movement, in a spectacular lightning attack, captured the city of Burao. Four days later the liberation of large areas of the northern capital, Hargeisa, was initiated. The oppressed at once abandoned their daily routine and swelled the specialist ranks of the SNM; there was overnight transformation into a popular peoples' army, sweeping all before it. Cities, towns and settlements were liberated. Political prisons were opened. Many Somali conscripts deserted the forces of oppression, laying down their arms or joining the Somali National Movement. Ninety-five percent of the northern section of the Republic has been liberated. Even though the liberation armies have temporarily withdrawn from certain urban areas for tactical reasons.

Today, after their armies' humiliating defeat, the junta has turned to unprecedented violence on the civilian populations. Rockets, heavy artillery, and aerial bombardment have all been deployed in a vicious pogrom against defenseless civilians. Not just the conurbations but even the columns of innocent refugees who sought to evade the area of conflict have been targeted. Even so, the countryside, roads, and most of the settlements in the north remain in the hands of the SNM. The cities of Hargeisa, Burao and several other settlements have suffered very severe material damage. Some 30,000 civilians have died but thousands more have picked up the banner of liberation the struggle still escalates. The port of Berbera has been encircled and, even as we discuss here, the environs of the town of Erigavo are witnessing a further extension of the liberation struggle. Small pockets of Siad's forces remain in parts of Burao and Hargeisa, but the tide of events is against them. Their morale is low, the desertion rate is high and their command structure weakens daily. Although on a lesser scale, resistance and open conflict have so mounted in other regions.

What kind of government seeks to destroy the nation's infrastructure, buildings and communications network? What type of government employs white mercenaries from South Africa to bomb innocent civilians: And pays them blood money in dollars for each fighter-bomber sortie? These monsters spare neither women nor children since they enjoy disrupting the African people's march to freedom and independence. Somali pilots have defected and ditched their planes, choosing political exile or imprisonment rather than attacking their brothers and sisters.

When representatives of the aid agencies and international organizations witnessed arbitrary executions, mass shootings and organized looting, they were whisked away from the scene. The government ministers and those diplomats still at their posts almost hysterically deny the facts, but the evidence is massive and incontrovertible.

Foreign aid workers have also testified to the bombing, shelling and gunning of innocent civilians, often on an ethnic basis. Desperately afraid of the wrath of the oppressed, members of the junta have mainly targeted one northern clan – the Isaaq – in an ugly pattern tantamount to genocide. That such is the deliberate plan of the junta has long since been exposed in the infamous 'letter of death' signed by Brigadier General 'Morgan,' sometime governor in the north and son-in-law of Siad Barre. Nor is it surprising that one ethnic group should be targeted. The Isaaq are not the first; earlier it was the turn of the Majerteen. No clan group is safe.

One of the regime's serious calumnies is to imply that the SNM seeks to divide Somalia along former colonial lines. It is entirely untrue. Siad and his unrepresentative junta have sought to rule through a calculated balance of disunity, ignoring the voice of the entire nation, which has cried out in vain for unity. The Somali National Movement is the response of all decent Somalis – not just Isaaqs; not just northerners – but all decent Somalis, to the current terrible crisis in the nation's history.

In this context, the Somali National Movement repudiates clannish and freely asserts that it has no antagonism to other clansmen and women. The SNM is dedicated to the total liberation of the Somali nation and makes no distinction in its offer of membership either by ethnic group or area of origin. In this context, it also extends its congratulations, good wishes and cooperation to all groups of Somalis who seek the overthrow of the regime. Somalis have repeatedly come together in Europe, the Middle East, the United States and Canada to expose contemporary tyranny. The Somali National Movement is particularly encouraged by the recent formation in Rome of the Somali United Congress – as it happens by largely Southern Somalis.

For the historical and geographical reasons, it has been easier to commence the liberation struggle in areas, which have suffered years of economic neglect, but the liberation struggle will extend to every corner of the regime. A new Somalia will arise from the scars of the struggle. There will be negotiations and consensus politics will be restored but note that this is not possible while one man holds absolute power - and that man is a selfish and unprincipled enemy of the people.

General Siad Barre has abrogated to himself all the powers of the state's presidency and the Party's secretary-generalship. He is also Commander-in-Chief of the Armed Forces, Chairman of the National Defence and Security Council, and the higher judiciary council president. He enjoys sole power to declare so-called national emergencies. This is a recipe for autocratic dictatorship and the economic rape of the state. It is alien to Somali tradition.

The Somali National Movement, on the other hand, remains implacably opposed to all criminal and exploitative groups of what clan, who seek to ill-treat or dispossess the underprivileged.

Primary responsibility for the tragic events of recent years lies with the dictatorial regime and its cronies, but western governments, which had aided and abetted the regime and paid scant attention to the appalling erosion of human rights within the country are also in part to blame. The United States and Italy have provided the machinery of modern war and associated military supplies. The United Kingdom has serviced centurion tanks and Hawker Hunter fighter-bombers. The government of China has supplied and serviced MiG fighter – bombers and continues to do so.

While civil war raged: The United States government in one consignment delivered 1,200 M16 rifles; some 2 million rounds of ammunition and 1000 grenade launchers; and when Congressional sources cited in the US Press criticized this, it was pointed out that "no one in the United States government thought (they) would be used to kill' the recipient government's own subjects. But they were and they are! U.S. Army personnel have also helped maintain jeeps and other light vehicles and there has been controversy over the location and use of a mobile 200-bed hospital currently in Berbera. The State Department has admitted that a U.S team has supplied radio equipment and repaired Somali government military communications – thereby clearly assisting the latter's attempts to suppress a popular, democratic uprising.

On the other hand, on the 28th of September 1988, nineteen members of Congress wrote to the Secretary of State to the effect that "unconditional assistance by the United States government . . . Is highly inappropriate (. . . and that) the State Department should demand a halt to violations of human rights, the release of political prisoners held without trial, and permission for "journalists, human rights groups and humanitarian organizations such as the

International Committee of the Red Cross to enter the northern regions of the country." On the following day no less than 35 members of Congress signed a letter, also addressed to the Secretary of State, recommending the suspension of economic and military assistance to the regime. We thank the honest American leaders.

As has become well known, the latest monstrosity is the arrival by plane in Mogadishu on 7 October of a shipment of chemical weapons, including sarin and soman nerve gasses of Russian origin (almost certain without the knowledge and approval of the Soviet Union) courtesy of Libya's Colonel Gaddafi! Our immediate reaction to the delivery of such dangerous chemical weapons by Colonel Gaddafi's regime, banned under the International Protocols since WWI, was the following: In the name of humanity, let there be no more arms or support for Siad Barre's genocidal ambitions.

The response of the West to appeals by the United Nations organizations, the UNHCR and the Government of Ethiopia for assistance to cope with recent major refugee flows has also been minimal. Over 600,000 have fled into the countryside to avoid the planes and the guns. According to the UNHCR, some 440,000 refugees have crossed the border into neighboring countries. Their desperate plight in barren, cold, windswept and shelterless areas is attracting international attention slowly. Yet some 200 to 300 a day are still arriving. One particularly irresponsible act of the dying regime has been to mislead the army and forcibly conscript earlier refugees in the camps into ethnically based militias. This is a cynical effort to set them against the freedom fighters and the general population. This type of action and the arbitrary seizure of food, medicines, and vehicles meant to alleviate the sad lot of the refugees has led to several Non-Government organizations and more recently the UNHCR to quite rightly suspend further help to the repressive regime. Now suddenly the very same junta is to have a new look. The constitution is to be amended. Political prisoners are to be released; the world is about to be told. If the Central Committee of the governing party really means its recent resolution on any amnesty for political prisoners, this is a positive step. SNM not only welcomes it, but it has also been putting it into practice, by capturing and opening prisons. But how to ensure that the prisoners will not be rearrested sooner rather than later, on the whim of the president or one of his henchmen?

Last week a spokesman for Said Barre's iniquitous regime announced imminent 'reforms' involving even the amendment of specific articles – 26, 41, 43, and 44 of the Constitution. The statement, however, does not bear honest examination. Article 26 is supposed to relate the right of individuals and others to certain aspects of the economic sector.

In 1979 constitution already stipulates many safeguards for the rights of the individual, but these have long been absolutely disregarded. Article 26 is supposed to safeguard against cruel or degrading treatment or punishment, including torture. Articles 28 and 29 are considered to safeguard the privacy of homes and the sanctity of private property. But arbitrary arrest is rampant; torture is a daily occurrence; houses are frequently burst into and property expropriated. Nor is article 31, on the freedom of worship, respected. Religious leaders have been the victims of harsh imprisonment and even execution for their views. In the present political climate in our country, Articles 32 and 33 of the Constitution are a mockery. They are supposed to ensure the provision of proper legal defense and to guarantee the assumption of innocence until the converse is properly proved in a court of law. Two decades of oppression, but particularly recent years, have seen these safeguards consistently trampled upon every human right repeatedly violated by the government and certain oppressive institutions it has set up.

Arrests, detentions without trial for long periods and blatantly unfair legal processes have been rife. Courts have been set up without trained, qualified or even experienced judges. Little or no legal representations are allowed. Hearings have been in camera and summary executions have been too frequently followed. Cogent and irrefutable evidence of this sad situation has been collected over the years and reported by many human rights organizations. One has only to glance at the wide field of international publications issued, for example, by the International Parliamentary Union, the Lawyers' Committee for Human Rights, The Committee for Human Rights of the National Academy of Sciences, The Institute of Medicine, Committee on Health and Human Rights, The Human Rights Watch, Amnesty International and the Centre for the Investigation and Prevention of Torture.

While it was thought safe to ignore such voices, they have been ignored, but today, when their cries have been reinforced by the spontaneous uprising of the Somali people the regime suddenly finds itself obliged to pay lip service to the need for reform. Political prisoners - whose existence has been denied again and again – are supposedly now to be released. Human Rights are to be 'guaranteed.' It is all too little too late.

Mention has not been made of the NSS - the National Security Services and para-military forces contribute a major instrument of terror, and indeed the backbone of the police state that Somalia has degenerated into. Its tentacles extend to every walk of life - government offices, community centers, schools, and even places of worship. Surveillance knows no boundaries. There is no privacy in the lives of our people. Remarks considered by ill-trained and often vicious minor officials to be critical of the government or disrespectful to Siad Barre, his family and his clan, can lead to detentions and disappearances. Godka – the 'hole' is the NSS detention center in Mogadishu dreaded as a house of harsh conditions maltreatment and torture. It has its parallel in every city and town throughout the land.

The wanton, cruel, and barbaric techniques practiced by security officers seeking information from private Somali citizens are horrifying. The files of evidence corroborating the testimonies of those freed, often by SNM forces, is a terrible indictment of the inhumanity of the evil men whom today seek international help to extend and consolidate their tyranny. What price is respect for the provisions of the Constitution when law 54 or 1970 was passed, revoking the customary Habeas Corpus legal recourse in cases of illegal arrest and detention? That law gave absolute power to the security forces to arrest, detain and extract information as they thought fit. It is still in force and is not mentioned by the regime's latest spokesman.

Nor is there a word on the National Security Courts, whose very name strikes terror into the hearts of honest men and women. Their arbitrary judgments have led to many deaths and sent many to languish and rot in solitary confinement, incommunicado in tiny unlit and unsanitary cells. The President of these so-called courts has neither legal training nor background. Yet, the special prosecutor and his assistants have the power to arrest and detain, search without warrants, and confiscate property. The president is, however, an army general and a member of the Cabinet and the ruling party's Central Committee - the only party allowed to exist. These are his qualifications!

Any fundamental change of the political system in Somalia demands the total abolition of such organizations as presently constituted. But this would involve the dismantling of the very framework, which alone ensures the survival of the regime. Of course, the Somali government violates the Universal Declaration of

Human Rights and the Covenants on Political, Civil and Economic Rights. That is also window dressing. The reality is far different.

What is meant by talk of a 'political solution to the 'northern problem? What problem? For Whom? And why are there no details? Why not tangible suggestions? This smack of empty rhetoric! Our people have been murderously shelled and bombed. While vital in this dry season, the border villages and even the livestock or nomadic people have been made the subject of dastardly attacks. Hospitals, local pharmacies, and homes have been looted. Why, in this new climate, is no one to be arrested? Why is no one charged? What credence can people place on such empty words?

Since the Constitution has been latently ignored in nearly all aspects for so long, there is absolutely no reason to believe that juggling with its provisions in Siad Barre and his cronies has been alarmed by the national and international outcry that their gross violations of human rights have proved. They seek to placate this and their real motive is further to prolong enriching - from international sources and taxpayers abroad – members of the family and its clansmen who have come to dominate the nation's economic activities.

Fortunately, it is doubtful whether the world's governments, the IMF, the World Bank and other concerned international organizations will be taken in - though there is the danger that a few might. After all, early last year the IMF named Somalia as a bad debtor. The regime has thus not qualified for new loans. It is not only at home that a sorry tale of treachery and broken promises has come to roost.

Thinking Somalis fully recognize that any reform of the economy must be essential, and there cannot be economic reconstruction when much of the country is out of the regime's control and all of it is bankrupted by a vain attempt by the junta, the family, and their hangers-on to retain their privileges and power. Today, the country's people are being decimated, agricultural land lied deserted, and industrial sites are wrecked or starved of raw materials. Herds of livestock, the country's economic mainstay, are destroyed or scattered. These are the realities that must be addressed – and soon.

Every Somali knows that this cannot be allowed to go on. There is an urgent need for new honesty and integrity in the government, which this tired, oppressive, corrupt regime cannot offer. It seeks merely to mislead donor countries and potential investors and imply that window dressing is genuine reform. Do not be misled. It is precisely because the Somali people themselves recognize that human suffering, economic mismanagement and corruption are bound to increase, and their plight deepens while the regime stays in power.

Though regrettable, it has been unavoidable. The Somali people have risen against all military odds and have already succeeded in ending the regime's power in many areas.

So please, do not hinder us. Rather, we call on all friends of the Somalis to understand our just cause and earn the undying gratitude of a proud, freedom-loving people, by helping us. If God so wills, the Somali Freedom Fighters triumph and victory for the peoples' struggle is imminent. Meantime the struggle continues. Long Live the Somali National Movement. Thank You

Amidst Siad Barre's Carnage, a Pilot Defied Orders to Kill, and Landed His Jet in Djibouti

We know how Somaliland looked like when SNM finally freed the country from the brutal regime of Siad Barre. That criminal regime claimed they were keeping the peace by ordering jet fighters to bombard the cities, killing children and women who were running away from the shelling artillery inside the cities. Only one man defied the orders given. He was not from Somaliland but had a conscience not to kill innocent civilians. That man recently came to Hargeisa and had a warm welcome from the people he refused to kill.

Mengistu And Siad Barre's Agreement

Siad Barre intended to break the will of the SNM diplomatically when he realized his inability to break them militarily. The essence of his agreement was to disarm the SNM and in that process subject the Isaaq clan to submission and humility.

On April 4th, 1988, an Ethiopian delegation headed by the minister of foreign affairs and a Somali delegation led by Ahmed Mohamoud Farah signed an agreement as written below:

1. The two countries to re-establish diplomatic relations;
2. To exchange war prisoners from the 1977/78 war;
3. To re-arrange the two armies at the border and each to be pushed 15 kilometers back into their territory;

4. Each country to stop supporting opposition movements operating in their country; and

5. To stop political propaganda on the air against each other.

Siad Barre's Resolve to Negotiate with SNM

In February 1988, SNM fighters took over three refugee villages in Togwajaaleh. The victories of SNM in late 1987 and the beginning of 1988 compelled Siad Barre to search for other solutions to his plight. Dr. Mohamed Abdi Gaboose speaking about that situation said: *That war pinched Siad Barre's government economically and militarily. Those close relatives of Siad Barre like Warsame Indhole and Abdirahman Jama Barre called the Isaaq government employees into a meeting--ministers, assistant ministers and generals in the army force. At the time, the Isaaq clan was not respected inside the government circles. Therefore, they were called at that time to ask them to bring the SNM back. After a lengthy discussion, the most important suggestion we provided was that since the Isaaq clan did not hold any important position in the regional governments such as hospitals, police force, post and telecommunication, banks and even if they wanted to withdraw money from their accounts in the bank, they did not know anyone to help them, we suggested that Isaaq clan be given prominent roles in all regional and local governments. Fairness and impartiality should reign if a peace agreement had to be reached. Those ideas were passed on to Siad Barre, who initially accepted them. It was suggested that he traveled to the northern regions to see for himself problems and tyranny, summary executions, rape, arbitrary arrests and destruction.* There were clear steps that some relatives of Siad Barre wanted to implement if there was to be a real peace agreement that included:

1. True peace agreement to be reached with the Isaaq clan while the Army and officers people complain about being transferred to other regions

2. To lift the state of emergency imposed on the northern regions; and

3. The young UFFO group and others arrested be released unconditionally.

Siad Barre carrying those clearly defined requirements of the peace agreement went to the IGAD meeting in Djibouti on 19 March 1988. Instead of implementing the suggested peace agreement requirements, he chose to strike a deal with Mengistu. That was the deal he had in mind when he went to Djibouti.

Meeting Between Mengistu and Siad Barre

The SNM armed struggle had severely hurt Siad Barre. Therefore, he tried every trick to save his administration, including steps to weaken and eliminate SNM. Accordingly, he signed a peace deal with Ethiopia. The moment the two leaders met, Siad Barre expressed his desire to create peace between Ethiopia and Somalia and that he was willing to give significant concessions to Ethiopia.

Ambassador Awil Ali Dualeh expressed that at *the inception, Mengistu was suspicious of Siad Barre's peace request and thought he was not honest about it. Because he could not believe the man who in 1977 carried naked aggression to free the Western Somali Front had a change of heart suddenly and was willing to let it go. He felt "this man could not be trusted." If he were not the same man that fought us in 1977 and was someone else extending peace between the two nations, he would have believed him, but he is not the same. He could not fathom the sudden policy change that Siad Barre was submitting. Mengistu never thought the burden SNM operations put on him would push him to sign those concessions.*

Siad Barre's Proposed Concessions

The essence of the peace deal was that he would sign off the Somalia western front and Mengistu had to kick SNM out of his country. He would open camps for them and won't hurt them. Since Mengistu found Siad Barre uncredible and could not trust him, he informed him he would take the matter back to his government and could not decide on then. But he also indicated to Siad Barre that he was interested in the peace deal he was willing to sign.

Siad Barre thought Mengistu rejected his peace deal, and it was at that time, he decided to implement the points suggested to him earlier.

The Meeting between Siad Barre and the Isaaq Clan

When he returned from Djibouti, he traveled by road. The Isaaq elders were called for a meeting with him. Ambassador Awil Ali Dualeh explains again: *In that meeting no Isaaq elder, intellectual, businessmen, or government officer in the country at the time was missing. Here is how they interacted with him:*

Haruuri: Siad Barre, what the Isaaq clan wants from you is very small. They want fairness and justice.

Suldan Abdi: I was Aqil in Ethiopia; what the Somali people that we share with language, religion and country did to us had never been done to us in Ethiopia that we differ with language and religion. Our government here treated us in a way that Ethiopia never did.

Aqil Bud-Jabay: Mr. Siad Barre, the army officers you sent here are all from the same clan with an orientation that the Isaaq clan hated them and wanted to topple the government. They land here angry and ready for a fight without considering their positions as government officials. If the people sent here were from different clans and regions, they would have balanced each other out. People from different clans would not have all agreed on one thing. If one transgressed, the other would have stopped him. Right now, look at the people surrounding you, your regional government officials. They are all from your clan. Siad looked around him and realized it was true!

Siad Barre quickly answered: When your youth threw stones, they chanted Down with Darood. When he mentioned that statement, all his officers looked down.

Aqil Bud-Jabay laughed and said: No! Mr. President, an Isaaq leader would never have avenged the utterance of angry students' chant: Down with Isaaq and he continued laughing heartily.

Mengistu's Telegram to Said Barre

When Mengistu left Djibouti, he passed through his forces in Eritrea. He met with his army defeated badly. Entire regiments surrendered. As soon as he returned to Addis Ababa, he sent his foreign minister to Mogadishu with a message for Siad Barre that he accepted the entire peace offer Siad Barre forwarded in Djibouti. Siad Barre was still negotiating with Isaaq elders in Hargeisa when the foreign minister traveled to Mogadishu. The meeting continued. At around one o'clock Abdirahman Jama Barre (then minister of foreign affairs) carrying the Minister's message landed in Hargeisa on a special plane and walked into the meeting with the message as Siad Barre was in the middle of the negotiation. The meeting ended abruptly, and Siad Barre's tone changed from conciliatory to tyrannical and hostile. Siad Barre suddenly announced that he would intensify his aggression.

Dr, Gaboose relays: *Siad Barre did not like the way he was spoken to. He called us into a meeting at Morgan's house, now Somaliland's presidential square. Twenty of us Isaaq clan sat at a round table. Only Morgan and Siad Barre were the non-Isaaqs among us. He threatened us and said: you are complaining now. We will intensify it and make it worse and then get up immediately.*

Ambassador Awil also in the meeting explains that: *the meeting continued to the next day. Siad Barre addressing the elders said: I am going to intensify the war not appeasing it. I am not going to release prisoners. I am neither transferring government officials nor lifting the state of emergency.*

Osman Jama, alarmed by Siad's remarks, got up and held Siad Barre's head and beseeched him: Mr. President, you came to a difficult place. You are the leader. Please withdraw from your decision.

Siad Barre: Start defending yourself and looking in the direction of General Ismail Ahmed Ismail who was sitting beside him said: 'let this one also buy your guns to fight.[1]

Meeting the Public at Hargeisa Football Stadium

In the afternoon Siad Barre was supposed to speak with the public at the Hargeisa Football Stadium. People were called and the stadium was packed. Ahmed Mohamoud Farah spoke and praised the Isaaq clan and how heroically they negotiated for independence in 1960 and then welcomed Siad Barre to the microphone. Siad Barre started his conversation with brutal and cruel words. He said: *These poor people (Ogaden) whose livestock you survived with and you were fattened with their ghee. They bring everything they have to you and can't sell it anywhere else why can't you be kind to them?* He continued with his speech. "The other day when I traveled to Borama through Gabiley I did not see anyone on the roadside. Who has farted on Gabiley? He continued. I am not afraid, but I am not returning to this place again. In one murmur, the entire audience whispered: May Allah never Grant your return. People suddenly moved like a wave. The stadium was packed, and it was easy to crush the limited number of red barrette army protecting him. He barely escaped the fury of the people. Ahmed Mohamoud Farah ushered him quickly into a small car and drove the car himself. Shortly afterward the bullets flew all over the place. Six o'clock that afternoon, he flew to Mogadishu. The next day Morgan called all the Isaaq elders who attended the meeting and told them that anyone who did not want to be arrested should leave that evening. They were not allowed to sleep in Hargeisa. They were collected at Shideh Hotel in Berbera to wait for the plane from Mogadishu to take them there.

---

(1) When SNM entered in 1988, he fired General Ismail Ahmed Ismail

Awarding the Contract for Handcuffs

To teach the Isaaq clan a lesson and to break their will, it was concluded to slam all doors on them. They were to be locked in dark rooms and tortured. Morgan believed that SNM members would be thrown out of Ethiopia to prepare handcuffs to lock up the fierce SNM commanders. Morgan, the commander of the 26th regiment requested the president to deliver handcuffs. Siad Barre was awarded a contract to buy handcuffs from overseas because, in their mind they were going to arrest the SNM members and commanders that would soon be in the hands of Siad Barre's regime. The man who won that contract, who is still in Hargeisa, told the author he did not know what the handcuffs would be used for. They were many. When the container came to Berbera Port, the ismaqiiq attack happened and everything came to a halt.

Man Proposes and God Disposes off: SNM's Planned Vulnerability Turned into Impressive Victory

The typical story of how the turtle got his thick skin applied. There was a time when the turtle did not have his thick cover. He was slow and unprotected. His flesh was vulnerable. One day all the carnivores met and decided to eat the turtle's flesh. They knew his vulnerability and wanted to feast on him. When the turtle heard about the grim news of the carnivores, he said: wasn't God available where all those carnivores were planning to eat me? Then suddenly God covered the turtle with a hard cover that none could hurt him. The analogy is that while Siad Barre and Morgan planned to slam the doors shut permanently on the Isaaq clan's men, women and children, Allah's disposal was yet to be revealed.

Abshir Walde [1] Approaches Ahmed Silanyo about Uniting SNM and SSDF

When Abdillahi Yusuf was arrested, Mohamed Abshir Walde held the chairmanship temporarily. Walde and Ahmed Silanyo have known each other for a long time. Mohamed Abshir Walde relayed that when he was the chairman of SSDF leadership, he suggested that Ahmed Silanyo unify the opposition

---

(1) Mohamed Abshir Walde interview he gave to Hassan Abdi Madar when he visited Hargeisa in January 2013

movements to topple Siad Barre as one force. Here is what he claims to have discussed with Chairman Ahmed Silanyo.

- To move the SNM soldiers and commanders to the central area in Somalia since the government fighters there were mostly Isaaq; and
- To move the SSDF soldiers and commanders into the northern fronts since the government forces were all Majeerteen. The idea behind the reshuffle was that the government forces wouldn't attack their clan members fiercely if they faced them in a war.

Walde relays that: *Ahmed Silanyo expressed that it was a problematic suggestion for him to accept for the following reasons:*

- *My soldiers are emotional and angry. They can see their country destroyed by hostile forces and if I come up with such an idea, I might lose them.*
- *Secondly, your suggestion would require us to start an awareness campaign.*
- *Thirdly, our sole supporters are our members in the diaspora who send us 50,000 dollars a month. If we change the direction of the struggle now, they will discontinue supporting us and we cannot afford to lose their support. Therefore, we need time to think about that.*

Walde relays that he informed Ahmed Silanyo that he does not have time to think about it. Tomorrow SSDF is electing a new chairman and I am not a candidate. I do not know what the new chairman would do if I leave.

How SNM Viewed the Agreement between Mengistu and Siad Barre

The agreement between Somalia and Ethiopia was horrifying. The biggest shock was how the two dictators suddenly shook hands on the agreement. Ethiopia, acting on the points of the agreement silenced Radio Halgan. They cut off telephone lines from the Guul Allah (SNM headquarters in Addis Ababa). When that awful news reached SNM, the leadership held an emergency meeting in Diridhaba to discuss the agreement between Siad and Mengistu and the steps already called by the then chairman of SNM *Ahmed Mohamed Mohamoud Silanyo.*

We converged in Diridhaba. Those of us elders and intellectuals inside Ethiopia met and asked ourselves many questions:

Are we going to stop the armed struggle?

What options do we have regarding the situation?

How is it going to affect us?

It was ugly and miserable to end the struggle there. There was no way to end the struggle. The only option open to us was "War Rush Operation." We were confident because we had the support of our people wherever they were and gathered courage from their support. We concluded to act on war. At that point, we decided to divide ourselves into two groups. I was among the group to speak with the Ethiopian government. The other group was assigned to prepare the war machine and start the war.

The Feeling of SNM Fighters

Ahmed Weysa'adde, one of the commanders of SNM explains his feeling about when he heard about the peace agreement between Mengistu and Siad Barre and the ensuing decision to move the (Qaaho) army back into Ethiopia for training: *After the two dictators agreed, the following action was to move the military away from the border. It was decided that neither Ethiopian nor any other army was to remain in Qaaho, and if you could enter an army in your country, that was your problem. (The request Ahmed Silanyo submitted to Mengistu became an opportunity). At the time, most people were reeling from shock, and those willing to sacrifice their lives saw an opportunity there.*

The two choices, to move into our country or move back were both difficult, but if we chose to move back to Ethiopia, we were not sure what the two dictators would do next. The time was 1988, and we were in the bush for seven long years. There were armies in three areas, east, central, and wes; II was with the main regiment. People were asking each other the question: What next? They could envision the next thing was going to be: Why are you armed? Return the weapons! If they unarmed us, the new reality would be: Remain in Ethiopia unarmed, travel abroad, or submit to the brutal Faqash and ask our enemy for mercy. Everyone could see the future.

The better option for us was: If we were going to be destroyed and killed, let our graves become inside our country. For the SNM, it was better for them to destroy themselves than to submit to anyone.

The Meeting between Mengistu and Ahmed Silanyo

When we went to Mengistu, he told us what we already expected to hear from him: *"We support your struggle. He praised us and told us that he was not against our struggle but also had problems. He has several war fronts and oppositions, and he wants to recall his army on the Somalia border and you SNM bring back your soldiers and remain in your camps. Give them training inside your camps and stop the war for a while. Let the war stop for a little bit."*

We told him: *We understand your plight but our fighters and people are inside the country. They are killed every day for no reason. The regime does not spare anyone, and our people have no protection. There is a genocide going on as we speak. Ahmed Silanyo remembers: I asked him: Mr. President, I remember what you told me the first day I met you. You told me you are a man who honors his word. What I wrote down as we spoke was that you keep your promise. Has that changed? No, he answered. Has your pledge to support our struggle changed at all? No, he repeated.*

This is our predicament. What should we do? I asked.

Let your army stop the fight for a little while and then we will discuss what to do later. He said.

Since we had made up our minds, we just told him OK. For us, it was fine to regroup our scattered army and collect them into two camps to avert the attention of both Ethiopia and Somalia. Regrouping was also beneficial for us because Siad Barre's army would come out of the ditches and let their guard down so that we could catch them unaware. We sought the opportunity to find Siad Barre's army to leave the border and move back into the country. Each army (Ethiopians and Somalis) required to move 15 km back into their respective countries. It was beneficial for us to replace the Ethiopian army after they moved back. We planned to hit as fast as they moved back before the Ethiopians returned their army. We were not going to lose anything if we did that.

I informed Mengistu that I wanted to send about 2000 plain clothed army into the country to protect our people; therefore, I requested him to give me a little bit of expense to support their food and gasoline. He accepted and granted us a little bit of money and some gasoline. We were doing our mission of mischief. We collected what he gave us and whatever else we could collect and entered the country. That was how the Ismaqiiq operation was to be achieved. I then flew to London. The fact was that we betrayed them otherwise nothing would have worked for us.

Ahmed Silanyo Meet with the Commanders

When we enter the country, we need a spokesperson to inform the world about it. I cannot speak inside Ethiopia; if the war operation did not find a voice internationally, it would become meaningless. Siad Barre's propaganda machine would run faster than the truth. They would hide the facts and inform the world that there was no war.

That is what happened, SNM entered the country. Silanyo left Ethiopia. Silanyo told the BBC that SNM was in a fierce fight inside Hargeisa and Burao with Siad Barre's army. He told the world about the new phase of the war. Siad Barre's propaganda machine announced on radio Mogadishu that a regional football match was being played in Hargeisa as the country fell into the hands of SNM.

SNM's Resolve to Enter Somalia

I have heard stories that SNM entered, and no leadership knew about it. That statement is false. I authorized the rush war operation and signed the document with my own hands. Even at the time some were skeptical about the rush, but we organized it and had no other option.

Silanyo: To Openly Deny the Rush War Was Our Decision

It was our tactic to deny that we ordered the war and announced that our commanders acted without our knowledge. SNM's return to Ethiopia would have been difficult if we did not do that. We did not want to sever our relations with Ethiopia. As happened later, our relationship remained as it were, and it was our tactic to play with both hands and we succeeded.

The Ethiopian Minister of Security Visited JiJiga

When the minister of security came to JiJiga and asked where was the SNM leadership, they told him they were not there. And he asked where the army was, and they told him, they had left. He wondered who asked them to leave. They responded nobody. That tactic worked very well for us.

When later it was inevitable to return and we insisted that it was not a unanimous decision, we asked them to continue supporting our needs as before; it worked as well. The ismaqiiq operation worked well for us. It has killed the agreement that the two dictators were trying to save their dictatorships.

The Resolution to Fight

In mid-May, Chairman Ahmed Silanyo transferred Ahmed Mire from the chief commander and replaced him with Jama Ali Elmi, then the commander of the Awaareh training camp. The Army Chief of Staff before now was Ahmed Silanyo. Also, a committee of five commanders was nominated to prepare the army for war operations. The chairman and a delegation he was heading traveled to the eastern front for several days and held meetings to inform the soldiers and the public about our new situation. On May 16, the chairman and his delegation reached a place called Kabo-Qor where the western army started their journey to target Hargeisa on 31 May. Ahmed Silanyo held a meeting with the army commanders and at the same time ordered Jama Ali Elmi to dispense the money the army was supposed to buy gasoline.

When chairman Silanyo finished preparing the army for war and gave instructions to move into war, he returned from the war front and held meetings with those available on the central committee and executive committee in Jijiga and Diridhaba. After he informed them, he received an invitation from SNM members in Europe to attend a big conference in London. Ahmed Silanyo returned from the war fronts on 18 May after he organized and prepared the SNM army for war and ordered the war operations. On 22 May 1988, he flew from Addis Ababa to London.

The Ismaqiiq (Rush) War Resolution

Ahmed Silanyo authorized the rush war operation when SNM military support of the Ethiopian government stopped. The agreement between Mengistu and Siad Barre indicated that SNM could not attack Siad Barre from Ethiopia. It was a frightful situation for Ahmed Silanyo and the entire SNM leadership, SNM soldiers, and SNM supporters inside and outside the country. At that time the movement was limping with a crippling conflict that started from the 5th SNM central committee congress in 1987. Musa Bihi Abdi explaining that situation says: *The man accountable and held responsible for whatever happened at that time was Ahmed Silanyo. Therefore, while he was dealing with tribal issues, the commanders who could have led the soldiers of the western war front were in jail and the movement was endemic with tribal problems; the agreement between Mengistu and Siad Barre also fell upon him.*

Leadership was in a very tight place. Everyone looked after his interest. Ethiopia looked after its interest. Therefore, SNM had to look after its interest as well. The new deal was for everyone to focus on its interest only. The new reality dictated that SNM should stand and walk alone. That is why at the end of May SNM resolved to engage in a bold war and face the brutal army of Siad Barre that fortified the border in multiple rows from the border to the middle of all the major cities in the north.

The ismaqiiq war operation was not planned earlier because the army was not ready. They were stationed in camps far from each other and did not have enough weapons for war. They did not have enough gasoline for their vehicles or the vehicles they seized from the public. They also had to move stealthily and efficiently to not alarm the two regimes now in agreement. All those obstacles and needs were there, each warning of the danger surrounding the act of war. However, the SNM army, leadership and supporters enjoyed something neither Mengistu's army nor the army of Siad Barre had; they had unshakable Faith and confidence in steel and the support of their population. They said 'yes' to death and 'no' to subjugation and humiliation.

Abdisamad Abdillahi Gamgam who was among the commanders of the ismaqiiq operation speaking about the situation surrounding SNM at the time explains: *The Ethiopian commanders called a meeting with the SNM commanders and told them they were going to start training for the SNM soldiers therefore they should be moved from the border and return into the barracks. We returned to the soldiers and informed them that there was no training to be given but they wanted us to be collected and contained in barracks and that was the agreement Mengistu and Siad Barre signed.*

Ahmed Silanyo Signed the Ismaqiiq (rush) War Operation under a Tree

Musa Bihi Abdi explains: *I was at the time attending a meeting that required Silanyo to sign the war decree and then leave Ethiopia. Ahmed Silanyo discussed in that meeting what he and Mengistu discussed about the soldiers to be returned to the camps, and he asked the congress for advice. The central committee in that congress was not complete. Those available discussed it further. It was decided to enter the country. Ahmed Silanyo agreed. He signed the ismaqiiq war authorization right there. The difficult operation was signed under a tree not even in a village.*

The Elders Should Not Join the Soldiers

The question came up what would the elders be doing if we resolved to take the war inside the country? I was among the commanders who did not want the elders to join us because they would burden us. Should we protect them or engage in war? Besides, there was no war in the world where civilian leaders followed the frontline soldiers. It was already agreed that Ahmed Silanyo leave the country to avoid imprisonment. Also, we knew the reason Ahmed Silanyo went to London. He sat in London for a while without a telephone and news, yet he carried the cause of the movement far and wide. We returned to the army and he left for Jijiga. If he remained for one or two more days he would have been in jail because he defied what Mengistu and Siad Barre agreed.

Abdisamad Gamgam explains: *When the ismaqiiq operation was signed, the biggest armies were the western and eastern regiments. The plan was for all the regiments to enter the country simultaneously at the same time. We had postponed several times because the regiment of the west commanders were in prison. They were not friendly with the Ethiopians therefore they still had not received the ammunition and gasoline. Their operation was slow-moving. The eastern regiment received their ammunition and gasoline right away.*[1] *But for the western regiment everything was delayed.*

Ahmed Mire explains that situation, says: *Ahmed Silanyo called his people inside and outside the country to war and his leadership was the one that compelled a decision for the fate of the people. Its strategic plan was to get ready and his leadership succeeded in taking big war operations into the country. Silanyo went to Dhoobo-Guduud and called for a meeting of the commanders and informed them of the situation. He told them 'you can see the situation we are in. They have turned the tables on us. The reality is for the SNM man to resign to his tribal, rural area, seek political asylum or submit to the brutal Siad Barre. The commanders resolved to start the war. Silanyo signed the ismaqiiq operation and that meant victory or death and destruction.*

Life is to live well or to disappear

It's the situation I am in

(Sayyid Mohamed Abdulle Hassan)

Moving the Regiment to Enter Burao on 27 May 1988

Abdisamad Abdudllahi Gamgam again: *The plan was to start the war on the 14th of May. As the war operation was being postponed several times, finally, the people got angry and thought we were joking and pushed the army hard, then there was no choice but to go ahead.*

Ahmed Mire commanding the army of 27th May, explains: *When we realized there was no help coming our way and even that it was impossible to synchronize all the regiments to enter simultaneously, we quickly decided to enter Burao as possible. I could never forget their sense of resolve to do it or die when I told the army of the daring decision to enter Burao. The courage, determination, and confidence they had accepted the decision had been fantastic and moving. The gasoline we had was only enough until we reached Burao. Our*

---

(1) Silanyo asked Mengistu for some resources to support some plain clothed army he wanted to protect the civilians under Siad Barre's siege but the other resources were the ones the army stationed in Qaho were using to move them back into the barracks after Mengistu and Siad Barre's agreement

vehicles and the vehicles donated by the people were about 30 altogether. Our consolation and comfort were that: our support, gasoline and bullets were all in Burao. Some of the army members that entered Burao were women. We told them: 'Oh girls stay behind from the front lines. These men are determined not to come back.' They argued and I decided to let them follow. Most of them survived. Before I moved the army from the Samater Ahmed location, I told them we only had gasoline to reach Burao. The weapon to fight was enough only to fight the first round of the enemy. Support, gasoline, and weapons were in our country. Are you ready to die there? In unison, they roared "yes."

We prayed the Fajr prayer in a place called "Barta." When the enemy saw us they aimed their canons at us. I ordered the soldiers not to respond to them. The enemy thought an army was on their back and started running away.

The Attack on Adaadley 28 My 1988

[Ahmed Weysa'adde on the Adaadley front said this much about SNM's plans of attack]: *Aim at any one of the Siad Barre's camps. It was not important which one. The goal was to attack the one that could give him the most brutal blow. Of all his camps, we chose Adaadley and we were 450 martyrs. Some chose Burao. The rest chose Hargeisa. The determination was: that everyone should face the place most difficult for him. One of the happiest occasions in my life was when we crossed the border.*

We succeeded in the operation. We were forced to do it and Allah swt gave us victory. Our situation was like that of Tariq Bin Ziad who burnt the boats his army used to cross the sea then looked back and told his army: 'the sea is behind you and the enemy is in front of you.' We had no place to turn but forward. Our choices were going back to Awaareh or facing our enemy inside Somalia.

We were three brigades of 160 SNM fighters each: Mohamed Ali, Mohamed Ismail and Hussein Guled (Dheere)

How did things happen? The army in Adaadley was composed of one division and two brigades. The two brigades fought with another two brigades from the Faqash and the third brigade overrun an entire division called 'Barkhad' from the faqash. We fought continuously for ten days. Forty-five martyrs died in that operation. Afterward some of our fighters moved to strengthen Burao while the rest moved to help the attack on Hargeisa. Initially, the plan was for the central and western brigades to attack Hargeisa together. However, when the planned synchronization of Burao and Hargeisa did not work, we crossed to Adaadlay to support the Burao attack.

The Attack on Hargeisa, May 31 1988

The Hargeisa army entered on May 31st. At about 2 am, they moved from Balli Samater. As Mohamed Elmi Gallan relays: "Although we were a large army, we were a drop in a bucket compared to the military we were going to face.

Our army moving toward Hargeisa was the one Siad Barre's army observed the most. They were prepared for us. Every entrance to the city was closed. The army reached Masallaha at 3:00 am. Since they were ready for us, three army groups were confronted from three different directions. They were fighting us fr7 am6-7am; at7:00 am they regrouped and an army with tanks hit from the back. It rained as well. SNM soldiers were determined to enter the city but every road leading to Hargeisa was closed. Finally, they crossed an old road made by the British not in use at the time between Hagal and Haraf which was empty of Siad Barre's army. They were three regiments and they had two goals:

1. *The group commanded by Mohamed Elmi Galan entered the army headquarters.*
2. *The army commanded by Aden Adde to enter Taar dheer, the headquarters for the second regiment.*

Siad Barre's army ran away and collected themselves near the airport. The biggest problem that faced SNM fighters was that the government army was prepared and waiting for them; Hargeisa was a big city. The SNM fighters did not have good communication devices. There was an SNM army that had captured vehicles and other heavy weapons and when they tried to join the other fighters, they were mistakenly taken as Siad Barre's army and were burnt there. Those circumstances brought the difficulty that could face every operation when the army loses each other, and a friendly fire occurs. The process took place at night.

Declaration of War: External Media War

Wars have many aspects. The most dangerous one is the propaganda of the war and explaining the reality on the ground at the war zones. Siad Barre's regime threw a more serious curfew on all the cities in the northern regions. He had abstained from local and international press to know and report on what was happening, especially, Hargeisa, Burao and Berbera.

The government press reduced its news to telling the people, some drugged bandits attacked the cities of Hargeisa and Burao and the government army dismantled them. Some were killed, others were arrested, and the country is back to peace.

Mohamed Abshir Walde commenting on Ahmed Silanyo's decision of war says: When Ahmed Silanyo signed the war act, he spoke with the army and told them, he was going to Europe. 'When I leave enter into the war and I would speak.'

When the war begins we need someone to speak for us. We need the world to hear our voice and can't speak while inside Ethiopia. Our fight would be meaningless if we could not find a voice to reach the world. Siad Barre's propaganda machine would run faster and he would hide the facts.

Silanyo left Ethiopia, and the war started. Amidst a fierce fight in Hargeisa and Burao,

Ahmed Silanyo spoke to the BBC.

Although Siad Barre tried to hide from the world the brutality he and his army committed in the north, the genocide that happened in Hargeisa and Burao were more extensive than what he could hide. SNM succeeded in grabbing the attention of the world and the free press. The international free press saw with its own eyes the genocide that Siad Barre's regime committed against the population in the northern regions. Michael Sailham who worked for the daily Nation and AFP wrote a long article about the circumstances on the ground in his article on 23 November 1989 entitled 'Horn of Africa Martyrs". He explained how SNM tactically was the strongest movement in Somalia but had little idea of how to take things forward if they gained victory over Siad Barre's government.

SNM Fighters Isolated the Cities of Northern Regions

An article written in English by Journalist Michael Sailham, published in the Daily Nation on November 23, 1989 stated: *The movement that is fighting to topple Siad Barre regime demonstrated major military victories but they were short of ideas when it comes to what they would do once they free the country. The SNM chairman Ahmed Mohamed Mohamoud Silanyo who is now located on the southern side of Hargeisa suburbs speaking with an AFP journalist said: The regime in Mogadishu committed cruelty unseen in the world before. There is no callous dictator equal to Siad Barre. We want an open transparent system, democratic government, free and fair elections and multiple political parties. Ahmed Mohamed Mohamoud Silanyo accused Siad Barre's loyal army of killing more than fifty thousand innocent civilians in the northern regions in the last eighteen months. Most of them died in heavy air bombardments aimed ruthlessly at innocent civilians and most targeted were from the Isaaq clan. In May, attacked all the major cities in the north. Although they were forced to exit those cities, they have captured an extensive area on the eastern side of the border with Djibouti and small towns like Sayla' and Loyaado. Four SNM brigades surround Hargeisa.*

A foreign journalist, reporting from the top of a mountain of a city empty of its inhabitants got th,is information from the SNM commander of the area. But Colonel Mohamed Ali Omar who abandoned the Somali army force for SNM did not say precisely how much army he was leading.

SNM exited Hargeisa in August for war tactics, but at night they poured logistical officers into the city every night. Siad Barre's army controlled a huge compound near the airport. 80,000 inhabitants in the area escaped for their lives. SNM army wanted to take control of the road between Hargeisa and Borama on the western side and Hargeisa and Berbera port on the city's eastern side. However, Siad Barre's army mined all the roads in and out of Hargeisa. One day early in the morning they showered bullets on the SNM fighters, a journalist and his cameraman traveling with them. The SNM fighters, though well trained and well-armed that were interviewed by AFP journalists were not able to speak candidly about their operations and SNM political options.

Ahmed Silanyo explains*: "Siad Barre viewed the Isaaq clan as a danger to his regime. The northern regions had many complaints like lack of development and aggression. We are at the point of no return."*

America recently tied its aid to Somalia to the way it enhances its human rights, but SNM's future will depend mostly on how much support they get from other Somali clans.

The Results of the Rush to War Operation

The atrocities of the brutal regime and the genocide that did not discriminate against citizens from SNM fighters compelled the inhabitants of Hargeisa and Burao to flee those cities. They were left as ghost towns. Those who remained in Hargeisa were Siad Barre's soldiers and the Ogaden refugees from the 1977/78 war with Ethiopia they used as militia. Those who stayed in Burao were Siad Barre's soldiers and a few people who could not run away. The brutal regime took the most atrocious steps of summary executions and mass graves to hide those killed. The mass graves dug daily in the northern regions are testimony to what had happened. The regime started to collect young and old, urban or rural residents, students, women and children, tied them together and killed them with heavy artillery aimed heartlessly at them. After killing them, they bulldozed their bodies into mass graves. Evidence of these mass graves mushrooms all over the cities of Hargeisa, Berbera, and Gabiley and in the remote rural areas. They are dug daily by heavy rains and are well documented.

Siad Barre: Mengistu, You Have Betrayed Me

25th of May Siad Barre was invited to Addis Ababa for the 25th anniversary of the African Union. The two leaders, celebrating their agreement on 27th May in the town of Soodra in Lake Tana learned that SNM captured Burao. It was a mouth-dropping shock. Siad Barre was the first to receive the bad news and when he got the telegram, he looked at Mengistu by his side and told him: you had betrayed me. Mengistu spoke with his security officers, and they also confirmed. Mengistu swore he did not know about it until that moment.

The Ethiopian officers came to the SNM office in Diridhaba. They asked the people there. Where was Ahmed Silanyo? Not here they answered. He went to London. Where was the other leadership? Not here. Where were the commanders? Where were your leadership and commanders? Not here. They crossed the border into Somalia! The SNM commanders rejected the idea of sitting in camps to train so they crossed the border without telling the leadership.

Siad Barre and his generals could not believe Ethiopia's explanation and the party mood turned into a grim reality. The hostility between the two countries was reasserted and SNM and Ethiopian relationship remained cordial and cooperative.

Tens of Thousands of Civilians Took Up Arms

After the daring operation, we could evaluate what the regime could do. We expected a mass exodus from the cities where the fighting took place. Ahmed Mohamed Mohamoud Silanyo explains that situation: *One of our victories was that many people left the cities of the war. We had already arranged refugee camps for them so that we could get humanitarian assistance from the United Nations as soon as they reached the camps. We opened the refugee camps before people left Hargeisa.*

Our victories also included how we had convinced the international community to stop aid to Siad Barre's cruel regime because of his atrocities against the people. Ahmed Silanyo sent a plea to the Secretary General of the United Nations and UNHCR to bring emergency support to the refugees. Refugee camps were opened in eastern Ethiopia for them. He also called neighboring countries to support the SNM operations. In addition to that, there were also continuous diplomatic steps taken by SNM supporters worldwide to gain support for the SNM cause and to inform international communities of Siad Barre's brutality.

Other victories included expanding the war beyond the Isaaq and Somaliland only and taking it to Suufka. In this place, many different clans shared so the war was a Somali war with Siad Barre. The refugees from the cities overflowed to the SNM headquarters and along the border with Ethiopia. SNM was empowered by the youth, both boys and girls and anyone who could carry arms volunteering and willing to fight with Siad Barre's army.

When SNM fighters withdrew from the cities, they did not go far. They remained on the outskirts of the cities. They controlled the roads between Burao-Berbera, Berbera-Hargeisa and Hargeisa-Borama. At night they used to enter the cities and control them. Siad Barre's army collected themselves inside their barracks. They mined the area around their barracks and the roads leading to their camps. The mines they left caused Somaliland the lives of many people and livestock even after the war with Siad Barre ended. Everybody believed that the demolished cities would be rebuilt, and real democratic government would replace the destruction. It was the people's victory. People's feeling was that Siad Barre's days were short and numbered.

The war uprooted businessmen, religious men and people who would never have left their country. It was the destruction of life and property. Warplanes and heavy artillery were used to uproot those people. If, in the beginning, the war was between SNM and Siad Barre's army, everyone took up arms at that moment.

The 6th Congress and the Controversial Central Committee Resolution of 31st March –28 April 1990

SNM Central Committee held an extraordinary meeting. It was suggested in that meeting that anyone who had not been registered SNM member for two years was not going to attend the 6th Congress, and anyone who was not registered was not going to be in the central committee. Hassan Moallin explains that the youth who already held positions in SNM were afraid of others in their clans, more powerful and *experienced in threatening their positions. Ahmed Silanyo was against that. To him, it did not matter how the clan member came to the movement. Whether he was a fighter, or a refugee who fled Siad Barre, what mattered was that they came. Let's embrace everyone with open arms.*

His strong position was that: 'SNM was the people's struggle, it is their country, and we need everyone. This is not a time for separation and to put restrictions and limitations on the people who came out to fight for the cause.

When the 6th congress took place, the majority of the participants voted for the idea that was restricting the newcomers.

Condemning the Controversial Resolutions of the 6th Congress

Ahmed Silanyo and Ibrahim Meygag opposed the resolutions strongly. After the vote, Ahmed Silanyo came to more than 500 men. Among them were the educated elite, respected elders, and politicians led by Sheikh Ibrahim and he told them: *We lost the vote and I want you to come up with some advice on what to do.*[1] *When the elders heard about Ahmed Silanyo's report, they took decisions right there:*

1. *The resolutions of the extraordinary meeting were null and void since the time of the central committee had elapsed.*[2]
2. *We, the elders would choose the members that would attend the 6th congress.*
3. *The chairman would be chosen at the congress and chair the meeting.*

Those points took effect and Musa Bihi Abdi was chosen to chair the meeting. The elders who were thrown out at first came back to congress.

The 2nd Extraordinary Central Committee Congress

In February 1989, SNM held an extraordinary central committee congress in Baligubadle. It was marked by the fact that it was the only congress that the SNM chairman did not chair. Mohamed Ibrahim Warsame Hadrawi, the chairman of the SNM standing committee, chaired that meeting.

Ahmed Silanyo presented the names of the preparatory committee, but it was rejected, and he was not happy about that.[3] He then suggested that the central committee handle the matter. The central committee chose five members to nominate the preparatory committee to be approved by the central committee. The nominated committee was one opposed to Ahmed Silanyo whose aim was to ensure that Ahmed Silanyo was not re-elected. As relayed by Hassan Moallin: *that committee made some serious legal and ethical errors, which has placed a question mark on their entire method of operation. The Guurti took over and decided on who was going to be attending members and the number of attendees.*

---

(1) 35 votes were for those favoring restricting those not registered with SNM for two years and 16 votes for those who wanted to embrace all. Ahmed Silanyo was among those who did not want to discriminate against the new SNM members.
(2) The unusal meeting was overdue because of the daring operation.
(3) (Dhahal Reeb, Boobe)

In Baligubadle, the central committee broke into two camps, one supporting the re-election of Ahmed Silanyo and one opposed to it. Many attempts to bring the two camps together did not yield results. When that conflict became impassible and the movement almost forgot its big cause, Ahmed Silanyo decided to withdraw. Abdirahman Alin speaking about that issue explains: *If Ahmed Silanyo did not start at that moment, the SNM movement would have collapsed. His decision to withdraw saved the movement. What was interesting is that, at the time, many people were encouraging Ahmed to stay. Clan elders, the Guurti and even Mengistu wanted him to stay. Also, half of the central committee wanted him to stay. Many people directly or indirectly expressed their support for Ahmed Silanyo believing that the country would soon be freed. It was not the time for him to relinquish the SNM leadership.*

Musa Bihi Abdi explains: *When all converged in Baligubadle, I was among those who wanted Ahmed Silanyo to leave. All the military commanders agreed that Ahmed Silanyo was a weak leader. I remember his words: we do not need conflict today.*

Silanyo Does Not Arrest Anyone

Ahmed Silanyo was accused of being a weak leader. He did not arrest criminals; he did not control thieves, nor did he do anything about crimes as serious as death. In his defense of all these allegations while in Baligubadle, he countered: *killing and imprisonment, I tell you, if killing and imprisonment of citizens did any good, it would have done good for Siad Barre (Afweyne) and the nature of a thief, I give you an example now. All of you are the cream of the people in Somaliland. You were trusted with the people's future. Everyone was given the utensils to eat with, a thermos to keep your tea warm, bed sheets, and blankets for your sleep and comfort. To the allegations of "I don't arrest thieves," I tell you, look at what you are sitting on now! Every one of you is sitting on a small plastic sheet. The rest he placed somewhere. That is all I will say about a thief's nature. Forget about thieves to be arrested or criminals to be killed; when the one entrusted with responsibility fails in his duties and we fire him, his entire clan flees the movement and threatens to take all their sons away from it.*

Silanyo Hands over SNM Leadership

For all those who pressured me to stay in SNM Leadership, I want to tell you, I had sacrificed a lot for the cause of SNM. I had sacrificed my responsibility to my family. A wife and small children I left a long time ago. They have a right too. I have given six years of my life to this cause, and many people see leadership as something big and powerful and are eager to take over. Surely, there are many people in the movement worthy of its leadership. Therefore, I have decided to withdraw from the run for chairmanship. My only advice is to hold the congress; you can manage alone because I am leaving you. We are in a war so I would advise you to choose a leadership that can take us through to the end of the war.' [1]

When Ahmed Silanyo withdrew, many others were running for chairmanship. Among them were Ibrahim Meygag Samater, Abdirahman Ahmed Ali, Mohamed Hashi Elmi and Hassan Essa Jama.

When Ahmed Silanyo insisted on leaving, his supporters asked his advice on a person to nominate. They told him: we would nominate whomever you suggest to us.

Ahmed Silanyo told them he was supporting Abdirahman Ahmed Ali. Once he relinquished the leadership, he chose to support his friends. Ibrahim Meygag did not have enough votes to support him because his clan had another candidate Mohamed Hashi therefore Ahmed Silanyo chose to support Abdirahman Ahmed Ali. Silanyo left SNM at a perfect place. Ahmed Silanyo's tenure with SNM was the most painful period for Siad Barre. The testimony to that was when Ahmed Silanyo resigned and left SNM, Siad Barre celebrated the end of the SNM movement. To him, Silanyo's departure marked the end of the movement.

That jubilation did not last long for Siad Barre; his regime was already paralyzed, and the national symbol was destroyed by dangerous tribalism and widespread corruption. In less than a year, armed struggles of all movements converged in Mogadishu and its suburbs. Siad Barre hid inside a military tank to leave Mogadishu on January 26, 1991. In 1991 all three major movements claimed significant military victories. SNM took over all the major northern cities including Hargeisa, Burao, Berbera, and Erigavo. On 26 January 1991, USC attacked the villa Somalia which resulted in taking over the capital Mogadishu. SPM succeeded in overrunning many military camps in the south.[2]

---

(1) Amina-Weris says: When Ahmed returned from Baligubadle, he remained in London for nine months and it was the first time in almost seven years, he remained with us for that long. After that he returned to the country to take a lion's share of peace building in the country.

(2) In November 1989 SNM &SPM released a declaration that they have same motives on internal and international affairs of Somalia. In 1990 SNM signed a similar agreement with USC. Again, SNM announced on 24 November 1990 that it united with SPM and USC so that they could have a united strategic plan to confront the military administration.

The Results of the 6th Congress

After a long argument, the 6th congress ended peacefully and successfully. Abdirahman Ahmed Ali was elected as the SNM Chairman, Hassan Essa Jama as the Vice Chairman, and Ibrahim Meygag Samater as the central committee chairman. The Guurti became constitutional and was going to become a vital institution in the future of Somaliland.

Ali Assey: Feeling of Emptiness – Poem

Ali Assey, a young man among the chairman's bodyguards speaks about his knowledge of Silanyo: *He was a bold man who visited any place SNM fighters resided. He was a fighter who came at a time SNM needed him. He was also a politician who knew how to keep different people together. When he arrived, SNM leaped into action. He was kind to the youth in the movement. He was an impartial man who treated everyone the same, a good manager who managed things calmly. Everyone including commanders, soldiers, politicians, and the members of the movement respected and held him in high esteem. He was a man who was aware of every state the movement was going through from east to west. He succeeded in connecting all aspects of the movement from soldiers to politicians. He moved the movement despite difficult circumstances.*

I was one of his bodyguards and when he stepped down and Abdirahman Ahmed Ali took over, I returned to my regiment. I have created a small poem discussing the change. I borrowed the title of the poem 'Gocanaya mooye' from the famous poet Ali Jama Habil. It speaks about the situation then. A central committee member by the name of Ahmed Yusuf Golhaye was killed in Harta Sheikha by mistake. He died by accident. Some SNM members became dissident, and dissidents being searched for when information was wrongly gathered, they were hiding in Harta Sheikha. Innocent men among them the deceased were sitting in a small hut chewing qat and did not know what was going on when suddenly their hut was surrounded and showered with bullets. Therefore, an innocent man was killed. Abdirahman Ahmed Ali was the chairman. It happened that none from the SNM leadership came to the place of the incident. SNM members felt the absence of leadership. I remember a similar incident when some commanders' car was seized in Allay Baday and the race of Ahmed Silanyo. He sent elders and soldiers. I was among those who went there. Therefore, I compared that day with this day. Today an important man in the central committee was killed by friendly fire and nothing happened to acknowledge his death. When I compared this day to the day of the car incident and realized the fight for the car was much more furious and faster than this one where an important man died and no action marked his death, I created this poem: Commemorating Ahmed Silanyo's Leadership

Oh, dear Ganay, I toss and turn and can't sleep
There is a reason I did not bite the food left for me
The 6th conference left us in an ominous state
A dark day for SNM members wherever they are
Alas! They removed our previous chairman. Alas!
Six personal qualities he had to stir my solemn recollection
*Any hostility happening between clans in the same environment
Or collective complaint regarding earlier transgressions
When the car of the men usually *accused was seized
Whether he sent elders or visited the places of the incident
The speed of his actions stirs my solemn recollection
When essential group decision was to be reached
Or, as usual a reporter from the *Bush House approached
His eloquence affected everyone, Muslim or non-Muslim
And his wise responses stir my solemn recollection
Really, he was a chairman for the entire Horn. Genuine
*Voices of the youth praising him stir my solemn recollection
When suddenly unexpected members landed late at night
Where food and qat were unattainable, whether he
Gave us from his pocket or pushed another to acquiesce
The *10b that satisfied our needs stirs my solemn recollection.

Explanations starred words.
Gabaray: People living in the same environment
Nimanka gaar loo eryado: Commanders and other leftist groups
Bush House: BBC Headquarters in London
Siad Deposed, Silanyo came: the praising songs during Silanyo's leadership.
Asir: 10b that in Ethiopia could buy a lot.

The SNM Plan after It Enters the Country

At the end of the 6th congress, it was clear that SNM would soon capture the cities in the north and Siad Barre's days were numbered. For that purpose, the SNM movement reached some decisions on what to do when it captured the country Musa Bihi Abdi who was the chairman of the 6th congress explains: *We agreed that war has many unanticipated twists and turns therefore, it was inevitable to reach some conclusions on the methodology of what to do after we capture our country such as:*

1. *What to do with the refugees still inside the country;*
2. *What to do with Siad Barre's defeated army when they surrender; and*
3. *How to deal with the clans in the northern regions that turned against our struggle.*

After a discussion on those and other issues, it was agreed that:

1. *Not to hurt the people who become refugees in our country after the 1977 war (all from the Ogden clan). It was agreed not to hurt them.*
2. *Not to hurt the defeated army of Siad Barre.*
3. *Somaliland to offer peace to the clans on the corners who did not support the struggle. Those points were adopted in an all-northern clans fraternity reconciliation conference held in Burao.*

BBC Interview with Ahmed Silanyo on Monday, May 30, 1988

The invasion of Burao and Ahmed Silanyo's interview with BBC (Waxsansheeg News): Friday 27 May 1988 was the day the SNM fighters, and the general public took over the city of Burao and toppled the repressive rule. 27 May and 31st May 1988 were the two days Burao and Hargeisa broke the dictator's yoke and marked the memorable victory of SNM and the freedom people enjoy today in Somaliland. These two days ended the summary executions of citizens, the curfews, imprisonment, women's rape, and the hardship the people of the northern regions endured. Neither local nor international press was available to report on what had happened. There wasn't freedom of the media in the country. Newsagents were not able to ask for information freely.

Communication was in the hands of the government and people couldn't exchange information without harassment and arrest. Therefore, it was as if something big had just happened in the dark and no one knew what it was.

(waxsansheeg news, Burao).

The only place people could find reliable news was the BBC Somali Service. Although they could not inform from inside Somalia or visit the actual sites of the war, they were able to interview both SNM and Siad Barre's regime about the situation. SNM spread its message to the entire world to inform them of the war situation. The most valuable information they got was a BBC interview with Ahmed Mohamed Mohamoud Silanyo.

Here is an interview with Ahmed Silanyo three days after SNM attacked and captured Burao. This interview was Ahmed Silanyo's response to news that the Siad Barre government categorized the attack on Burao as the work of a small group of pirates that killed some civilians and confirmed the situation was under control and the security of the city was in the hands of the army. When that interview was completed, the BBC announced breaking news informing the world of the capture of the town of Hargeisa nd discussed it on its weekly program: 'This Week in Africa.' Here is the interview:

Question: *When did you capture Burao and how did you do it?*

Answer: *Burao was captured entirely on the 28th and not the 29th. As you might know, SNM has been a movement fighting inside and outside the country for a long time. When we thought the time opportune to attack with the help of the population, we took a surprise attack on many parts of the country including the northern regions, and the city of Burao was captured.*

Question: *Did you attack other cities or only Burao?*

Answer: *Many other cities were also attacked and until now the fight is going on in many places. The news we have now confirms the capture of Adaadly, a small town near Gabiley and many small villages were freed by the people themselves, towns like Odweyne and other rural villages.*

Question: *Is Sheikh one of the cities you have captured?*

Answer: *I am not sure about Shiekh as I speak, but I can confirm that fights are going on now in many places, including between Berbera and Sheikh.*

Question: *Can you tell us the number of the army that attacked Burao?*

Answer: *That was a large army that had made it possible to capture Burao, the second capital city of the north and the third largest city in Somalia, where many Siad Barre's army were stationed. The ease with which the two cities were captured shows the confidence and determination of our fighters and the weakness of Siad Barre's army*

Question: Can you guess the number of the SNM army, one thousand, two or three? How many do you think?

Answer: I don't want to say how many there were. There were large numbers of civilians who converged from all the corners of the city, so all I can say is that there were many.

Question: Did the civilians who live in Burao join the fight?

Answer: The fight did not happen inside the city, but the attack started at the military barracks. When the city was captured, Siad Barre attacked with planes killing many people and destroying large property, but the fight did not happen inside Burao.

Question: You have downed those two planes as was indicated in your news release?

Answer: One of the planes was downed in Burao, and the other in Hargeisa.

Question: In your estimation how many of Siad Barre's army did you kill in Burao? How many were dead?

Answer: Frankly speaking we don't want to say we have killed that many. But I can say that it was a fight and some of Siad Barre's army surrendered while others ran and some joined the SNM struggle.

Question: How many of your SNM army died?

Answer: Six of our fighters died and seventeen of them were injured.

Question: News from Mogadishu is saying that 600-800 of your army attacked the city and none of them survived.

Answer: Our fighters captured Burao and now the SNM flag is the only one flying. As I said yesterday, we will show you. We would show you if the regime agrees to let the free press into the country.

Question: The news we are getting indicates that after SNM fighters entered Burao, they collected citizens from other regions and killed them summarily.

Answer: That news is false. Everyone sided with the fighters no matter what region they came from. The people together fought the Siad Barre army. They sided with the SNM fighters and fought side by side with them. It was SNM who was protecting the people from the regime. What had hurt the people were the planes throwing bombs at the poor civilians. It is Siad Barre who is killing the people as he has always done and now he is aiming to finish them all. It is Siad Barre's *regime that exploits tribalism and regionalism, and it is his regime that commits genocide for revenge. SNM's policy is not like that. Its war is legitimate and includes all Somalis, incorporating brotherhood and nationalism.*

Question: *Mr. Ahmed Silanyo, what is the next step you are planning to take?*

Answer: *Our next step is to free as many parts of the country as possible from this decadent regime. Fights are going on now in Hargeisa and many other cities in the country. I hope we will continue the fight until the entire Somalia is free from this depraved government.*

Question: *What land are you planning to free?*

Answer: *As is clear in our constitution, we are Somalis and the land we are planning to free is the land called Somalia.*

Question: *The northern regions, right?*

Answer: *The northern regions are part of Somalia, and we will free them. We will also free the rest of Somalia. Fights are already going on there.*

Constitutional Guurti: Aydaroosh 1988

When people emptied the cities in1988, everyone including the elders, business people and clergy left the country. Hassan Moallin explains that when those elders met, they decided to take up arms and fight since there was no way out of war.

The men who settled those issues included Sheikh Ibrahim and Sheikh Ahmed Nuh. They met again in 1989 and completed the formation of the Guurti, ensuring the membership of all clans to be included. No central committee meeting was held between when the people left the northern cities and the meeting in Baligubadle.

At the Baligubadle SNM congress, it was suggested to constitutionalize the Guurti, which has created a big conflict. Many people turned against the idea, especially the idea of making the Guurti an integral part of the government. Those against the idea lost the argument on the premise that the country suffered by the decision of young and rash men who surrendered our independence to Mogadishu. The elders should heed that and not allow it to happen again. Therefore, when SNM captured the country, the guurti was constitutional. Ahmed Silanyo supported the guurti to become constitutional. Ahmed Silanyo and Ibrahim Meygag were the backbones of the guurti becoming constitutional. They were also advisors to the elders and constantly reminded them to exercise patience with their young men and work on peace.

The Guurti tried to mediate conflicting parts. Hassan Moallin explains: We tried to negotiate a conflict between Ahmed Mire's group against Ahmed Silanyo's group, which took us longer than 21 days. We thought if this mediation took us this long, how long would older and more deep-rooted conflicts take?

The SNM Guurti Conference in Hargeisa

That was the first meeting the guurti held inside the country. It happened at the Hargeisa dry stream in February 1991. It was when SNM captured the land and any remnants of Siad Barre's army were cleared from the country. The guurti took the first steps to peacebuilding that was vital to the country. It was the constitutional guurti that was formed earlier. They were elders who were free from the kind of conflict that regressed SNM, they were able to evaluate the insurmountable amount of work in front of them and decided not to wait for anyone else to solve the problem, so they tackled them. They held their meeting in the middle of the Hargeisa dry stream as soon as they entered. It was their most important meeting. Three hundred eighteen members from all clans that participated in the war joined. The Musa Ismail clan in Erigavo was the only clan missing from that meeting. The rest of the Sanaag region was there and Sheikh Ibrahim was the chairman of the meeting. A debate started earlier on what direction to take the country started again, such as: whether we leave the union with Mogadishu or remain with Somalia. Many clans supported leaving the union. That argument continued for five days. Finally, the guurti prepared itself. They converged in a Hall at the presidential compound and wrote seven points for the press. Hassan Moallin who had worked closely with the guurti explains that situation: *We held that first meeting in 1991. As soon as we entered the country while SNM was around, the elders had their meeting in Hargeisa with the participation of all the clans in the SNM movement. It was held at the presidential compound. The president was there and did not attend. That conference was the foundation for the six reference points that later guurti conferences were based on. When the guurti completed its conference and announced its resolutions, they called Abdirahman Ahmed Ali for a meeting in which Abdirahman Ahmed Ali told them to stop the secession from the union and let Somaliland remain part of the federal government.* [1] The conference that happened in Hargeisa was an Isaaq meeting. It was the first significant meeting not usually acknowledged. The resolutions of that meeting were:

---

(1) Hassan Moallin

1. *Somaliland is a sovereign state.*

2. *Adopts Islamic Sharia as its constitutional law.*

3. *Isaaq to forgive and forget the clans against the struggle and Somalilanders to forgive each other.*

4. *To adopt a system of government encompassing all its clans so that we did not divide our people into the ruling and ruled. After that meeting a government nurtured by all clans in Somaliland was to be built.*

On February 15, another meeting was held in Berbera with the attendance of the clans from the eastern and western corners of Somaliland. The peace accord was signed there. It was agreed that every clan bring peace to its environment. Every clan took the responsibility to work on the stability of its territory. No outsiders would come to bring peace. It was their responsibility. It was acknowledged that peacemaking and peace and reconciliation are mandatory. Clans should work on integrating people in Somaliland and build on things that unite them. Each region was responsible for building peace at the grassroots of its environment.

After that meeting, the guurti announced another meeting in Burao in May 1991.

Silanyo's resignation in Baligubadle not to create a chasm was part of the discussion.

It was the Guurti that had taken over the decision. They stopped the feud that was going on for three years. They were the ones who stripped the power of the commanders controlling the different militias. The Guurti was fundamental to peace.

CHAPTER FOUR

SORTING THROUGH CHAOS: PERIOD OF CONFLICT RESOLUTION, PEACE MAKING, AND PEACEBUILDING

Somalia After Siad Barre: Ahmed Silanyo's Paper on Transitional Government

Although the USC movement in Mogadishu announced a government without consulting anyone, the SNM movement that captured the northern regions did not speak about that move. Ahmed Silanyo ignored the steps taken by the USC in Mogadishu but still thinking about steps to be taken before any hasty actions toward shared government are thought about also wrote about the need to clarify how the Somalis could share anything. He wrote a paper entitled: The proposed Structure of Transitional Arrangement.

From:	*Ahmed Mohamed Mohamoud Silanyo*
Address:	*42 Compton Road, London, 7QD*
Date:	*19th March 1991*
TO:	*Chairman of Somali National Movement, and the Operational Committee*
	Chairman of the Central Committee
	Chairman of the Political Committee of the Central Committee
CC:	*Secretary of the SNM Office in London*
Sub:	*Proposed Structure of Transitional Federal and Provincial Government.*

My Congratulations to the freedom fighters, SNM martyrs and all those who volunteered to free our land and the fantastic way the Somalis defeated the regressive regime of Siad Barre. Building a constitutional government, democratically based on free and fair elections is imperative It is equally important to start a debate about what kind of government we want to build for our country, whether it will be federal or not. Those issues need study and profound observation, calm and calculating thinking that would take time.

For that purpose, it is essential to complete the country's freedom. To do that, we need to build constitutional institutions. First, we need to develop a system of transitional government. That must be built on reality and not based on past actions. Unfortunately, it seems the situation we are in now forgets about future endeavors. Still, we have not yet built a system of transitional government or delineated our plans for the national and provincial government.

The only information I am receiving is the ambition of those working on bringing back the old characters and systems that have already burnt this society. They are those who ignore the reality of the country and its history. They oppose the movement's victory and the struggle they went through. When I understood what is going on in our country I decided to give you my advice and I hope for your consideration.

Thank you.

Victory and Freedom

Ahmed Mohamed Mohamoud Silanyo

Member of the SNM Central Committee

Somalia after Siad Barre 18 March 1991: Proposed Structure of Transitional Arrangement

Table of Contents

Introductory Notes

1) Proposed Structure of Transitional Arrangement
2) Concluding Remarks and Further Recommendations

Part One: Introductory Notes

Today, symbols such as the national flag are all that remain of the Somali state. There is no government or central authority of any form of existence. This is a tragic situation that should never have come to pass. But it did and ought to be rectified. However, if we have to build a nation-state again, on the ashes of the destruction and disintegration left by Siad Barre, and build it on a firmer foundation this time, we should. We should, perhaps, take a little time to ponder over it.

Hasty decisions to form a national government for its own sake could be self-defeating. We learned from our past that national authority per se is no guarantor of law and order, or social and political harmony and, therefore, not necessarily synonymous with the preservation of the national interest.

Any attempt to establish such an authority without a reasonable degree of consensus or, at least, without consultations among the principal actors is doomed to failure. That is why the unilateral step was taken in this direction recently in Mogadishu by a group of perhaps well-intentioned individuals [has not worked], as transition must be viewed as a process that needs a careful and pragmatic approach.

Political equations in Somalia, in terms of clan relationships, regional balances and personalities have undergone a radical change. To maintain the integrity of the nation, ensure a smooth transition to a democratic system of government under stable conditions, and avoid confrontations and chaos, it is necessary to come to terms with the new political realities. No attempts should be made to re-impose the old patterns or dig up icons of the past from their political graves. Within this context, we must evaluate the latest dramatic development of events in this country and bear this in mind in the formulation of policies for the future.

Thus, it is true that the humiliating defeat of Siad Barre last month was a matter of self-congratulation and cause for jubilation for all our people who had suffered for so long at the hands of a most brutal and vicious regime. However, the event undoubtedly also represented the two victorious liberation organizations, the SNM and USC and their fighters, the culmination of a long, bitter and bloody struggle against the ruthless tyranny of a tenacious dictatorship. Accordingly, their pre-eminence must be accepted, and the legitimacy of their present authority recognized.

For their part, the two organizations must demonstrate,

1. They do not intend to monopolize power but stand pluralistic and participatory forms of government at all levels.
2. Their respect for and strict adherence to human rights principles. In this connection, the liberation organizations must prevent any form of reprisals against individuals or groups of individuals on account of their regional or clan background, or on the pretext of injustices committed in the past.

3. Their readiness to set about the establishment of transitional arrangements will lead to a constitutional government and free elections at the earliest possible opportunity.

4. Speedy establishment of law and order in the areas under their respective control.

5. Their determination to complete the process of liberation. It is now against this background that the following framework for a transitional government in Somalia is submitted.

PART TWO: Proposed Structure of Transitional Arrangements

Summary of Proposed Structure

A) **National level**

1. *Council State ad interim*
2. *Transitional Government with limited Responsibilities.*
3. *Autonomous Organizations*

- *Currency Board*
- *Commission of Relief and Reconstruction*
- *Special Tribunal(s)*

B) **Regional Level**

1. *Provisional Regional Administrative Council, Northern Regions (the former Somaliland Protectorate)*
2. *Provisional Regional Administrative Council, Southern Regions (the former Italian Somalia)*

A Broad Indication of the Nature, Composition and Functions of the Proposed Transitional Framework:

A) **The National Level**

1. *The Council of State*

- *Composition: A limited number not exceeding ten numbers*
- *Nominating Authority: Half of the members will be nominated by the SNM*

and the other half by the USC

Nominations by the two organizations do not necessarily have to be restricted to their membership.

- *Functions: Performance of duties of a ceremonial nature generally reserved for the head of state. Giving assent to government decrees. Supervised and guidance of government activities without interference in its day-to-day operations.*

- *Powers:*

a) *Appointment and dismissal of the prime minister*

b) *Approval of nominations for Cabinet positions and possibly other selected senior posts.*

c) *Establishment of high military command at a national level in the event of external threat but only with the consent of the two regional councils.*

2. **The Transitional Government**

- *Composition: It must be broad-based and reflect comprehensive national representation plus a balance between the two regions.*

- *Responsibilities:*

a) *Creation of conditions necessary for returning to constitutional government and holding free elections at the end of the transitional period.*

Most of these are calling Constituent assembly whose primary responsibility will be the drafting of a new constitution.

b) *Conduct of foreign affairs/international relations*

c) *Posts and Telecommunications*

d) *Civil Aviation and National Airlines*

e) *Establishment and supervision of autonomous organs with operational independence, such as a Currency Board, a relief and reconstruction commission.*

f) *Assisting the provisional regional authorities to coordinate their policies and standardize procedures where and when necessary.*

- *Powers a) Power to issue decrees and pass regulations about all matters falling within their area of responsibility.*

B) **The Regional Level**

1. *Provisional Regional Administration Councils Composition. This must reflect a fair representation of the different communities in the region.*

- *Nominating Authority: The SNM and USC, after consultation in some appropriate form with the communities to be represented*

- *Responsibilities: All aspects of the administration and government of the respective regions, except those that fall within the domain of the central authorities or are otherwise retained by the liberation organization themselves.*

Autonomous Organs

1. Currency Board: It will be responsible for the re-organization and regulation of the national currency.

2. Relief and Reconstruction Commission. Its responsibilities will include:
    - *Assessment of national emergency relief requirements and the longer-term needs for rehabilitation and reconstruction.*
    - *Coordination of relief effort on behalf of the Somali authorities.*
    - *Liaison with international organizations and other groups active in the field.*

3. Special Tribunal(s) Their duties will include:
    - *To initiate appropriate legal action to safeguard national assets outside the country and recover those already plundered by the previous regime.*
    - *To prepare legal actions about crimes committed against the country and the people.*
    - *To collect and safeguard documents, files and other records relating to the above matters or others of a similar nature.*

Part Three: Further Recommendations.

1). Cooperation between the liberation movements must be established against the remnants of Said Barre's forces. There should be no cease-fire until they are crushed or disarmed.

2). Establishing coordination mechanisms between them is essential to widen the areas of cooperation and consultation.

3). A time limit must be specified for the duration of the transitional arrangements. This should not exceed two years.

4). Once transitional arrangements are in place, the liberation organizations should take a backstage role and concentrate on transforming into political parties and working out their strategy for the future. This does not affect the continued existence of organized units of their fighting forces until the latter are eventually absorbed into a permanent force after establishing a constitutional government.

5). The SNM has done well to start successful consultations and to reach an understanding with the various communities of the North at a regional level. It must also extend an immediate invitation to the USC for discussions about transitional arrangements at the national level, as well as appropriate ways to bring the liberation process to a speedy and successful conclusion.

BBC Interview with Ahmed Mohamed Mohamoud January 30, 1991, 1709 GMT

(From the Focus on Africa Program)

Other movements did not welcome the new situation in Somalia. Robin White asked Silanyo about his reaction to the new government of Ali Mahdi Mohamed in Mogadishu.

Ali Mahdi Mohamed became transitional president three days after the USC took over Mogadishu and after four weeks of intense fighting on the streets of Mogadishu. Siad Barre seems to be on the run but Omar Arteh Ghalib whom he appointed as prime minister is still doing his work as usual. The new government asked government soldiers to submit to the struggle movement centers, SNM in the north, USC in central Somalia and SPM in Southern Somalia but SNM seemed upset about what was happening in Mogadishu while SNM was whispering about where to join.

Robin White asked Ahmed Silanyo a senior SNM leader about what they were unhappy about.

Silanyo: *In any event, the question is not about us being unhappy. It is a matter of principle. Let me tell you in advance; I know at least seven decent, respectable people, and I have lots of respect for them. I can understand the situation in Mogadishu. But the principle before all of these is an agreement among the freedom movements even before Siad Barre was thrown out of power. The agreement was for each movement to free its area where it has the strongest support and any government temporary or otherwise to be one that was discussed and agreed upon and that has not happened.*

Robin White: But the new president Ali Mahdi Mohamed wants to speak with you about

	anything you want now. Are you going to talk to him? What do you like to discuss with him?

Silanyo: *Citizens elect presidents or nominations by groups. Therefore, this was not consulted by SNM. How can we accept it?*

Robin White: *Are you rejecting to recognize the new president and the new prime minister?*

Silanyo: *I am not accepting him. There is no question about that. SNM controls part of the country just the way other movements control some parts of the country. We strongly support USC, for example to build peace, law and order in the area of Mogadishu or other areas they control. That is very important and what we want to do in the areas we control. However, we will not accept a government Siad Barre built or personalities that have nominated themselves.*

Robin White: *Is it possible that non-Somalis believe that since you ousted Siad Barre you have already started squabbling?*

Silanyo: *No, No the matter is not a dispute among us. We are going to agree. I am hopeful of that. The problem was Siad Barre and his army. But there is no reason to rush to the presidential election until everything settles. Leaders of the movements have not met yet. We are not fighting among ourselves. Far from that!*

Robin White: *So, you are not going to run for president, and you will not attack USC since you control the country's largest area?*

Silanyo: *No, No, that won't happen. We will come together and build a transitional government or whatever else we agree on.*

Chaotic Time (The Meeting in Burao in 1991)

In 1991, Burao hosted the solidarity conference of all clans in the north. When we entered the country, there was ruinous damage from the clan civil war. Finding a decent location for a meeting or anyone to host a meeting was even tough. Burao succeeded in hosting the guild of all the clans in the north and the first SNM conference since we entered the country. The mayor of Burao at the time, Mohamoud Hashi Abdi, said: *When a place to hold the meeting of all the clans in the north could not be found, Burao took that huge responsibility to host it. All the other regions did not come forward because their local governments did not have money, but in Burao we had established a revenue collection system right away; therefore, our local government hosted the delegates in the meeting and invited them in late April.*

Ahmed Silanyo Came to Burao

Two successive meetings took place in Burao in April and May 1991. The first was the all the northern region clans' solidary conference that was meant to bring peace among all the clans in the north following earlier discussions in Hargeisa and Berbera. All the notable clan elders attended that conference and after that conference, the SNM central committee congress was a legislative body approving all the resolutions of the solidarity conference. The central committee congress evolved into the parliamentarian meeting when all the missing clan delegates that were not SNM were added.

Ahmed Silanyo came to the SNM central committee congress. He traveled through Hargeisa and said, '*When I saw the extent of the damage to the city my eyes welled with tears*. When he arrived, he worked with the leadership to bring the clans together. He was among the envoys discussing with the head of the clans, and political leaders representing different regions because that was when the foundation of Somaliland was laid down. That SNM central committee congress was the first political gathering the central committee converged since returning to the country. It was also a time when things that were not agreed upon happened in Mogadishu. Manifesto Group headed by Ali Mahdi Mohamed announced its arbitrary government. And in that manner steered away from the planned political agenda of the freedom movements. Manifesto's decision annoyed SNM especially when Ali Mahdi announced on the BBC that the fight with Siad Barre began in the central regions, ignoring the long and fierce struggle of SNM completely. When the BBC asked him what kind of support Somalia needs from the international world, he answered Nafto (Diesel Fuel), nicknamed Ali Nafto.

Ali Mahdi did not mention the long struggle SNM engaged with Siad Barre's regime for ten years. He did not acknowledge the death and devastation of property in the northern regions caused by Siad Barre's regime long before any struggle began in the central regions. Although many people did not like how we united with the south in 1960, the steps taken by the manifesto put the nail in the coffin of any hope of a united Somalia. Still many politicians hoped to share a government of some kind with Somalia. For that purpose, some men who believed Somaliland to remain with the union in a federal system attended the meeting. However, most of the people supported secession. People were suspicious of many politicians: Ahmed Silanyo, Suleiman Mohamoud Aden, Ismail Buuba, and Abdirahman Ahmed Ali. The men who believed in the federal government were Jama Mohamed Ghalib and Ismail Dualeh. It was an emotional time for Somalilanders and those who believed in federalism were treated harshly. Especially Jama Mohamed Ghalib who stated his belief clearly. He was given a hard time and showed hostility.

Silanyo Defends Jama Mohamed Ghalib

As relayed by Mohamoud Hashi Abdi, then mayor of Burao, Jama Mohamed Ghalib was hated for his idea of federalism. One day the SNM fighters annoyed by his thinking were ready to use force to silence him. Silanyo realized the tense situation and the likelihood that Jama Mohamed Ghalib might get hurt for his idea of federalism. He stood up and said: *in my opinion the two Somalis should part company, but I respect the view of my brother Jama Mohamed Ghalib and others who agree with his statement. The choice would be the choice of the majority of the public. That is how leaders in the world work.*

To Jama I say; you see and hear the thinking and debate in this gathering and I say to the public, you need to respect the views and opinions different from yours and to the arrogant men around I say: don't threaten Jama. He was a vital organ in the SNM struggle.

Ahmed Silanyo Reveals Two Secrets (Silanyo's Secrets)

Today, I will reveal two secrets I had not told anyone before. The first one: When I was in Baligubadle, you asked me about 10,000 dollars and I did not say how it was spent. I led SNM for close to seven years. I endured a lot during that period. I hid many things because of the people's security, like the men who helped us inside the country. We never mentioned their names and one of them was Jama Mohamed Ghalib.

At The conference in Baligubadle, I was asked to account for 10,000 dollars. I requested the supporters in Abu Dhabi to send me an open cheque for that amount and they sent me one. That was the first time I took a route outside the SNM system. The supporters expected me to talk to them and ask them for something, but I never asked anything personally. I never asked them for personal things or asked them to send me anything. The SNM money came through the finance secretary and the bank of Djibouti. At the time there was no money-remitting agencies. This was the only time I asked the supporters in Abu Dhabi for money directly and it was the first time I had ever done that.

I asked them to send me 10,000 dollars fast. I was paying that money for a cause vital to the movement. It was not for my personal use. Today I am telling you where that money went. I gave that money to General Demise, the Ethiopian army commander on the eastern side of Hararge whose wife was diagnosed with cancer.

At the time, I was desperate to meet that man and wanted to ask him for ammunition and support. He was a difficult man dealing with us and we used to wonder if he was an underground supporter of Siad Barre. The man I used to stand in line for hours in Herer and Diridhaba waiting to see walked into my office one day unannounced.

General Demise: *Chairman, I need to make an appointment to see you*

Silanyo: *Sit down. Don't worry about an appointment. Let's talk now*

Gen. Demise: *My wife is sick with cancer. I love her very much. I am a High-ranking military officer and I have medical insurance but Russia is where I have to take her and there are better places than Russia when it comes to cancer treatment. England is where my wife can get better treatment and we don't have good relations with England. The only way I can take her to England is to get an invitation from a doctor in England, for her to carry a check of $10,000 U.S dollars and to show a hotel reservation. Therefore, I am not a poor man; I have money but need hard currency and I heard SNM gets foreign currency. I need you to give me 10,000 dollars in exchange for its equivalent of Ethiopian birr.*

Silanyo: *Give me some time.*

Ahmed Silanyo said he spoke with the SNM supporters in Abu Dhabi and asked them for a blank check of 10,000 dollars to be sent directly to him as soon as possible. He also spoke with his wife Amina-Weris and Abdillahi Omaar in London and told them to make an appointment for the wife of general Demise. Abdillahi Omaar made an invitation from a specialist for her and her nephew who was traveling with her and paid all the fees. Abdillahi Omaar also reserved a hotel for them. We fulfilled General Demise's request so quickly and he was very grateful.

When in Baligubadle the central committee asked me about that money, I did not answer. Mohamed Hashi says: *When Ahmed Silanyo was harassed in Baligubadle and asked to explain what he did with that money, I was there. It was the only accusation his opposition submitted. At the time Silanyo's response was: 'today I am not going to discuss it, but I used that money to do work for the movement. I won't say what I did with it today but I swear to Allah I will explain it some other time. The man who received the money is still alive in Ethiopia.*

When Silanyo was speaking in Burao, Mengistu was overthrown, and general Demise was killed. Mengistu killed him and other generals on suspicion of a coup d'etat. He was fighting in Eritrea and Mengistu killed him.

The second secret he revealed that day was about Jama Mohamed Ghalib. Of all the Isaaq informers inside the country, he was the most valuable contributor to SNM. He was the man who sent me sensitive and highly confidential information. He was the man who sent me the information about the summary executions that had awakened the world to Siad Barre's crimes against humanity. When he sent those letters, he was the minister of the interior.

He used to send papers through different routes. Whenever he traveled to England or Italy, he called Ahmed Silanyo directly and gave him all the secrets the SNM movement needed.

Talking to many men in the meeting who were unaware of what was happening, Ahmed Silanyo said, *there were men here who did not contribute any action or deed to SNM. Still, Jama was that man and it is not fair to dismiss his record for his present opinion. It is not right to threaten him for voicing his opinion.*

The conflict between Ahmed Silanyo and Abdirahman Ahmed Ali

Abdirahman Ahmed Ali and Ahmed Silanyo were friends. From the time in Baligubadle, they agreed that the Somaliland government's future would be that of a president and a prime minister instead of a president and vice president.

When SNM freed the country and at the conference in Burao, Abdirahman Ahmed Ali asked Silanyo to work with him and become a prime minister for his government. Ahmed Silanyo declined and told him that it was inappropriate to come back into the leadership when he had just left the chairmanship.

He told him it was not pleasant to appear again when those opposing him were here and would see him as leaving through the door and entering through the window. At this moment he did not want to take up that position but he was going to work with Abdirahman to build a president and prime minister government.

Although Silanyo declined the offer, Abdirahman pressured him through some elders of his clan such as Mohamoud Ismail Waraabadde, Awil Haji Nur, Abdi Shaybe and others to talk to Ahmed Silanyo. He also requested the elders to make peace between Silanyo and those SNM leftist groups. Those men were Omar Hiinwaal, Ahmed Mohamed Seidi, Mohamed Kahin and Jama Saleh. Finally, Ahmed Silanyo was convinced, and he accepted.

After the solidarity conference of all the clans meeting in April 1991, Somaliland seceding from the union was announced. The legislative body (SNM central committee) approved 18 May 1991 as the new National day. When Abdirahman's plan to appoint Silanyo as the prime minister became known, some elders from the west of Burao and even from Hargeisa disagreed.

Abdirahman Osman Alin says that there *was an agreement between Ahmed Silanyo and Abdirahman Ahmed Ali that when SNM frees the country, the new government system becomes president and prime minister and Silanyo to become prime minister. However, it was difficult. Abdirahman was advised against that decision. He was advised that if he stepped into that, Hassan Essa Jama, vice president, and Ibrahim Meygag, the chairman of the central committee, would leave him if Silanyo returned as prime minister. Also Ahmed Silanyo would become a threat to you.*

Abdirahman Ahmed Ali thought Silanyo was a man he could work with. He wanted to reward his friend who had supported his election for the chairmanship, and he felt it was wise to have him as prime minister he was honest about it; but when the elders advised against it, he accepted. The proper thing to do then was for Abdirahman to inform Ahmed Silanyo of the change of heart, which was the source of their conflict.

When the two systems were finally brought to vote, the presidential system only won by seven votes. Abdirahman built his government on the presidential system appointing Hassan Essa Jama as vice president.

Ahmed Silanyo and Abdirahman Ahmed Ali were still friends and worked together despite their differences. Perhaps another source of conflict was when Ahmed Silanyo tried to mediate between Abdirahman and Mohamed Kahin who was then the minister of Defense. Still, he soon realized that Abdirahman was not open to the advice Ahmed was offering him and especially when the war between the clans erupted and he realized that Abdirahman was not a man who could take the country out of the clan war.

When the clan wars started in Berbera, the BBC's Robin White asked Ahmed Silanyo on the "Focus on Africa" Program why there was a war among SNM members and where Somaliland was going to move from that problematic situation.

BBC: Is There an Army Fighting on The Road Between Hargeisa And Berbera?

London BBC World Service in English

15:15 GMT 26 November 1992

{From Focus on Africa Program)

Robin White asks Ahmed Silanyo about the fight in Berbera during Abdirahman Ahmed Ali's administration and an ongoing organization of a conference in Borama:

The President of Somaliland's government has been in turmoil lately. The country he rules is moving into chaos. There have been wars between clans that inhabit Berbera and Hargeisa and that Abdirahman Ahmed Ali is fanning the flames. Ahmed Mohamed Mohamoud Silanyo who used to be the chairman of Somali National Movement, the movement that freed Somaliland handed over to Abdirahman Ahmed Ali. He was also one of the mediators who tried to make peace between the clans. Robin White asked Ahmed Silanyo who is now in London to accept that there is a war in Somaliland.

Silanyo: There is no doubt an internal clan war is going on in Somaliland but it is not as bad as the situation in Southern Somalia. Though it is not as bad as you think, nonetheless it is an internal conflict.

Robin White: How many people, do you think died in that conflict?

Silanyo: It is tough for me to estimate the number of casualties in that conflict confidently but I think they are not less than one thousand people altogether.

Robin White From the way I understand, the conflict is about the power struggle between the two Sa'ad Musa and Habar Yonis clans. The competition is all about each clan getting the most significant share. Now is one clan getting more than the other and is that how you have agreed?

Silanyo: I prefer not to put it that way. How I see a conflict of this kind could not be considered clan war. It was not a war that a clan attacked another. Still, it came as a result of government mismanagement and irresponsible move in which the *government sent an army to attack Berbera so that it should be brought under government control. Still, it was done in a way that only one clan militia was sent and not a militia of all clans and that is how the war started and exploded. Fortunately, the great effort of many people now put an end to it.*

Robin White: Are you blaming the president for what happened?

Silanyo: *I know about those issues ... the president cannot ignore his role in this conflict. It is not only he; his entire government and many other people have to take the blame for it. The fundamental error was to send an army from one city to another. Also, they were from one clan and not a national army. Frankly, that is how the war started and they cannot run away from the responsibility for that purpose.*

Robin White: You supported Abdirahman Ahmed Ali when he ran for office. Have you withdrawn your support?

Silanyo: *True! I supported him though I was not the only one who helped him, now I withdrew my support because I had never thought things would come to this— i.e., when I realized his leadership is not the leadership needed by the country and the people. If we ignore everything else, the chaos resulting from this conflict is squarely on his shoulders, so I withdrew my support to him.*

Robin White: Are you working on throwing him out of power?

Silanyo: *The issue has nothing to do about ousting him. I am among many people trying to bring peace and tranquility back into the people and country. Our goal is to instill calm. In any event his term of office is almost finished.*

Robin White: What do you mean by his time is finished?

Silanyo: *I am talking about the time left from his term of office, which will end in April.*

Robin White: Are there going to be elections held to choose a leader?

Silanyo: *There will be elections for a new leader. Also in January, there will be a national conference to be held by the Guurti.*

Robin White: Do you think he will be pressured to leave in that conference?

Silanyo: *I am hoping for a change of leadership that will bring peace and stability to our country.*

Robin White: You were once the leader of SNM. Would you be running for office again?

Silanyo: No. I made it clear that I won't run for office now no matter the conditions. I will do whatever I can for my country, but I won't run for election.

Robin White: Is anyone you know who would take over the leadership?

Silanyo: No, I don't have anyone in mind and even if I am thinking of one, I am not saying it here.

Saeed Mohamed Mohamoud

Saeed was Ahmed's youngest brother. When the clan wars broke out in Burao, he was among the peacemakers who stood at the battleground between the warring tribes waving a white flag for peace when a flying bullet hit him. He died instantly. Saeed lived in Liverpool and Ahmed Silanyo's kids knew him.

Amina explains *how her kids heard the news one day while she was told on the phone that Saeed was killed in Burao. Kulmiye came to me and asked: 'Mom how come my uncle died? Didn't we defeat the Faqash? How come my uncle died? I heard you saying my uncle died in the war! Are we still at war? With whom are we fighting?*

Amina told him. Yes, my son we defeated the Faqash but our soldiers are sometimes careless and they fight the way you and your younger brother Ali do. He answered. 'But we don't take guns!

Safeguarding the Weapons Depots

Ali Mohamed Abdulle (Bikalo) relayed that when the SNM entered the country a period of chaos and confusion ensued. Clan wars, bandits and chaos reigned. Everyone built his roadblock. They fought with rockets as enemies and people died. The fighters killed innocent civilians. Saeed Mohamed, Silanyo's brother was among those waving for peace and was killed by a strayed bullet. Finally, in Burao the angry civilians fed up with what the fighters were doing ran into the streets in significant numbers throwing stones at them and chasing them out of the city. Though armed militia killed people, they finally ran away from their weapons and weapon centers. Ali Bikalo who witnessed all that says: *After the people chased them out, they tried to enter the weapons depot and burn everything inside those depots, but other people intervened. There were big weapons depots and the artillery that was stored there was nationalized and now used by the Somaliland army. At that stage when people converged in front of the weapons depot and wanted to destroy everything, Ahmed Silanyo came to the place. He spoke with the people from the top of a car and told them not to enter the weapons storage. He convinced them some infiltrators had come to disrupt us. They are thugs and we will capture them. The reason we left, fought and died for is here. These are the weapons we captured from the enemy. If you destroy them, then the enemy will come back. I am telling you that those claiming to be maimed in the war and running around have not served SNM and did nothing for SNM. They are young hoodlums. Anyone who was bitten by a killer snake in his village or hit by a camel now asserts to be hurt in the war. That is not true. They are not the real SNM freedom fighters. They are not the SNM fighters who have sacrificed their lives for your freedom. Please do not destroy our weapons. He moved from one depot to another to calm the people and convinced them, that the guns in those depots showed our victory and should be saved for us. Suddenly, the angry crowd that was no less than ten thousand angry individuals had a change of heart. Ahmed Silanyo's speech melted their hearts and they turned away from their determination to burn the depots.*

Pillars of Islamic Faith and Pillars of Government

Parliamentarian Abdillahi Ismail relays: *I was there when Ahmed Silanyo spoke to the people in Burao at the Daallo compound. It was when Abdirahman Ahmed Ali was the president. There was an argument that Ahmed Silanyo was an opposition to the government. All the ministers from the HT clan resigned. It was alleged that Ahmed Silanyo told the people not to pay taxes. Ahmed Silanyo was overthrowing the government. Rumors like that were flying all over the city of Burao. In Burao, the HT and HY were not on good terms. All kinds of people gathered at the Daallo compound to hear Ahmed Silanyo's speech. He gave a phenomenal speech that touched everyone who listened regardless of clan. It was a speech that had built the Solidarity of the clans and brought them together. In the middle of his speech, he turned to another subject. He said 'we are Muslims, and our clergy is present. Just the way our deen has pillars, so does our government. The Islamic Faith has five pillars of Islam and six pillars of faith. Our government also has six pillars. One of the pillars of the government is to pay taxes to the government. To collect taxes, there should be police. To recruit police, there should be law and order. If we send armed men without the law to control them, they will kill and finish the people. To collect the taxes, we need law-abiding police. There should also be a symbol to collect taxes. The government should also have a symbol to recognize the government.*

For those of you who are old enough, the symbol of the Somaliland protectorate was the picture of the queen of England. It was the government's symbol to collect taxes. After independence, a receipt with the two leopards symbolized government. They were the signs to recognize the document's authenticity and the way to collect taxes. Now we need to use the Somaliland flag as the symbol of government but what the insignia will be has yet to be decided. We won't be a government until we develop a government insignia. Dear Burao inhabitants, I want to tell you, Burao is where the struggle began. Let it be where the paying of taxes begins. The earlier disgruntled clans walked out of the Daallo compound holding hands with a feeling of brotherhood.

Ahmed Silanyo's Car Was Seized in Berbera

The clan wars were about to erupt in Berbera in 1992 and the city was shaking with emotions. Militia from the HY clan seized Ahmed Silanyo's car driven by his driver, while Ahmed was not in it. They took the keys from the driver and drove away. When a large HT clan army stationed at the Russian hospital got angry and moved to return the car and capture whatever else they could find, Ahmed Silanyo stopped that move and told the HT army, 'the car was mine. *SNM army is the same to me no matter what clan. I don't want my car to be the source of war. You are not going to capture those who took my car. You and they are the same as me. If they use that car with something beneficial for the public, there is no problem. I used this car for the good of the general public. It won't happen that some have taken my car while others fight to get it back. I would never allow that to happen. Go back!'*

Silanyo: 'Position is the Source of Conflict'

Political chaos and hostility reigned. People started condemning the Somaliland politicians for the conflict. That generalization and characterization of politicians as bad people greatly bothered Ahmed Silanyo.

Ahmed Silanyo speaking about that era says: *At the time of Abdirahman Ahmed Ali's government when conflict erupted somewhere people used to say: 'it's all about position.' I did not care about those fighting for positions. As Allah is my witness, I left the country. People used to call me and ask me if I was coming back. I used to tell them I would come back when the story of fighting over positions ended. SNM was a different story. I was elected twice and I did not want either one of them.*

Silanyo's Advice for The Meeting in Borama

Today, I would not advise HT clan to seek the country's leadership.

Mohamoud Hashi who was there in that meeting says: "*For the Borama meeting people came from regions and clans. It was a period people were fed up with Abdirahman's leadership. The delegates from the eastern regions had about 60 representatives. They were composed of Togdheer, Sool and Sanaag regions. Ahmed Ismail Dukhsi was the leader of those 60 representatives and Mohamoud Hashi was the secretary. Those delegates called Ahmed Silanyo in London and told him they had sixty votes and needed only some thirty votes. Did he want to be elected?*

Ahmed Silanyo called those delegates and told them not to tempt him. And his advice to them was not to nominate any HT candidate and would not advise them to seek the country's leadership today. The conflict among the Isaaq clans is still alive. We were part of those blamed for it since we were part of the conflicting debate. If Abdirahman Ahmed Ali returned to the leadership, it would be a problem; if I came back to the leadership, it would also be a problem. Therefore, we need a leader clean of the conflict. We need a non-allied leader who could unite the two factions and cement the relationship.

Suleiman Mohamoud Aden speaking of that situation explains: *In the Borama meeting, we asked Ahmed Silanyo to become a candidate. I was not going to be accepted in Borama, but Ahmed Silanyo was able to succeed. He could have become a real contender to Egal. Many of us called him in London and asked him to come.*

He told us. How can those who chased me away from the place call me to become a candidate? No. I am not coming he said. He did not realize that the situation had changed. After he rejected our suggestion, I chose to stand for election. At that time, I was not going to succeed. Mohamoud Hashi reiterates that when Silanyo rejected our suggestion, the eastern delegates chose to support Mohamed Haji Ibrahim Egal. At first, the delegates from the east side of Burao did not want to support Mohamed Haji Ibrahim Egal, but Ahmed Silanyo's advice convinced them.

Mohamed Haji Ibrahim Egal: Ahmed Silanyo Is More Worthy of President

Ahmed Silanyo spoke at the ceremony where SNM fighters were surrendering their weapons. In 1993 when the government of Mohamed Haji Ibrahim Egal was inaugurated in Borama, Ahmed Silanyo spoke at the occasion. He said: *The first fight was the struggle to free our country from tyranny, and this struggle is the one to build a nation and anchor a government to stand on its feet. Let us not kid ourselves; this struggle is far more bitter than the first one, more difficult, carries more hardship, and has more responsibility. I pray to Allah that our martyrs know the value of those who sacrificed and lost their lives, and their martyrdom should not go in vain. We will remember them when the country and the people are rebuilt. We would build our country and people when we build a government and the government could not stand alone if the people don't support it and if the security of the country is not in its hands, if law and order are not in place and if its citizens do not support it. My plea to the SNM members is to be sensitive to all those requirements in building a government.*

Ahmed Silanyo referring to what Mohamed Haji Ibrahim Egal said earlier, in which Egal said, 'Ahmed Silanyo, who led the SNM and the struggle to free the country was more worthy of becoming a president answered: 'The SNM struggle was not to benefit from its fruits. It was always our aim when we freed the country to let the people choose their president. The people made their choice and chose a president. We are going to support him. We are working with him. Finally, I am asking the people and the president to honor the name and the work of SNM. I don't want to hear that SNM destroyed the country. I don't want to hear that SNM is handicapping the country. I don't want to hear SNM fighters did nothing for the country.'

Ahmed Silanyo A Member of Parliament

Ahmed was not in the country when in the Borama meeting he was included in the Parliament. MP Abdi Jama Gagale, a colleague in the parliament, remembers: *'Ahmed Silanyo was a mature man who never came to work late. He was not arrogant. He used to sign a paper in the morning and was at work until lunch and he was available for all the debates. He was included in all the appointed special committees. He was instrumental in peacebuilding and bringing closer together those in conflict.*

A Delegation Mohamed Haji Ibrahim Egal Sent to Ethiopia

As relayed by Abdirahman Aw Ali Farah bilateral relationship between Somaliland and Ethiopia became difficult. President Mohamed Haji Ibrahim Egal and the Ethiopian movement that took over the government of Ethiopia could not understand each other. It had become necessary for the two parties to understand each other and strengthen their relationship. When President Egal was asked about his relationship with Ethiopia, he said he could not understand the movement that took over Ethiopia. He was asked what happened to Dr. Abdul Majid. Did you not meet him? He answered "that is not Somali. He is Ethiopian."

Abdirahman Aw Ali Farah, the vice president for President Mohamed Haji Ibrahim Egal, confirmed that President Egal and the Ethiopian government could not understand each other. Maybe the cause of the misunderstanding was because of the disparity of age between President Egal and the Ethiopian administrators. President Egal asked his vice president Abdirahman Aw Ali

Farah to take a delegation to Ethiopia for better understanding.

Abdirahman asked Ahmed Silanyo to become part of his delegation. When he told Mohamed Haji Ibrahim Egal that Ahmed Silanyo was part of his delegation, Egal asked his vice president, "why are you taking Ahmed Silanyo with you? He is in the opposition. Abdirahman responded that they (SNM leaders, including Ahmed Silanyo and Abdirahman himself) know the Ethiopians well. They were movements at the same time. Ahmed Silanyo was the chairman of the SNM, a similar movement; therefore, it was essential for him to go with me.

As Abdirahman Aw Ali Farah reiterates, Ahmed Silanyo and that delegation were instrumental in smoothing the bilateral relationship between Somaliland and Ethiopia in opening diplomatic offices and managing the border security. They traveled to Eritrea and Ahmed Silanyo was the speaker for the delegation.

Aide Memoire by Ahmed Mohamed Mohamoud Silanyo

This is a speech Ahmed Silanyo read at an international meeting in Nigeria in 1994 about the recognition of Somaliland. He discussed what Somaliland had already achieved and the help it needed. It was noted in (Adan_1) on October 8, 2008. Here is the Aide Memoire presented by Somaliland on February 14, 1994, to the consideration of the government of Nigeria.

First: *A territory known colloquially as Somalia is not an international entity. As such, if the Security Council is referring to the Somali Democratic Republic, it should say so.*

Second: *For this Aide Memoire the colloquialism Somalia is regarded as the territory of the Somali Democratic Republic, less the sovereign territory of the Republic of Somaliland that, on 18 May 1991, restored the sovereignty, granted to it by the United Kingdom of June 26, 1960.*

Third: *Somalia's constitution has enshrined in it the sacred duty to unite all Somali-occupied territories in the Horn of Africa. Its flag, consisting of a five-pointed star on a blue background, is a manifestation of this constitutional imperative for the formation of a "Greater Somalia," consisting of Somalia itself, the Republic of Somaliland, the Republic of Djibouti, the Kilil 5 (Eastern Ethiopia), and the Northern Frontier Province of Kenya.*

Fourth: *The Republic of Somaliland, formally known as the state of Somaliland on independence, voluntarily merged with the UN Trust Territory of Somalia to form the Somali Republic on 1 July 1960 and subscribed to the Greater Somalia precept, though no Act of Union was signed because it was soon realized the merger was an error of judgment. Military authorities in Mogadishu suppressed an attempted military coup d'état in 1961 to restore the sovereignty of the state of Somaliland.*

Fifth: *The Republic of Somaliland rejects the implied wording preamble to Security Council Resolution 897 to the effect that the boundary of Somaliland contiguous with the boundary of Somalia's Northeast region is not inviolable.*

Sixth: *the international community cannot have both ways: a condemnation on the one hand of Somalia's desire for the unity of all Somali-occupied territories as inscribed in its constitution, and rejection, on the other hand, of the reversion by the Republic of Somaliland to the borders existing at the time of self-determination, and by inviting the attention of only of its independence.*

Seventh: *by disregarding Somaliland's pursuit of the equally cogent principle of self-determination and by inviting the attention of only to Somalia's sovereignty and territorial integrity with its implied application to the Republic of Somaliland, the Security Council has created for itself and the Republic of Somaliland, a prejudicial political situation in Somaliland's relation to Somalia. Sovereignty is reposed in Transitional National Council in Mogadishu (in accordance with the 27 March 1993 Addis Ababa Agreement), and this future Council may now seek to exercise its supposed sovereignty over the Republic of Somaliland by duress, encouraged by Security Council Resolution 897.*

Eight: *moreover, the reference to the Addis Ababa Agreement is the preamble to Res. 897 as constituting 'the basis for the resolutions of the problem in Somalia is a parody of the realities of the situations that exist between Somaliland and Somalia. Representatives of the Republic of Somaliland were not a party to the agreements referred to, and the Government of Somaliland rejected the premise that this agreement constitutes the basis for resolving the problems in Somalia.*

Ninth: *Given the hostile attitudes toward the Republic of Somaliland adopted by some political leaders in Somalia (but not the public), a threat to internal peace and security is now a probability following the prejudgment of the issue by Security Council Resolution 897.*

Tenth: *Another consequence of the prejudicial preamble to the Security Council 897, referred to above is fear among UN and NGOs that their current plan for development in the Republic of Somaliland could be unilaterally jeopardized by the future Transitional National Council of Somalia which, usurping the sovereignty of Somaliland, could in pursuance of a policy of intimidation, deny these agencies the right to reside in Somaliland.*

Eleventh: *the compelling reasons for the restoration of the sovereignty of Somaliland have no parallel in other countries and are therefore, exceptional, creating no precedent.*

Twelfth: *the case for Eretria's secession from Ethiopia, though dissimilar to the case for Somaliland in that Eretria was a bit of a sovereign state before it was involuntarily federated with Ethiopia, was based on the right to self-determination following an overwhelming desire by the people of Eritrea for independence, as expressed during the internationally monitored referendum. The Republic of Somaliland expects no less from the international community, having an even stronger case than that of Eritrea in that Somaliland voluntarily merged as a sovereign state with Somalia.*

(No act of union was ratified) and is equally entitled to withdraw from this informal union.

Thirteen: *if it should be thought that the Republic of Somaliland is taking advantage of continuing stability and insecurity of Somalia by seeking international recognition, the facts are otherwise: the restoration of Somaliland's sovereignty was deeply desired in 1961, evidenced by a referendum on union with Somalia. The final victory over Siad Barre's murderous and oppressive regime was achieved in 1991, followed by massive chaos in Mogadishu. The same year, the restoration of Somaliland's sovereignty was declared at the national congress following a huge public outcry for such promulgation. Since then, the Republic of Somaliland now with an elected government following a four-month deliberation during the first half of 1993 by representatives of every clan has continuously urged international recognition. It is an old and exceptional phenomenon based on the people's right to self-determination and the right to have their former sovereignty restored by voluntarily withdrawing from the merger with Somalia. It is not a will-o'-the-wisp conjured out of the air to take advantage of Somalia's agonizing situation.*

Fourteenth: *The Republic of Somaliland has requested the United Nations and bilateral aid donors to assist with funding and monitoring a countrywide referendum to satisfy an international desire to ascertain the people's wishes. The Security Council is a de facto authority in Somalia and is thus incumbent on the members of the Council. First, show the wishes of the people of Somaliland according to the principle of self-determination and, secondly, promulgate and abide by the wishes.*

Fifteenth: there is of course urgency in seeking international recognition for one supremely important reason, among others. For three years, the Republic of Somaliland has been deprived of assistance from the World Bank and the International Monetary Fund because of the absence of this Recognition.

Sixteenth: the government of the Republic of Somaliland without dependence on the United Nations has re-established its police force, judiciary, and prison system and is currently receiving, voluntarily and without duress, all heavy armaments which have hitherto had irresponsible young men. There is no reason why the international community thwart the international Recognition of Somaliland.

The Conflict Of 1994: Abdirahman Ahmed Ali called for Federalism

1. Abdirahman Ahmed Ali announced in Addis Ababa that Somaliland withdrew from its separation of the Somaliland state and agreed to Federalism.

2. There was a meeting organized by the HY clan in Burao, supporting what Abdirahman announced in Addis Ababa. The story took a serious and dangerous turn.

Ahmed Silanyo's Role in Calming the Conflict Of 1994-1996 And Restoring Peace

Internal Conflict erupted in Somaliland on 15 November 1994. Soon after Abdirahman Ahmed Ali announced that Somaliland no longer believed in reasserting its state sovereignty and wanted federalism, a group from his clan held a meeting in Burao supporting him. That created considerable confusion and threatened the country's security and Somaliland's choice of state separation. Somaliland population saw these steps as ones to dismantle the agreement people reached in Burao in 1991and Borama in 1993. The Somaliland clans got upset about those actions and decided to defend Somaliland and its decision to disunite Somalia. The quick eruption of the 1994 war eliminated the chance for negotiation, mediation, and reconciliation.

In the town of Ainabo started, the HT clan held a meeting called Aynaan. Ahmed Silanyo was among the first invited to speak at that meeting. He did not hesitate but candidly told the members in the meeting that they should work together on how to stop the dangerous conflict in Somaliland. His speech was valuable and passionate and stirred people's feelings. He urged the HT clan to stand up for peace and go anywhere and everywhere in search of peace. They should go to Gaashaamo and talk to the Gerhajis clan. They should go to Burao where the conflict was most fierce and speak with HY and negotiate peace and they should go to Oodweyne and do the same for the sake of peace. Let the HT clan become the beacon of peace for Somaliland. Ahmed Silanyo's direct message was taken wholeheartedly, which compelled HT clans to travel to Gaashaamo.

A small war between some HT and HY clans happened in the south of Gaashaamo and Baalidhaye. It was worrisome for the conflict to escalate to the rural areas. The Ethiopians did not want the war to cross the border to Ethiopia. Therefore, they worked hard to impose peace on both conflicting clans. The HT clan from Ainabo went there for Peace. Meetings were held in Baalidhaye. The HT clan hosted the meeting, and the conflict was resolved. There were other meetings hosted by the HY clan followed by other sessions.

The political and traditional wing of the HY clan met in Eilhume and disagreed on how to negotiate peace. One group headed by Suldaan Esa Hersi-Qani wanted to bring peace to the government and travel to Hargeisa. In contrast, others headed by Suldaan Osman Suldaan Ali Madar and Abdi Aw-Dahir did not want to go to president Egal but wanted to discuss peace with HT clan in Burao claiming that the peace process was initiated by clans in Burao and not by President Mohamed Ibrahim Egal.

Finally, most of the HY leadership clan went to Beer, where 180 delegates from each clan remained for two months plus other guests. Garaad Abdulqani Garaad Jama and other clans were also invited. Ahmed Silanyo was the oldest and most vital person in that Beer meeting.

In Hargeisa, the 1996 Guurti conference was held. The Guurti and newly added members to the guurti were nominating a president and vice president. However, the HY and HT clans' delegates, plus their guests in Beer disagreed with how the members have selected and the fact that they were holding political meetings while the peace was still being negotiated. They were concerned about two things: a) the Timing of the guurti conference in Hargeisa was inappropriate when the clans were still negotiating peace and could not attend and b) the way the President was handpicking the delegates was not appropriate. Clans from Sheikh, Borama and Las Anod commented that the Hargeisa conference was unnecessary.

The argument about the Guurti congress was how its delegates were selected. The clans did not select members but were called by Mohamed Haji Ibrahim Egal and the guurti members. It seemed to many that the whole congress was something Mohamed Haji Ibrahim Egal and some Guurti members organized without consulting anyone. For that purpose, the congress was vehemently opposed because those organizing the congress did not consider the requests coming from the clans' conference in Beer and other clans who requested the congress to be postponed.

Finally, the clans in Beer sent Suldaan Abdillahi Suldaan Ali Musa and eleven other delegates to Hargeisa. Their request was to convey the message of postponement from the rest of the clans until the meeting in Beer was completed and they could attend the congress in Hargeisa, but they did not succeed because their request was rejected.

The Strong Opposition to Beer Decided To Hold Its Own Clan Conference

When the meeting in Hargeisa continued without consideration of the requests of those in Beer, the opposition decided to hold their meeting declaring their resolutions. It was a deadlock that could have jeopardized the future of Somaliland. They wanted to start another meeting in Yarowe and select a new government. At the conjecture, Ahmed Silanyo spoke fearlessly to the meeting attendees. He asked them the hard questions: *'do you want to take the road of Ali Mahdi and Aideed in Mogadishu? If so, why do we want to negotiate peace?'* Most of Ahmed's friends asked him to build a government and his answer was: *'there would never be two governments here. Are you suggesting that every two rows of houses have a government? No!'* Then, they suggested they should fight but Ahmed Silanyo rejected that saying: *'I won't be called the Ahmed Silanyo who fought and killed for power. We know how a war begins but no one can estimate how it ends.'* Ahmed Silanyo's wise thinking and intervention were welcomed and all the opposition in Beer traveled to Hargeisa.

SNM Was Limping When It Entered the Country

When Ahmed Silanyo and the rest reached Hargeisa, many of his SNM colleagues were still upset, as Ahmed Kijaandhe explains: *The opposition in Beer was furious and believed Ahmed Silanyo betrayed them. One evening a group of his SNM colleagues called him at the house of Abdirahman Aw Ali Farah. They were Osman Dool*

Quule, Dayeb Guray, Abdirahman Aw Ali Farah, Ibrahim Dhegaweyne, and Mohamed Abdillahi Absiye. They were angry about how Ahmed Silanyo reverted the HT opposition. They told him he was the opposition leader, and he was the one they wanted to lead the country. We want to oppose Mohamed Haji Ibrahim Egal, who seized control and usurped power.

Ahmed Silanyo responded, "Listen, my friends, you remember our relationship in SNM. We were always in conflict, but we entered our country still hanging together. Despite our conflict, we never had two chairmen leading SNM. Here is Dhegaweyne who wants to capture Berbera. It would be better for us to hand over leadership to Mohamed Haji Ibrahim Egal wherever he wants to take it. On the other hand, he tested them and asked. "If you want me to compete with Mohamed Haji Ibrahim Egal, I have all the votes of my HT clan. What votes can you get from your clans? Some of those who called him just left still enraged with him."

Mediating Between Ahmed Silanyo and Suleiman Mohamoud Aden

HT clan nominated Ahmed Silanyo as a candidate and Suleiman M. Aden resigned from his ministerial position and declared his candidacy. It was necessary to mediate between the two candidates. Therefore, the 24 delegates from the east cast their vote and 22 chose Ahmed Silanyo but Suleiman Mohamoud Aden rejected their choice. Then, the clan selected 33 elders to settle things and choose one unanimous candidate from the three declared candidates: Ahmed Mohamed Mohamoud Silanyo, Suleiman Mohamoud Aden and Robleh Michael Mariano.

Ahmed Silanyo asked the other two candidates to let him run this time. He asked them that he was chosen and that they should give him a chance and allow him to be the candidate. Robleh Michael Mariano accepted his plea and withdrew his candidacy.

Ahmed Silanyo then addressed Suleiman Mohamoud Aden directly and asked him to concede because he had just resigned from a position he was holding from the time of Baligubadle. Still, he did not hold any position since that time. He also asked him to allow him to finish some of the unfinished business he had planned since SNM and asked, 'do not compel our HT clan to choose one over the other.'

Suleiman answered thus: '*I don't have much time left for me because I am as old as you. So let our clan members select.*

Ahmed Silanyo spoke again: *Suleiman, whether I win, or you win, a conflict will result and that will continue for a long time. Don't put our clan into a state of conflict. Let's respect our clan members and stop any cause for conflicting factions.*

When Ahmed Silanyo realized that Suleiman was not ready to concede or consider his plea, he announced that he would withdraw for peace. He was also going to support Suleiman's candidacy. At that point, the whole clan prayed for Ahmed and praised him.

Suleiman reflects on this many years later: *Some elders came to me and asked me to concede for Ahmed Silanyo and I asked them why I should concede for him. And they said: we are supporting him.* Suleiman insisted on remaining a candidate and refused everyone.

Ninety Stronger Than Iron

Suleiman was supported. Ahmed was among five elders helping him but lost the election. Mohamed Haji Ibrahim Egal was chosen as president again and Suleiman got ninety votes dubbed as the ninety stronger than Iron. Those who voted for Suleiman were the most valuable and respected delegates.

Egal invited the 90 that voted for Suleiman, and he told them that. 'I got the quantity of the votes, but the quality of the votes went to Suleiman; therefore, since I became the chosen president and we don't have a multi-party system, I don't want you to become an opposition but to work with me so that we can build our nation together. '

Mohamed H. I. Egal, Sh. Ibrahim Sh. Yusuf and Ahmed Mohamed Mohamoud Silanyo

When the congress, where Mohamed Haji Ibrahim Egal was elected ended, Ahmed Silanyo wanted to leave the country. President Egal called him. He also called Sh. Ibrahim Sh. Yusuf Sh. Madar who was Silanyo's long-time friend. He asked him to work with him and not to leave his government.

Ahmed Silanyo called his supporters and told them what President Egal had suggested but he told them that since I came here to run for president and things did not work for him, I don't want to take a ministerial position but wanted to leave the country and congratulate the president.

His supporters stopped him from traveling and advised him to accept President Egal's request. If he wanted to work with him as an experienced elder, then take the ministerial position and work with him in that capacity. The country is now coming together, and President Egal would not stay for five years. You have been building the country for a long time. Continue with that and work with him.

Ali Bikalo explains that although it was tough for him to accept a ministerial position, he took his supporters' advice, got the minister of finance position in Egal's administration, and did a lot in that ministry.

Establishing Financial Policy

President Egal appointed Ahmed Silanyo, as the minister of finance. There was no financial policy. Revenue collection was not structural. Merchants advanced loans to the government and cleared their goods without paying any taxes for seven months or more. There was a great disparity between the tax exemption they received, and the loans owed to them by the government. It was a deal that severely encroached on the government revenue, but at the time, the country's circumstances compelled the deal and the government was grateful to the merchants. Somaliland had no other way to receive money. Somaliland stood alone on its own.

Ahmed Silanyo, the economist faced that complicated situation head-on. He had to devise a plan of action for the government to get systematic tax collection.

Ahmed Silanyo organized a system of using vouchers and billing. Merchants were to write vouchers for their goods while the government provided an IOU for future payments of goods bought. When Ahmed Silanyo created that billing and payment system, he called all the merchants who loaned money to the government, explained the new financial system, and told them: *What the government needs is now under my responsibility. I will give you the guarantee to pay and you will be paying the proper tax for your goods at the port of entry. In other words, I will pay back your loans to the government and you will pay the taxes you owe the government.*

Ahmed Silanyo and the merchants agreed on that system of operation. They agreed to pay taxes and collect their loans through those proper channels. That system of financial process in place until today in Somaliland is the one Ahmed Silanyo introduced when he was the minister of finance.

President Egal's Attempt to Dissolve the Parliament

While Ahmed Mohamed Mohamoud Silanyo was the minister of finance, President Egal tried to dissolve the parliament, opposing him at the time. He informed his cabinet ministers about the plan and started the process of dismantling the parliament. As parliamentarians Mohamoud Baday and Hassan Moallin recall, President Egal forwarded an agenda to dissolve the parliament for approval. *The ministers unanimously agreed to the agenda. As they were clapping for the agreement, Ahmed Silanyo who arrived late to the meeting because of work elsewhere walked in and asked: 'what is this issue you all agreed to?' He was informed about the agenda to dissolve the parliament. Ahmed announced: 'that is impossible!' President Egal told him the entire cabinet agreed to the idea. Before Ahmed answered, some ministers said; 'Mr. President, Ahmed only voiced his opinion.' Ahmed Silanyo then jumped in outrage and said: 'this is not an opinion. It is a principle, and we will not accept it and will fight it to the end.'*

After the ministers debated with Ahmed, President Egal said: 'Wait, Ahmed is more than my cabinet minister, so don't argue with him. Giving the respect due to Ahmed, President Egal let the matter drop for that day.

Eventually, President Egal, , after consulting with the chair of the House of Parliament, accepted it was impossible to dissolve the parliament then. Therefore, he said 'Ahmed and I won't fight over the issue anymore'.

Demobilizing of the Clan-Based Militia in Togdheer

Ahmed Silanyo's contribution was not limited to the duties of the ministry of finance. He participated in the peacebuilding. He and Vice President Dahir Riyale Kahin visited the Togdheer region to incorporate and demobilize clan militia in Burao, build the police force, create an operational regional administration, and bring Ainabo and Oog under Togdheer financial and administrative umbrella.

From Ainabo to Oog, the police force Management was to come under the Togdheer region and not Sool as before. Therefore, operationally and in tax collection the police force came under the Togdheer region since the government institutions were stronger there, and they succeeded.

President Mohamed Haji Ibrahim Egal: 'There Are Terrorists in Burao'

President Egal announced that the cities of Burao, Yarowe, and Las Anod were harboring the Al-Itihad terrorist cells and allowed the Ethiopian government to attack them and clear them from the area.

The Ethiopians suspected the Al-Itihad movement was attacking them from those places and Al-Itihad received its support from them. They also believed there were training camps there for the Al-Itihad army. President Egal's remarks confused the country. Those areas became soft targets for Ethiopian attacks. Ethiopians could easily abduct people from those areas or even kill them. It was a danger the president confirmed. [1]

Mediating President Egal and the Clerics

Ahmed Silanyo reminded the president of the danger in his remarks on the eastern regions. He told him. *"Mr. President, your remarks were harmful to the people you were ruling. It was inappropriate to call them terrorists and ask a foreign enemy to attack them."* Ahmed Silanyo intended to close the door on the misunderstanding because he knew there were no terrorist training camps in those places.

Ali Bikalo explains that situation says: *There might have been individuals but there were no organized armies. It was wrong to counter opposition with hostility.*

Ahmed Silanyo met with the clerics in Burao and brought the clerics and the president together. He intended to clear any misunderstanding. He brought fifteen clerics from Burao to meet the president. The president invited them to the presidential compound for lunch. They remained there until evening. Hassan Moallin from the parliament and Osman Qootali the then minister of interior were among the government representatives in the meeting. President Egal acknowledged his mistake of pointing the finger at his population and authorizing a foreign government to clear it when there were no terrorists. On the other hand, they reassured him of peace in the region and informed him of how the population supported him and his government. The president was reassured, and the misunderstanding cleared.

---

(1) President Egal's remarks followed some earlier opposition comments of some cleric. Ethiopians turned their attention to those specified places and there was likely going to be chaos

President Egal told the clerics that he was grateful to Ahmed Silanyo and that he was not just a minister in his cabinet but an elder who helps him with running the government. Ahmed represents him with full authority from him.

The conflict ended there, and they held a press conference signed by all parties stating there were no terrorist cells anywhere in Somaliland. Hassan Moallin reiterates that Ahmed Silanyo had always been instrumental in solving problems detrimental to peace. People were always calling for clan wars during that time, but Ahmed Silanyo sided with peace and built consensus from the ground.

Ahmed Silanyo's Resignation from the Ministry of Planning

Although Ahmed Silanyo was the minister of planning for a short period, he had established the three-year development plan that was the first of its kind in Somaliland. He organized an international donors' meeting where the government demonstrated Somaliland's development and discussed the obstacles.

Ahmed Silanyo gave a memorable speech about the needs of Somaliland. Soon after, a delegation headed by him traveled to Nairobi to attend a meeting of the Somali Aid Coordination Committee in Nairobi. That was the first time a minister from Somaliland participated in that kind of meeting and the first time they met the World Bank and IMF.

At the end of 1999, Ahmed Silanyo resigned from his minister of planning position. President Egal did not accept his resignation. When Ahmed Silanyo insisted on leaving, President Egal asked Sh. Ibrahim Sh. Yusuf and other elders convince him to change his mind. Finally, Ahmed Silanyo accepted the elders, remained in his position for a while longer, then submitted his resignation in 2000.

Ahmed Silanyo remained outside the country for a while. Still, he was always involved in the issues of Somaliland's sovereignty and the problems in Somalia through debates and interviews held by BBC.

The Conflict That Resulted From the Multi-Party System

At the end of 2001, President Mohamed Haji Ibrahim Egal established the UDUB party when his five-year term of office ended. Those who called themselves the SNM reformists were the strongest among the many sprouting opposition groups. Suleiman Mohamoud Aden, Hassan Essa Jama and Musa Bihi Abdi started among them. Later there was another "Ummad " movement established in Awdal. Abdirahman Aw Ali Farah and others were among the founders of Ummad. Later they found the ASAD coalition that remained an opposition until 1997 when they lost the nomination. ASAD became a problem for President Egal's administration. The party members were mistreated. When Suleiman Mohamoud Aden returned from abroad, he was harassed at the airport in Hargeisa, searched and announced publicly that he got money from foreign countries and for that purpose he was sent to prison in Mandheera.

The conflict between Clan Elders and President Egal's Government

President Mohamed Haji Ibrahim Egal was accused of misleading the country that has just come out of the clan system and moving into a multi-party system.

Clan elders met in Burao and the resolution was for President Egal to dismantle the UDUB party in 40 days and call for a clan conference to be announced. They called for all clans to attend a follow-up meeting. Egal tried to snuff the conflict. Clan elders were called, and when they arrived from Burao, the government and opposition both rushed to welcome them. Most of the clan elders entered the house of Suldaan Barre. President Egal attacked Suldaan Mohamed Suldaan Abdulqadir and Suldaan Mohamed Hersi-Qani in their own homes and arrested them and others. Also, Abdalla Farah Harbi who drove Boqor Mohamed Ali-Arab to Suldaan Barre's House was arrested. Therefore, there was a big demonstration and a confrontation between police and the public where some people were wounded, and others killed. Heavily armed police surrounded Suldaan Barre's house. Musa Bihi spoke about that issue accusing President Egal of using unnecessary force on unarmed clan elders.

Ahmed Silanyo's Mediation

Opposition groups announced that they would not recognize President Egal's government after 23 February 2002 and a national meeting to be held at the end of January instead of an election. On 12 January 2002, the Guurti approved an extension for President Egal's government. Opposition Groups Rejected Guurti's decision to extend President Egal's Term of Office. The confrontation hit a deadlock. Clan elders insisted on rejecting Egal's government, and the government did not yield from attacking and arresting them. Ahmed Silanyo returned from London on 9th February 2002.

He met with President Egal and emphasized the dangerous path he was leading in the country. Egal gave him permission to mediate and do what he could. He started with Hargeisa and then met with the clan elders in Burao and finally with the coalition of ASAD. Ahmed Silanyo and a delegation went to Burao and were greeted by a wave of supporters greeting him with 'welcome Mujahid.'

To break the deadlock, Ahmed Silanyo advised Egal to change his method of governing and the clan elders to stop the clan meetings they announced.

On February 20th, 2002, three days before the opposition's specified day, Ahmed Silanyo officially announced that he wanted to mediate between the government and the opposition. Suldaan Mohamed Hersi-Qani immediately welcomed the idea on behalf of the clan elders. Suleiman Mohamoud Aden also agreed to the mediation. Egal became suspicious of Ahmed Silanyo's effort of mediation. It appeared to him as if Ahmed Silanyo was building his political status. President Egal held a press conference that Ahmed Silanyo was not representing him and he did not have any confidence in his mediation. He accused Ahmed Silanyo of siding with the opposition and his clan.

President Mohamed Haji Ibrahim Egal Dies and Dahir Riyale Kahin Becomes the New President

President Egal became ill and was evacuated to South Africa. He died there on May 3rd 2002, while the HT clan elders met in Burao to discuss the political stalemate. The meeting attendees were Ahmed Silanyo, Suleiman Mohamoud Aden, Ismail Ali Abokor, Ahmed Hassan Musa, Hassan Abdi Khayre, Mohamed Kahin Ahmed, and Yusuf Mohamed Ali (Tuke). They were discussing how to bring the two sides together. The meeting stopped and ended there. In the afternoon of the same day, the chairs of the two houses nominated Vice President Dahir Riyale Kahin as president. [1]

The opposition members of the Parliament rejected the nomination of Dahir Riyale Kahin, questioning how the transition was conducted. A small group of opposition members of the parliament visited Ahmed Silanyo in his house and complained about how the chairs of the two houses conducted the process. Still,

---

(1) President and Vice President's term of office that was going to finish on 23/2/2002 was extended for one year. The new term began on 24/2/2002 to 24/2/2003

Ahmed Silanyo advised them not to continue their opposition and succeeded in stopping them from taking any actions against that decision in case of negative consequences. He told them: *'your opposition might appear differently. It can dismantle Somaliland. This new president was a vice president of the country. He comes from the border clans. If opposition arises on legality grounds, it will present a different picture. Don't act on your feelings and don't write anything about it.*

Again, Ahmed Mohamed Mohamoud Silanyo stopped that conflict which could have created a big problem in Somaliland. The opposition attended the funeral on the day of Egal's burial on the 5th of May. The conflict between President Egal and the opposition died there. Only eight months remain before the extended year to President Egal's term of office expires. It was mandatory that Dahir Riyale held an election within eight months.

CHAPTER FIVE
SOMALILAND ADOPTED
A MULTI-PARTPOLITICALAL SYSTEM, AND AHMED SILANYO STARTED THE KULMIYE PARTY

The time to register new parties ended. Six parties noted their intentions. They were: BIRSOL, HORMOOD, UDUB, UCID, SAHAN, and ILAYSKA SOMALILAND. The Guurti decided to extend the registration period for one month in case anyone is still interested in registering. The ASAD coalition registered as the ASAD party.

Building KULMIYE from the Ground

When Ahmed Silanyo resigned from the ministry of Planning in 2000, he returned to England. At the time, he mentioned that he had given up on politics, but at the end of 2001, he announced that he would participate in the presidential election. He came back to Hargeisa on the 9th of February 2002. Ahmed Silanyo's decision to come back to politics annoyed Suleiman Mohamoud Aden and the ASAD party because both men were from the same clan, and Ahmed Silanyo would get a big chunk of votes from ASAD party whose members were mainly from the SNM movement. Suleiman got very upset about Ahmed Silanyo's return to politics.

Suleiman Mohamoud Aden discussing that issue, said: *I had never been more annoyed. Ahmed Silanyo announced he retired from politics. He returned when President Egal died. Why did he come back to me? I was so upset. I had never been more upset. I did not rest from my ambition. I was after President Egal, yet when President Egal died, he just appeared and announced his candidacy.*

As Mohamoud Hashi explains: 'Ahmed Silanyo was in London when President Egal died and the diaspora encouraged Ahmed to return to the country and save the country since President Egal is no longer there. Ahmed returned to the country and the multi-party system was in full swing. He called Mohamoud Hashi and Hassan Moallin and told them: *'as you can see the multi-party system is taking root. Therefore, I want to establish a political party. He also told them he met two men with two small parties and each of them offered that if he joined his party, they would give him the position of chairman.*

Ahmed asked them for their advice and asked them to support him even if he joined one of those parties. 'We agreed to go with him.'

Then they suggested that instead of joining a small party it would be better to establish a party of our own. Mohamoud Hashi and Hassan Moallin were both parliamentarians and they suggested they could start a motion to extend the registration deadline. Ahmed encouraged them to do so. Abdulqadir Jirde also promised to support their motion if they were sure Ahmed Silanyo would find a party and encouraged them to submit the motion.

The following day 15 members of parliament presented the motion. Abdulqadir Jirde, as the chairman supported the motion and explained it to the members. That was how the motion was voted for and approved. Ahmed Silanyo invited young people to the party. He injected new blood into the political system. Among the young people he recruited to politics were Abdulaziz Mohamed Samale, who was recruited as the chairman of the Maroodejeex region, Khader whom Abdulaziz Mohamed Samale replaced, Dauud Mohamed Geele, Abdulkarim Hinnif, Mohamoud Hashi, Ali Mohamed Hassan, and Ali Bikalo. These men were the young men who matured in the compounds of Kulmiye. Some became parliamentarians.

The party's flag and insignia were discussed among the supporters. Many names were suggested, such as KULMIYE, GUULEED and WADAJIR. Finally, the name Kulmiye was agreed upon as the party's name. Abdi Giire suggested the name Kulmiye. It reminded people of the nostalgic songs in 1960 when the first Somali flag was hoisted and people sang "Kulmiye has been hoisted, let's congratulate it. For that memory the name Kulmiye was unanimously approved. On 12 May 2002, the party with all its requirements fulfilled was submitted to the registration committee for approval. Mohamed Jama Guun, who was the head of the registration committee, announced the new Kulmiye party.

One of the elders who spoke at the inauguration of the party was Haji Abdi Hussein, who said: *'dear Ahmed, you have always led this country. You went through a hard and difficult struggle for your people. Although I have never confronted a sitting government and don't like others to do that, I know the party you created and announced will succeed. I know you can lead this country and I know you can create the most effective party in the country.'*

The party's temporary leadership was chosen where Ahmed Silanyo was selected as the chairman, Mohamoud Saleh Nur "Fagadhe' as 1st vice chairman, Shine from Awdal region as the 2nd vice chairman and Dauud M. Geele as secretary general.

The first central committee meeting was held on 20th August 2002. Among the new supporters of the party was Sirad Ali Yusuf as 2nd vice chair. She became the first lady in Somaliland appointed to a prominent position in a political party. Then, the next move was to establish regional and district offices quickly because the election date was coming soon on December 14.

In the beginning, it appeared the race was between the Kulmiye party headed by Ahmed Silanyo and the incumbent UDUB party led by President Dahir Riyale Kahin.

Many people predicted the political struggle of Ahmed Silanyo and his record in fighting for the country expected the Kulmiye party to succeed in the election. However, despite Ahmed Silanyo's political experience, President Dahir Riyale Kahin had the advantage of being the reigning president and presiding over the government agencies and had loyal individuals in the judiciary system, Guurti and members in the parliament.

Dahir Riyale was a candidate for the UDUB party. It was the first political party that started in Somaliland. It had the support of government agencies at all levels, national, regional and district. That has created the UDUB party to flex its power everywhere in Somaliland including the border regions. Dahir Riyaale was also not part of the conflict between President Egal and the opposition. When he temporarily took the Oath of Office, the conflict between Egal and the opposition groups dissipated. Every source of the conflict died in its tracks. Therefore, Dahir Riyale had an advantage over other parties.

His Name and Reputation Represented His Politics

The only thing Ahmed Silanyo had under his belt was his name. The record of his struggles especially the one against Siad Barre. However, his name and legacy alone would not win him an election. Elections spent money and Kulmiye did not have money and no wealthy patrons were supporting it. The government harassed him particularly because it saw him as the only candidate challenging UDUB. In hindsight, if you look at the almost identical results of the two parties (a difference of 80 votes), it indicated that the public saw him as the leader that had sacrificed for his people. At the same time, UDUB was the party leading the country and had used all its power and resources to defeat Kulmiye. There was a difference of 80 votes that separated them. It was a deadlock that could have created an election nightmare, but Ahmed Silanyo conceded and solved the problem again!

The Bali-Alanleh Ballot Box

When the ASAD party did not make it to the race, Suleiman Mohamoud Aden joined the UDUB party. He accused Ahmed Silanyo of the failure of ASAD. He decided to fight Ahmed Silanyo. The fight had many faces but the glaring one was the Bali-Alanleh ballot box that Suleiman obstructed in 2003. It was the ballot box that brought about Ahmed Silanyo's election defeat. That ballot box was one in which the Kulmiye party had many votes. Suleiman Mohamoud Aden refused to allow that box to be counted for Kulmiye. As Abdillahi Ismail who was a commissioner in Burao explains: *'Suleiman entered his already running car and told the people trying to convince him to allow the box to be counted, 'who told you there was ever an African sitting government that had lost an election' then asked his driver to move. Then, the election commission asked the Burao commission to send the disputed ballot box to Hargeisa. And the Bali Alanleh box, which was the box that could have determined the victory for Kulmiye was never opened and that is probably how Kulmiye lost the election.*

Disbelief in 2003 Presidential Election Results

The presidential election took place on 14 April 2003. It took five days to announce the results. Many movements had created suspicion in the minds of Kulmiye supporters. They were leading the votes from the ballot boxes they counted. Their numbers were promising and impressive. Abdirahman Abdulqadir speaking about that situation says: *I went to Ahmed Silanyo before the results were announced and told him that there are suspicious movements. Therefore, I would advise you to declare you are a winner then he called Abdillahi Jawan and told him: 'if you don't announce the results, I will declare myself a winner. I could see you are up to something,' Abdillahi Jawan responded 'we will announce [it] shortly; please wait.'*

Until 11:00 am we felt we had won. People's enthusiasm peaked, and they sang the song 'A dawn has appeared, a good day and a beautiful morning'. People converged at the house of Abdirahman Aw Ali Farah, close to the election commission building. As people were celebrating, they walked in Haji Abdi Hussein, better known as Haji Abdi-Waraabe, saying:

'Don't take revenge. Don't avenge.' At that time, Dahir Riyale has already given up hope. There was no one in the presidential building. Suleiman Mohamoud Aden and the Guurti led the Corruption of the 2003 election results. It was Suleiman who changed everything when he returned from Burao.

Abdirahman Aw Ali Farah says, 'we celebrated and sang our songs. Our results were correct, but they were corrupted later on. The Guurti was the culprit. Some people point the finger at the parliament, in the end what was meant to happen happened. What the potential president decided was the best course of action. The alternative would have been war. The choices were to fight for power or protect the country and Ahmed Silanyo chose to protect the country. The choice to protect the country gives Ahmed Silanyo credibility of character.

Some people disliked him for conceding. But if he did not concede, the alternative decision would have been revenge, war and destruction of the country, or keeping the country safe and intact. He chose the latter. Many people did not like conceding. Abdillahi Hussein Balaaki says: 'Candidates were congratulated at the house of Abdirahman Aw Ali Farah. I was sent to Gabiley to celebrate with the supporters in Gabiley. I was at the Gabiley control when the police at the checkpoint asked me what had changed. They told me the commission announced the results and UDUB won the election. I turned around. We believed Kulmiye won until the surprising results were announced. When earlier Kulmiye counted their results as they were coming in, they were 120 votes ahead of UDUB even when a problematic ballot box from Dhalaah (Sanaag) was counted for UDUB. At the same time, the Bali-Alanleh ballot box was not counted for Kulmiye. In other words, the ballot box from Dhalaah (Sanaag) that was written off as a bad ballot box was counted for UDUB while the good ballot box from Bali-Alanleh was not counted for Kulmiye. Still, Kulmiye led the votes by 120. The election commission announced UDUB as the winner on 19 April 2003 by 80 votes. They also announced that if anyone had a complaint about the results, they should go to court. On 27 April, the election results were submitted to the court. On that day, the chairman of the election commission Ahmed Haji Ali Adam, was called. When he was shown the final result figures and the votes kulmiye party was leading UDUB; he said the matter was in the court and he was expecting the court to catch any calculation errors so he advised them to take the numbers to court.

Abdirahman Abdulqadir remembers that: *Ahmed Silanyo knew nothing would come out of the arguments, but he respected the kulmiye militants who would not let the matter rest.*

In the afternoon, people were shocked when the BBC Somali service announced the Somaliland presidential election results and the UDUB's narrow victory. Ahmed Silanyo was interviewed and mentioned that the Kulmiye party won the election but there was corruption and they will take the matter up to the courts. He confirmed that elders were part of the corruption. The BBC reporter asked if kulmiye would form a government since they believed they won the election. Silanyo answered 'no' this country won't become like the territory of Aideed and Ali Mahdi.

Silanyo told the BBC that he did not believe he lost the election, but he also told them that Somaliland would never happen to build two governments under the flag.

Ahmed Silanyo's philosophy was that he would never take the path of war. His famous aphorism that he would not sit on a chair gained by fight and bloodshed remained resolute. Though he knew he had won the election, he was fully conscious of the need for stability and peace in his country and prioritized that. His desire to become a president was one that he needed to serve his country, not himself.

Abdirahman Abdulqadir explains: '*before the matter was taken to court, Kulmiye nominated a committee of seven members to evaluate. Among them were Abdi Aw Dahir, Muse Bihi Abdi, Daaud Geelle, Abdirahman Abdulqadir, Abdalle Haji Ali and Ahmed Silanyo. They held a heated debate. They broke into two groups, one that wanted to avenge the corruption and fight to the end and Ahmed Silanyo, who advised them to let it go. The Kulmiye supporters were pressuring Ahmed Silanyo not to concede. It was not easy to accept. A sense of disbelief and anger hovered over the Kulmiye supporters; the number of votes separating the two parties was not credible. Kulmiye took its evidence to the court and the chairman of the court promised to correct any calculation errors and do justice for all.*

Ahmed Silanyo's Feelings When the High Court Announced for UDUB

The constitutional court announced the victory of the UDUB party. The press asked Ahmed Silanyo in front of the court his feelings about the announcement and his response was: "*as Kulmiye party I want to declare right here that we don't see the court's announcement as just and fair, and we disagree with the announcement because of many reasons we would explain later.*"

The chairman of the Kulmiye party Ahmed Mohamoud Silanyo also said: Frankly speaking when I tell you my *opinion and the opinion of Kulmiye party members we believe that the people of Somaliland are both inside and outside the country voted unanimously for Kulmiye.*

Ahmed Silanyo advised the Kulmiye supporters to stand on the side of peace. He also told them that the central committee would meet and declare its resolutions about the issue. He mentioned that although they would give details of their resolutions later on, he wanted to inform the public to focus on two conflicting statements from the government and the UDUB party. One was the statement from the minister of the interior that the court would announce the results as the commission submitted to them. The other was the statement UDUB sent to the court earlier in which they conjured that the election results were corrupt. At the time of the writing, it was expecting Kulmiye to be the winner and wanted to poke holes in the expected statement of the court. I like the public to think about these two statements when they want to evaluate the outcome.

As Abdirahman Abdilqadir says: "*The results announced by the court were different from the counted votes the election commission submitted to the court. I believe that if the votes had been counted again, the results would have been different. Added to that was the ballot box that the court refused to touch. To do a recount would have been a logistical nightmare not to mention there was no policy about voter recounting and serious impartiality of all concerned.*

For that purpose, doing a recount would have brought its own set of problems, such as impatience of the Somaliland public and inflammatory rumors that usually fly without being checked that would have made a recount impossible. On the other hand, Ahmed Silanyo was unwilling to let emotions take over, and as usual, he preferred to advance the public's interest before his interest.

Awil Ali Dualeh, a minister in Dahir Riyale's administration and an adamant one, also agrees: '*our tender institutions were incapable of facing such issues and it was those situations that had compelled wise men like Ahmed Silanyo and others like him to accept the announced court results. However, the Kulmye supporters never doubted that their party had won the election.*

Calming Kulmiye's Militant Members

Kulmiye supporters were very emotional about the issue. The central committee of eight members met to advise on the course of action. It was not easy for the central committee members and the Kulmiye supporters to swallow that outcome when they believed they had won the election.

They did not want to accept the results. Still, chairman Ahmed Silanyo looked at it differently: since the court that had announced the outcome had been chosen by the president. As *a result, he was not expecting any justice from that court, and since he did not want to start a war in the country, his only option was to accept the results.*

The two opposing opinions between the chairman and his supporters shook the party's foundation and were big enough to collapse Kulmiye. At this stage, Ahmed Silanyo swore to Allah he would not accept to rule from a chair brought by bloodshed. He reiterated that he ruined one administration. He would never ruin another. He gave this example to convey the gravity of his message: *'if you want to save a kidnapped individual from his captor and kill both of them, what have you achieved? NOTHING! You have killed both therefore you defeated your purpose. Since Ahmed Silanyo decided not to fight the election results, his next challenge was to keep his party supporters together and save Kulmiye from collapse. He needed to calm the nerves of his angry members who outnumbered the group that did not want to fight. His leadership was challenged by how to keep them from acting.*[1]

Therefore, he used harsh language in his interviews to gain their confidence and spoke publicly about the election results.

The annoyed Kulmiye members were so far from peace, they even discussed playing the military option if the legislative institutions did not correct the situation. A military option was never the path for Ahmed Silanyo but at least he listened to them and allowed them to vent their anger.

Ali Mohamed Bikalo explains the situation: *Ahmed tactically planned anger should never overcome them. In order not to lose his members he acted as if he too was not compromising the mistakes done to their party. In the end he wanted to say that he was the man they were fighting for, and he did not wish to redress with bloodshed. Although we know we won the election, it is still not worthy of killing our people and destroying our country.*

Some of the Kulmiye members suggested a coalition government. The idea was UDUB's: the two parties got equal votes and it was logical to share the cabinet ministers equally. (Some men were expecting to become ministers)

Ahmed Silanyo did not confront those who might have wanted to share a government. But he advised the central committee to study the issue carefully. However, some other members rejected the idea of sharing a government with UDUB claiming that anyone who becomes a minister in Riyale's government had done nothing other than becoming a loyal worker for him since he has to work with his policies. He would no longer be a member of the Kulmiye party.

---

(1) At the time of clan wars in Somaliland, a Aqil said: when the armed youth feel injustice, they take up their guns to find justice. I don't tell them to stop but I take up the gun myself and stand on top of a car and say some hard words....

Eventually, it was agreed that since Kulmiye accepted the loss of the election, it was not appropriate to share a government with UDUB. Instead, it would be better if the Kulmiye party regenerated and built itself as a strong opposition.

Guurti Interference

Although Somaliland moved into the democracy of a multi-party system, the idea of democracy was always diluted with traditional rules and compromise for the country's sake. It was no secret that the Guurti and the chairs of Parliament met with the election commission and the announcement of the results was delayed after that. It is also known that the Kulmiye party and UDUB party votes were very close and for that purpose, the Guurti and parliament elders felt to side with UDUB.

The words of Haji Abdi Hussein, who was heading the elders that could not be denied, were: Ahmed Silanyo, we decided against you. Remember, it is not for Faysal Ali Waraabe that I sided with. It is Dahir Riyale Kahin who I sided with. The border clans in the east are not here, and I did not want the clans in the west to isolate because of this election. We leaned on your feeling for Somaliland. You have always been a president so remain patient.

Accepting Election Results

Finally, the conclusion was as the Guurti and parliament were pushing. Haji Abdi Hussein told Silanyo that they sided with UDUB because they knew we don't have the support of the eastern regions and we do not want to lose the western regions. We leaned on you for the sake of the country and peace. You have always played a presidential role; Keep doing that for your country.

Ahmed Silanyo told his members, I won't accept a seat gained by bloodshed. We are a party, and we will concede as a party for the sake of our country. We are going to rebuild our party.

This is how the Kulmiye party, without losing a single member and even gaining more supporters, ended the election story. Some UDUB supporters joined Kulmiye when they could not find themselves in the new government. UDUB members left their party, but Kulmiye did not lose any members. Forty-nine members of Kulmiye and UCID opposition parliamentarians collaborated to oppose Dahir Riyale's government. Some of his cabinet ministers like Abdillahi

Mohamed Dualeh and Aden Waqaf were not approved by the Parliament. Others like Awil Ali Dualeh and Ismail Omar (Ismail Yare) barely got approved. Those who were not approved before were approved at a later date.

A Period of Calm Sorting

A period of calm and careful deliberation replaced the election upheaval. When the election of 2003 passed, the party as an institution and its members as individuals started planning their political future. Ahmed Silanyo found a period of re-evaluation and reconstruction of his political ambition. He was thinking about stepping aside for the Kulmiye members with political aspirations.

The Members Kulmiye Eliminated from The List of Parliamentary Candidacy in 2005

In the 2005 parliamentary elections there were two members that Ahmed Silanyo suggested be included in the list of candidates, but the preparatory committee excluded them from the list. The two members were Anab Omar Ileeye, a woman who was the head of Kulmiye's women's wing and Ali Abdi Sa'iq who is from the minority clan of Tumaalo. Both were hard-working loyal members of the party. Ahmed Silanyo supported them to run for election, but they were excluded from the candidacy.

Ahmed Silanyo was upset about that and saw it as unjust. He visited them in their own homes to comfort them.

Ali Abdi Sa'iq speaking about that situation explains: *I could not believe it when I realized Ahmed Silanyo was coming to my house. I walked to him when I realized he was coming. We knew he did not exclude us and accepted his good deed.*

Ahmed then went to Anab Omar Ileeye's house to console her. She was distraught and asked Ahmed: 'you know how hard I worked for Kulmiye. Did I deserve to be excluded from the list of Kulmiye candidates?' Ahmed then told her: 'I thought I sacrificed for his country like no other but when I ran for the presidential election, I lost it and accepted it. I advise you to exercise patience.'

Ahmed's statement was a great consolation for Anab. Realizing how the Somaliland voters treated Ahmed Silanyo in the 2003 election, her anger dissipated. Ahmed Silanyo is a man who gives great consideration to the people who work with him.

For many reasons, elections do not happen at the specified time. Lack of proper education, lack of experience and lack of resources could be major hindrances to holding elections on time. In addition, reigning presidents take advantage of the problems to extend their terms of office. All this causes the public to lose confidence in government institutions, especially the president's office.

Kulmiye Prepares for the 2008 Elections

After the parliamentary elections, the Kulmiye party prepared itself for the local governments in 2007 and presidential elections were expected in 2008. The Kulmiye party prepared its agenda for the public and its supporters:

1. The program for development if Kulmiye wins the election.
2. To hold the Kulmiye meeting before the election and nominate a new Leadership.
3. To hold the central committee meeting to nominate Kulmiye's president and vice president candidates.

If You Lose the Kulmiye Chairmanship Would You Accept?

A reporter from Jamhuuriya in London asked Ahmed Silanyo the following question:

Mr. Chairman, you are the founder and leader of the Kulmiye party. We know you barely lost the 2003 election. Now you are holding an internal party election. If you lose it, how would you take it?

Ahmed Silanyo: I would accept it, one hundred percent. I would take it. I have never lost a race and refused to accept the outcome. I have been in many struggles in many places, and I volunteered to step down most of the time. Now I would accept and support whoever wins over me. And I am telling you, again. Our party is democratic and guided by democratic principles.

The 2nd Congress of Kulmiye Party

Hargeisa (Somaliland.org) The 2nd Kulmiye party meeting was held at Ambassador Hotel in Hargeisa on 29 March 2008. More than 650 delegates composed of members, observers and guests attended. Delegates were 573.

Guests were invited from UDUB, UCID, QARAN and Election commission. Observers included the Ethiopian ambassador to Somaliland and representatives from the United Nations and other local and international agencies. Also invited were famous poets like Mohamed Ibrahim Warsame Hadrawi and Mohamed Hashi Dhama Gaariye. Ahmed Mohamed Mohamoud Silanyo presented the names of the new committee nominated to lead the congress pending the approval of the delegates attending the congress.

1. Abdulaziz Mohamed Samaale, Chairman
2. Ahmed Haji Ali Adami, Vice Chairman
3. Hassan Guure Jama, Vice Chairman
4. Layla Osman Haji Yusuf, Vice Chairperson
5. Hussein Ahmed Aideed, Secretary

The attendees overwhelmingly approved. Five hundred sixty-nine delegates accepted four rejected.

The Central Committee Chooses the Candidates for President and Vice President.

On 26 August 2008, Kulmiye's Central Committee meeting was held in the City Plaza Hotel in Burao. The most important outcome of that meeting was nominating the president and vice president candidates. The presidential candidate was Ahmed Silanyo and was uncontested. The vice-presidential candidacy was among four people. They were Abdirahman Aw Ali Farah, Ahmed Haji Ali Adami, Abdirahman Abdillahi Sayli' and Ismail Mumin Aar.

The issue of contention was whether the voting was to be one round and the one candidate with the most votes to be nominated for the vice presidency or the voting to be two rounds and the two candidates with the most votes to compete for a second round. The two ideas were voted for and those who wanted the voting to be one round only won by two votes. At that moment, Abdirahman Aw Ali Farah and Ahmed Haji Ali Adami left the meeting. At the same time, the voting process for both positions would still take place: the delegates overwhelmingly voted for Ahmed Mohamed Mohamoud Silanyo without any competition.

For the position of vice president, there were four candidates. However, Abdirahman Abdillahi Ismail Sayli' won after Abdirahman Aw Ali Farah and Ahmed Haji Ali Adami and 50 of their delegates boycotted the conference. In contrast, candidate Ismail Mumin Aar conceded for Abdirahman Sayli'. One hundred twenty-nine delegates voted for Ahmed Silanyo to become the presidential candidate while 123 delegates voted for Abdirahman Abdillahi Ismail Sayli' to become the candidate for vice president. Also, in that meeting the party constitution was approved and the chairman of the party was going to transfer the chairmanship to the vice chairman of the party Musa Bihi Abdi, and when, chairman Ahmed Silanyo wins the presidential election.

Let Us Bring Back the Annoyed Members

When Ahmed Mohamed Mohamoud Silanyo was nominated as the candidate for president, he first thanked the central committee members. He started his speech: *I want to congratulate the central committee. This central committee meeting was one that the public was waiting to see happen. There was much interest in the outcome of this meeting. Many who did not like the development of Somaliland did not appreciate this meeting. Many others hoped for this meeting to succeed. Today, I am thrilled that those who like the success of Kulmiye and the party supporters, its members and those who love their country welcome the outcome. It is natural for members who have political ambitions to run a race. It is what we need to do politically and the democratic process to lead the country. If we need to step into democracy and lead democratically, we should show it inside the party.*

Democracy means for a person to express his opinion and feelings freely. It is the process by which everyone clarifies his ambitions. It is his legal right. However, it also requires that we follow the democratic principle; Meaning: the person who wants to stand for election to accept the outcome. There are members of the party who want to stand for the party and national elections. Some won and others did not win. I won, and I want to tell my colleagues that I am sorry if they did not win. I want to ask them to do as Ismail Mumin did and let's all congratulate each other. We have to work together on how to bring back our colleagues who did not win. We need to forgive each other and work loyally for our country. We should lead our country with the law and constitution. We would lead to what is beneficial for our people. Insha'Allah, Allah would give us the victory. I pray to Allah that we succeed and Allah swt to direct us in the same direction. May Allah swt make us those who work well for our country.

Responsible Opposition

Many people believed that the multi-party-political system would not work in Somaliland unless Ahmed Silanyo led the Somaliland opposition. The testimony to that was that he was able to lead a party that crossed the clan and regional boundaries. He has created a party that has encouraged the educated elite to participate. Ahmed Mohamed Mohamoud Silanyo was the man who refused to rule from a chair gained by bloodshed and conceded for a questionable 80 votes.

It is vital for the democratic rule to build a responsible government just as it is vital to have responsible opposition. It does not always happen in third world countries to have a responsible opposition and responsible government working for the good of the country. Even if the government is weak but the opposition is strong and conscientious, a lot could be done to correct the government's mistakes. In a democracy, the opposition can be described as the mirror where the government could see its imperfections. If the government is willing to do well, it takes advantage of what the opposition is saying about it

Ahmed Silanyo established responsible opposition in Somaliland when he was the chairman of Kulmiye. He taught a lesson future opposition could learn from. A lesson all opposition groups could learn from was when he conceded only 80 votes and convinced his party members to accept the loss regardless of how it happened.

Opposition Before Ahmed Silanyo

The opposition before Silanyo was impatient, aggressive, and intolerant, ready for confrontation while Ahmed Silanyo's opposition style was patience, compromise and negotiation instead of confrontation. One of his aphorisms was that there is no one more protective of the country than us. Ahmed Silanyo believed that just as different sounds of singing birds are attracted to the ear, are also different political opinions beneficial to a country.

Ahmed Silanyo said: *Ever since I gained consciousness and ever since I gained political ambition, I believed the only way to get a decent government was that of the multi-party system through which frank and fair elections were held. In Somaliland, political movements took many turns.*

First the dictatorship, after we toppled that dictatorship, there was aggressive opposition ready for confrontation, then the civilian opposition that Ahmed

Silanyo started. Often African governments cause the opposition parties to lose control and divert attention from the democratic route.

When the Kulmiye party once tried to hold a memorial for SNM on 29 April 2009, the government did not permit them to hold it at the liberty garden. When they moved the memorial to the compound of Kulmiye offices, the police surrounded the compound to intimidate its members. Ahmed Silanyo then tried to walk to his house when the police turned their guns at him to stop him from walking. Despite all that, Ahmed Silanyo never allowed anyone to divert him from peaceful opposition.

The Direction We Want Our Country to Take.

Here is Ahmed Silanyo speaking about the dangers of delayed elections.

We are a poor country, but we have the foundation to build on what is good and eliminate what is not suitable for us. We are not saying that everything is good. No. Suppose we don't do a study of our situation now and the direction we are heading and do not think carefully about the direction we want to take. In that case, we risk falling into the same dilemma as Somalia. We can even fall into more dire situations. May Allah forbid us from taking that route. The peace we have can be lost. So can the democracy we have and we can also lose the brotherhood and unity we have. The democracy we need to achieve is one in which we control our emotions. Our democracy is in danger if we don't stop postponing elections. It is now four or five times that elections have been delayed. Who is responsible? It is not the citizens on the streets or you members sitting here. It is the responsibility of the government.

Did the Current President Take Office by Force?

Chairman Ahmed Silanyo awakening the public to their democratic rights, said: 'did the incumbent president *take office by force? He was elected and he must follow the democratic principles that brought him to office. He has to ensure he does not lose the path to democratic rule.*

We are against change by guns and bullets. We don't want that. We don't support that. We need our parties and government to work democratically. We need to follow our constitution and laws.

I Am Not Reporting to Anyone

Ahmed Silanyo commenting on what Dahir Riyale said to the press once when he returned from overseas says: The sitting president said to the media, 'I am not reporting to anyone.' The question the press could follow up with would have been 'then why did you travel on our expenses?

A Somali man asked a British officer for money. The British officer told him he did not have then he asked him for a cigarette when the British officer told him he did not have one, the Somali man got annoyed and told him then if you don't want to give me anything, give us our flag (or grant us our independence) and then leave our country. In other words, what he meant was; 'you are benefiting from our country. When a president represents the people, his trips abroad are for the public. People have a right to ask about his achievements because he spent their money.

Our Party is Democratic

I want to tell those who say our party members conflict that we are not in dispute. Still, the ideas of democracy are evident in our party and therefore serve as the guiding principles to follow in all our political engagements. We are not in conflict, but we are holding healthy debates. We are well and alive. We voice our opinions freely. We are not fighting but competing with our ideas, which shows our party is democratic just the way our country is democratic.

Universities are Where Ideas Begin

There was a time opposition parties were denied entry to the university.

All over the world, the university is the fertile ground for independence and independent thinking. It is where ideas begin. It is where freedom of thought takes place. When the president ordered the opposition parties not to visit and speak at the university again, where did he want them to speak? He does not want to hear the truth. That means to curtail the freedom of thought and control the university.

Our Country Does Not Need Problems

Ahmed Silanyo trying to calm the emotions of his supporters said: *the change we want to make is evident. It is indisputable. Our country does not need conflict that escalates to war. It does not need destruction and flying bullets among us. We don't need to call outsiders, declare that Al-Qaida is among us, and call them to bombard us. We don't need to call anyone to our country. We need peace and the democratic process to advance peacefully.*

We need our country to become and stay independent. If those we elected to lead us in that direction fail to do so, we have a process in place called elections and we can change them through that process. We do not need to gain what we want by bullets, but we can achieve it by the ballot. We have to work within our democratic boundaries to fight for the elections to take place.

The Leader Should Be Reliable and Trustworthy

Ahmed Silanyo advising people to choose their leaders carefully, says: *What kind of leaders do we need? Let me advise you. Do not accept anything that is darkness. We need to test our leaders. We have to avoid anything that would lead us to a dark future. We need to elect wise leaders. The voters in this country are predominantly youth and children and none of them was elected. Why is that?*

The other night there was a debate on television and most of the female callers who were supposed to ask meaningful questions were harassing the women in the debate and asking them why were they sitting among men. Therefore, some of the issues need time, training and change of attitude. We feel that we must go to work on those issues that need public awareness.

Ahmed Silanyo Speaking in Washington

Here is the answer Ahmed Silanyo gave when he was told all his audience was not Kulmiye supporters: *This country traveled through many struggles to become part of the democratic and independent world. The insignia of our flag says, 'there is one God, Allah and Mohamed is his Prophet.' We know how many of our able men and youth died. Their lives were not lost in vain. Somaliland is thriving. Our country and people are both well and working. Our country is poor in some ways, but we have oil, agriculture, livestock, and fish. It is a country with great potential if it gets exemplary visionary leadership and employs educated people with integrity who are honest about achieving what we need to succeed. If we hire people to work in a transparent and law-abiding system, we can take our country to prosperity.*

What Does Kulmiye Have for The Youth?

We have already said that the largest voters were women and the youth. You need to make those elected accountable and ask what they have done for you? You can make us accountable when you elect us. That is when you can ask us what we have done for you.

Once upon a time, when I was a young boy in school in Sheikh, we wanted to give a list of demands to the school administrators. I was the student chairman. We met for a week and came up with a long list of things we needed and things that were not adequate, such as we did not have brooms. We did not have proper towels. Date ration was not enough, and so forth. I took the long list to the British school administrator. He was sitting down, and I was standing up. He looked up at me and said: You are the chairman. Right? I said, yes. He asked me how long were you meeting to come up with this list? And I said a week. Then he told me: this is the list of demands you submitted to me and I will consider it and give an answer of what I could do about it. Have you ever thought about what you could do about the school or what you could do for the school? I was flabbergasted by his request. I have only thought about my needs but never thought about what we could do for ourselves or the school.

That philosophy helped me a lot during my university years and even in my career. In the real world, people don't ask for things but submit an agenda and a plan. I traveled all over the world when I was the minister of planning; they always asked me what you have done for myself. International practice is to add to what someone comes up with, not handouts.

I tell you this story to inform you that we want to work with you, but we want to work together. It is not to point fingers at each other but my advice to you is to collaborate and for you to bring us your needs and your agenda so that we can work together now as opposition and later if we become a government.

Ahmed Silanyo Speaking About the Genocide

I wonder why when genocide is mentioned some people get upset. Is genocide something to hide? Why do some people get angry? I promise you the genocide won't focus on a clan. When we discuss genocide, we are not talking about any particular clan but the guilty individuals who committed the crimes against humanity. I swear to Allah that I won't forgive those who committed genocide and will follow them wherever they go. Under international law, it is a solemn obligation to follow those who commit crimes against humanity. I am repeating what I said here before. It is an obligation under international law that those who commit genocide are never given responsible jobs because they would likely commit the same crime again. Nothing stops them from committing the same crime again.

When I spoke at Malko Durduro, the people we mentioned were Gani and Morgan. Some people mentioned that Morgan and Gani helped them. That shows that if they could help some people, they had the power to do so. Who knows the story of the dead? If they could talk, they would have told us how they were killed and would tell a different story from the story of the one telling us how Morgan or Gani helped them. I want to remind those insisting that Morgan and Gani helped are giving an indirect testimony that genocide actually happened. You are proving that those men helped you survive the genocide. You are proving that atrocities happened, and you survived them.

Encouraging Opposition

The responsible opposition led by Ahmed Silanyo encouraged the public. Somaliland's artists started their creativity again after a long period of silence. National songs and songs for the Kulmiye party abound. Even ringing tones of the mobile phones rang with: *'Kulmiye, Kulmiye, we are all Kulmiye.'* Some international trainers who came to the country were so impressed with the support of Kulmiye when they learned that even the mobile rings sang for Kulmiye and mentioned that in all their experience, they had never seen an opposition party whose support was so strong. Among those young creative singers were the 'African Stars', who had become so popular in all the Somali-speaking nations.

Shotgun Aimed at Ahmed Silanyo

It was 29 April 2009 and the 28th anniversary of SNM. Kulmiye party planned a memorial at the liberty garden in Hargeisa, but the government did not allow them. They moved to the Kulmiye compound to continue but police surrounded the compound. They held their celebrations in a tense environment surrounded by armed police. MP Mohamoud Obsiye explains: *when we finished our celebrations, I asked the chairman Ahmed Silanyo if we could walk together to his house and he answered: 'let's go. It is a good idea.' The chairman and about ten more took off on foot. When we were about the halfway point walking, the police blocked the way and surrounded us with guns. One officer came out to aim at the chairman and his walking group. I became worried but the chairman did not stop. He carried on walking, and we walked along with him defiantly. Another officer started shouting at the earlier officer and told him: 'what are you doing? We were instructed to stop anyone advancing to the streets and even shoot them. The officer answered. You dare kill him and see what happens and leave the place. It was a dangerous situation, and the chairman could have easily been killed.*

Mr. Omane who later became the Somali ambassador to South Sudan, discussed this situation well: Dahir Riyale Kahin's irresponsibility *to order such an incident*. Kulmiye supporters were also very upset about the event. They thought letting the chairman walk on the streets in that tense situation was wrong. But the debate among Kulmiye supporters was that we had exercised our right to silent demonstration instead of fighting. Unless we did that, we could not get rid of dictators who would be willing to hold on to power for more than 20 years. We should never shy away from seeking our rights democratically and peacefully.

Electrifying Election In 2010

The best and most educated elite joined Kulmiye to work with Ahmed Silanyo. Kulmiye crossed the limitations of kinfolk and regionalism. Kulmiye also succeeded in attracting people of different views but united in working under Ahmed Silanyo's leadership. The election of 2010 was marked by waves of people shaking the Kulmiye flag and posters of Ahmed Silanyo's photo chanting, "We need change."

National Election Commission Announced Election Results

National Election Commission announced the vote results on 1st July 2010. On 26 June 2010, the public voted for the presidential election. UDUB, Kulmiye and UCID were competing. National Election Commission announced the Kulmiye party as the winner.

NEC announced the results in a celebration held at the Mansoor Hotel in Hargeisa where the parliament, Guurti, political party representatives, national election commission members, clan elders and other guests were present.

The Chairman of the National Election Commission announced that the Kulmiye party received the most votes 266,906 votes, UDUB received 178,881 votes and UCID received 92,489 votes and as such Ahmed Mohamed Mohamoud Silanyo would become the president and Abdirahman Abdillahi Ismail vice president of Somaliland.

Ahmed Silanyo speaking to international and local press mentioned that this victory is for the people. He wanted to congratulate the people. He would be a president both for those who voted for him and those who voted against him. He sent special thanks to president Dahir Riyale Kahin who did not win the election and also wanted to congratulate Faisal Ali Warabe his UCID opponent. Shortly after the announcement, waves of people gathered on the streets of all the cities and villages in Somaliland elated with the election results.

The Elation of Dr. Abdishakur Sheikh Ali Jawhar

'He, Ahmed Mohamed Mohamoud Silanyo weaved together a winning coalition of opposing ideas, interests, views and tribes. He organized an efficient and lean electoral machine. He raised the highest funds and worked the hardest to win over those who doubted his leadership. He was not afraid of surrounding himself with strong personalities with their agendas and their followers. He danced around the competition, "floating like a butterfly, stinging like a bee" like Mohamed Ali Clay. He won the knockout punch, and his opponents could only hold their heads in wonder when the dust settled. Long live the president.' Abdishakur Sheikh Ali Jawhar

Dahir Riyale Congratulated Ahmed Silanyo

'This was a race, and, in the end, one was going to win and the winner was Ahmed Mohamed Mohamoud Silanyo and the Kulmiye party. I want to congratulate him and the Kulmiye party. I will remain in the country as an opposition and hand over the presidential responsibility to him as soon as possible in accordance with our constitution.

President-Elect Silanyo Praises Incumbent President Dahir Riyale

Ahmed Mohamed Mohamoud Silanyo praised the outgoing president and what he had done for the country such as holding democratic elections. Accepting election results is testimony to his real leadership.

Silanyo also mentioned that he would establish a close relationship with Ethiopia and send a message to Somalia to solve its problems. He said: *'my neighbors in Somalia need peace more than anyone else and it is them that cannot achieve peace. We pray to Allah to give them peace.*

Ahmed Silanyo's election was the 2nd peaceful democratic handover of power since 1991.

Selection of Various Committees and Duties Specified

As soon as he won the election, Ahmed Silanyo consulted Kulmiye and Somaliland intellectuals. Since he believed his victory was the victory for the people of Somaliland, he consulted the most significant number of people for his work agenda. The three committees were:

1. Committee to advise on the size and structure of the government Kulmiye is planning to build
2. Committee to protect and audit government property during the transition
3. Inauguration Committee

President Silanyo nominated a committee of thirteen members to advise on the size and structure of his new government. Musa Bihi Abdi was the chairman of the committee composed of intellectuals, politicians and merchants while Edna Aden Ismail was the

vice chairman of the committee.

In a press conference on 3rd July 2010, Ahmed Mohamed Mohamoud Silanyo specified the committee's duties as advising on the government's size and structure and the number of autonomous agencies to be established. When the committee advising on the size and structure of the new government completed its work, the president asked them to advise on the jobs they would do in order of priority for the first 100 days.

On 12 July, Ahmed appointed the inauguration committee, whose duty was to organize the handover ceremony.

On the 15th of July, he appointed the committee to look into the complaints from the eastern regions.

On 25 July, Ahmed Silanyo appointed the audit and protection of government property committee. Their duty was to protect government property during the transitional period.

IRIN News of United Nations Office in Somalia and Somaliland Interviewed Ahmed Silanyo

Hargeisa, 2 July 2010

The Kulmiye Opposition Leader, Ahmed Mohamed Mohamoud Silanyo won the presidential election of Somaliland held on 26 June 2010. He got a few votes short of 50%. It was the first democratic election in that transfer of power changed hands peacefully and he will take office next month.

Q: What is your priority [when you take office]?

A: I have many things to do on my agenda, but firstly I will build a small effective cabinet. Secondly, I will lift the state of emergency that unconstitutionally sent many people to prison. I will release all the prisoners who were not arrested through the courts except those who were accused of theft and terrorism.

My cabinet ministers will be fewer than the present one. I am going to ensure that the Judiciary system is independent. Likewise, I will find a solution to the problems of the Sool and Sanaag region and try to bring stability to the regions. It is also on my agenda to build a relationship with our neighboring countries and strengthen our cooperation to eliminate terrorism and piracy.

Q. What are you going to do about corruption in Somaliland?

A. That is one of my top priorities. It is one of the big problems in our country. We are to work against corruption, and we would not have mercy on those who are corrupt no matter what happens. We will reorganize the Judiciary system to create new steps to punish the corrupt officials. We will also establish a committee to fight corruption.

Q. Somalia was in chaos for more than 20 years. Do you have any ideas on how to solve their problems?

A. We wish those Somali brothers anything that could bring them peace and stability because their problems can also affect us, and we are sad about what is happening to the Somalis there. We are hosting thousands of refugees from Somalia. We fully support the international communities' role in bringing Somalia peace and stability. We also fully support the role of the United Nations and the international community in their efforts to bring peace and stability to Somalia. We will become part of the global world and I hope we will take a vital role. We will study how we can directly help Somalia without jeopardizing our sovereignty.

Q. Thousands of people from the central regions who had run away from the problems there came to Somaliland as refugees. What is your plan for them?

A. These Somali refugees coming from Somalia, known as internally displaced people, were welcomed here warmly. They are boys and girls who are our brothers and sisters. Now many people from Somalia live in Somaliland. Most of them are not in refugee camps. They live with us. They are part of society and they will remain so. We are asking the international community to support our guests with everything they can do for them. Also, we will protect them and their stay will be the most important thing we will do. Insha'Allah.

Q. *The number of Somaliland youth going elsewhere in search of work sometimes putting themselves at risk is increasing. Does your government have a clear plan against that?*

A. *It is a big problem in our country. It is in our program to create jobs as best we can to stop these kids from dying in the sea. We will establish a better life in their own country where they can get proper education that can lead them to work. We will promote international investment so that they can find jobs inside their country.*

CHAPTER SIX

AHMED SILANYO BECOMES PRESIDENT OF SOMALILAND FROM 26 JUNE 2010 TO 13 NOVEMBER 2017

Ahmed Silanyo's Inaugural Speech

We Are Not Taking Off Our Shoes Until We Fulfill Our Campaign Promises

Ahmed Silanyo started his first speech after winning the election with a congratulatory message to Somaliland's people wherever they were. He also congratulated the national election commission on how clean and transparent they conducted the election. He also thanked the international community for its support, especially the EU and USA. My special thanks to our neighbor Ethiopia for its unwavering support of our election process and its role in mediating the conflict of 2009. It was not the first time Ethiopia helped us when we needed help. I say to Ethiopia, we know what you have done for us and we are capable of returning favors. Likewise, I want to send my greetings to our neighboring Djibouti that expressed happiness for our success and development.

- I want to thank the two candidates of UDUB and UCID and their supporters. I promise to give them the respect they deserve as national institutions and would open my doors for their consultation. Finally, I want to thank the supporters of Kulmiye who brought this victory. I want to say to them THANK YOU. I am telling you that what we promised to do for our country and people begins today. Therefore remember, we will not take off our shoes until we finish what we promised our people. Today's victory is not for Kulmiye only. It is a victory for Somaliland. Today is:
- Victory for the long enduring and unwavering freedom struggle of SNM

- Victory for Baligubadle, The Center for the struggle
- Victory for Berbera, clan peacemaking foundation for Somaliland
- Victory for Burao, Centre for reasserting Somaliland's Sovereignty
- Victory for Borama, the base for nation building
- Victory for the peaceful coexistence of different clans in Erigavo
- Victory for Odweyne, the leadership region
- Victory for Gabiley, knowledge cultivating Home
- Victory for Las Anod, the home of Liberty
- Victory for Sayla, Home for Culture and Civilization
- Victory for Hargeisa, The capital of Somaliland
- Victory for Democracy, the only way for people to realize their vision
- Victory for Peace
- Victory for our army who would no longer work without hierarchical rank
- Victory for our youth who would not die in the seas anymore
- Victory for our Ulima (Religious Scholars), safeguarding our moral integrity
- Victory for civil servants who would no longer be punished for their political views
- Victory for mothers in the marketplace selling fruits
- Victory for the Guurti (fathers of our constitution) and parliament
- Victory for Justice and administration of justice
- Victory for civil societies in support of nation building
- Victory for the merchants both men and women
- Victory for the general public in need of reliable public services
- Victory for our rural citizens isolated from the country's resources

Brothers and Sisters, I will be your president whether you voted for me or not. I promise to serve you loyally, fairly and justly.

Finally, I want to promise you that I will heed your advice. I need your support. The Somali proverb says: *one finger* cannot wash a face." Work with me and pray to Allah to make it easy for me.

Allahu Akbar

Unity for Somaliland, Long-Live Somaliland.

Berbera Thrives with Ahmed Silanyo

When Ahmed Silanyo became president, he took his first work trip to Berbera for two days in January 2011. His trip was a testimony to his interest in building the coastal town of Berbera. Government employees awoke to a new government whose motto was to build the country's big cities. The president opened several newly developed projects such as new roads inside the city and developments for the port and the airport for the first five months into his administration. Ahmed Silanyo announced that he was putting much effort into building the economy of Berbera. He praised the mayor and port administrator.

The Mayor of Berbera Abdalla Mohamed Ali reporting to the president and his delegation explained: "Mr. *President, when people ask me 'why didn't you build roads before now? I tell them this is one of the pillars of Ahmed Silanyo's vision and we are fulfilling his vision.*

What we see in Berbera today is Ahmed Silanyo's true vision for Berbera. Allah has allowed him to realize his dream of renovating the city and its port. The people of Berbera welcomed him wholeheartedly and thanked him for doing his first official duty to Berbera five months only after he took office. Speaking to the people of Berbera, Ahmed Silanyo reiterated that he has big plans for Berbera and all Somalilanders expect a lot from it. He informed Berbera inhabitants that the port has great potential to build our economy and can take an integral part in our development therefore he is going to give it the priority to make it international.

Somaliland and DP World Signed a Contract

Although Siad Barre's regime regressed Berbera, its potential could not be hidden. Somaliland's fighters who always fought for its development and freedom of Somaliland found the opportunity to realize their vision of development.

Ahmed Silanyo the longest-reigning chairman became the 4th president of Somaliland in 2010. He worked very hard to find investment and development for Berbera port. Despite lack of international recognition in Somaliland, it has always been his vision and burning ambition to develop the Berbera port.

Ahmed Silanyo speaking about the importance of Berbera port says: *For a long time, we have been searching investment for economically viable places in our country and most vital of all these is Berbera port. I want Berbera port to become a big modern port that can serve the people of Somaliland and neighboring countries. We need the money and knowledge to develop to make an international port. It would be a wasted resource if it lacks the means to compete with other ports in the region. In our desire to develop it, we contacted Bollore--a French transportation company, DP World owned by the United Arab Emirates, and Prime Africa, owned by Saudi Arabia. To ensure the best service for our needs, we sought the advice of World Bank experts who had given us a comprehensive study and valuable advice. We are still working with experts to help us achieve the best choice for our purposes. Nobody is more interested in developing our country. We are the elected officials who swore for the country. If we succeed in finding a suitable investment for it, we are sure our port will raise the value of our dock and create jobs and innovation. We are not going to lose anything. We can only gain from foreign investment. I urge you not to frustrate the development we are trying to achieve.*

DP World won 30 years contract to modernize Berbera port. This is a multi-purpose project. Berbera port would become an essential addition to the Horn of Africa business. This 442-million-dollar project has three parts. The first phase is to build 400 meters quay extension and an extension of 250,000 square meter of port space and facilities to load and unload containers. The quay extension will start 12 months after the contract is signed and will be completed within 24 months. There will be a commercial center and a free zone.

Sultan Ahmed Bin Suleiman, CEO of DP World said: *'we are happy to put our foot inside Africa when we invested heavily in Somaliland. This deep-water port will attract many lines traveling to East Africa. The port development will enhance the economic development of the country and the entire region.*

Berbera will help us advance into the upcoming African markets in the coming few years. It will also open the sea to Ethiopia which is a landlocked country and the largest market in Eastern Africa.'

Minister Saad Ali Shire: *'we are happy with our agreement with the DP World. DP World Berbera would make imports and exports easy for the merchants. DP World sold 14% of its 65% share to Ethiopia and Somaliland sold 5% of its 35% share to Ethiopia. Therefore, the contribution of DP World is 30% for Somaliland, 51% for DP World and 19% for Ethiopia.*

On 6th August 2016, the agreement was forwarded to the parliament and approved the deal with yes--69 yes votes and four votes disagreeing out of the 73 parliamentarian votes.

The international press wrote a lot about Somaliland and DP World agreement. This agreement came after a lengthy discussion lasting six months and has a particular interest for Somaliland, reported the journal "This is Africa. "In its interview with one of the best supporters of Berbera port, Lawyer MacCue who helps Somaliland get international recognition and international investor for Berbera and attracted more than 2.5 billion in investments.

MacCue: Berbera project is the largest project that has received direct foreign investment since Somaliland regained its independence. Mr. MacCue reiterated that foreign investment would help Somaliland gain international recognition and the countries these investors come from would become interested in Somaliland.

Military Base

Somaliland signed an economic and military agreement with the United Arab Emirates in March 2017. This would be an economic and social opportunity for Somaliland. The people of Somaliland welcomed the agreement as noted on the "National' website.

Somaliland rented out the Berbera airport for 25 years. It is estimated that the cost to develop that airport would be one billion dollars. The most important aspect of that project is the Berbera-Wajaale Road (Berbera Corridor). Also included in that project: an international cargo airport, big water reservoirs all over Somaliland, and projects on water, energy and health. United Arab Emirates will open markets for Somaliland so that Somalilanders can work in UAE, establish businesses, and sell their products in UAE. The workers in the airport would be Somalilanders. The two sides would collaborate on security and defense. UAE would train the coast guard and would defend itself from foreign aggression.

Ahmed Silanyo and Burao-Erigavo Road

One of Ahmed Silanyo's long-held ambitions was to connect Erigavo with the rest of the country. He thought about the idea in 1974 when he was the minister of Planning. As an economist, when he thought about ways to develop the economy and thought about the natural resources of regions in Somaliland, he was attracted to the Sanaag region. He saw that region as the place where the economy could be developed. Therefore, connecting Erigavo to the rest of the country was vital.

Silanyo Prepared a Proposal to Build the Erigavo Road in 1978

What I particularly want to record into the books of history is something I witnessed: Ali Bikalo, who was one of those who started Kulmiye and Silanyo's helper for a long time explains: *At the local government elections in 2002 Chairman Ahmed Silanyo and I went to Sanaag. We reached there at dusk on a Ramadan day. We invited the people to Hotel Sanaag. In this hotel we are in now, I opened it in 1978 when I was the minister of Commerce. I traveled that road with a big delegation. Then, I thought about the need to build that road and submitted a proposal. The proposal I submitted was to build the road from Erigavo to Ina-Afmadoobe. Siad Barre took the proposal and built the money with Garoowe-Bosaaso road. This was one of the reasons for the conflict between Siad Barre and me. I know the road to Garoowe also needed building, but the proposal was not for Garoowe but Erigavo. I have been thinking about Erigavo road since then, and if I become president, it would be the first item on my agenda.*

We were at a party at the time and talking about tomorrow. Then I thought about that idea to be used as a campaign promise for the people in Erigavo. Ahmed gave an appealing speech in Erigavo and people were so enthused that they lifted him and carried him for a distance. In that speech he did not mention his dream about the Erigavo road. After we left the crowd, I asked him if he forgot the most important part of what could have helped our campaign. He asked me what was that? I reminded him the Erigavo road. He answered me with a calm voice. My friend to build Erigavo road is my principle not a slogan to get votes from the public. Then I stayed quiet.

Mohamoud Aden Dheri: *Our government continued from the time the colonial came to Somaliland. No one thought about building the Erigavo road. Neither the British colonial ruling system nor the Somali governments attempted to build it after independence. That is a period of 135 years with no one finding the courage to build it. Ahmed Silanyo was the first to try it.*

Feelings of People in Sanaag About the Erigavo Road

Hassan Absiye: I am an elder. *From the time of the British protectorate to all the Somali governments, only this government found the courage to face it. I want to thank the president. Vehicles used to travel on that road for two days and two nights to reach Erigavo. I thank you for a job well done. Sanaag region was cut off from the rest of the country. Now movement has been increasing since it was built. Both small and big cars are coming. We are no longer isolated. Thank you, Mr. President.*

Dr. Salah Warsame Aden from the diaspora: *Sanaag was isolated. Travel was 20 long and arduous hours and now only a few hours. Ahmed Silanyo left us a long-lasting legacy. He took Sanaag out of isolation. We are thankful to the president. Roads are vital to the economy.*

Egeh Ahmed Ismail from Sanaag: *We have a road now by Allah's will. The long journey is now cut in half a day from Burao to Erigavo. Our gratitude goes to Ahmed Silanyo for his courage and nationalism.*

When Determination is Combined with The Will of Allah It materializes

For 46 years Ahmed Silanyo wanted to build a road connecting Burao and Erigavo when he was the minister of planning and the minister of commerce in Siad Barre's administration and even when he was chairman of Kulmiye. First, he tried to find investment and foreign aid but when that became difficult, he faced it head-on and laid the foundation in September 2013. Thus fulfilling his long-held dream.

It was long dilapidated
Sanaag was in dire need
Disconnected from the rest
Mayd, Hiis and Sanaag projects
Were unapproachable indeed
Blessed men laid the foundation
Let's responsibly unite and
Help with honest endeavors
Erigavo Road is now prominent
A place becomes habitable
When it builds thoroughfares
Vehicles flow smoothly
Deers in the wilderness
Share with friendly tourists
They blessed President who led the way
Fulfilled forty Years held dream
A Mujahid stood up for it
Help him with labor please

Ahmed Mohamed Mohamoud Silanyo told me as Abdirahman Artan: *If I win the election, my first official duty would be to ask China to build our Erigavo road. Frankly, he went to China but his request did not materialize. After China he went to Kuwait and the Gulf states to submit proposals for the Erigavo road. When nothing materialized from his search for aid, he turned to his government and the people of Somaliland to put their money, mind and manual labor into building that road. He is an economist who cannot underestimate the amount of money it would cost the people to build a road 280 km long. However, he also knew that when our people combine all they have to do something, they always succeed:*

Bashe Mohamed Farah, Chairman of the Parliament says: *Ahmed Silanyo first wrote the proposal of building Erigavo road and when Siad Barre diverted the money to Garowe- Bosaso road, the desire to build it never left him.*

Siad Barre notoriously played one clan against another in his entire administration. When people in Sanaag heard the Erigavo road was being built, elders from every clan in Sanaag preferred the road to pass through their place. Elders from Las Anod wanted the road to travel through Erigavo, Huddun and join the other tarmac road at Las Anod. Some other elders from Burao wanted the road to travel Erigavo, Sarar, and join the tarmac road at Ina Afmadoobe.

Some elders headed by Farah Harbi used to go to Siad Barre and tell him: Let the road travel through Sarar. Then the Las Anod elders would visit him and ask, 'are you taking the road through Sarar?' Siad Barre would say: 'Am I a lunatic when I take the road through Isaaq heartland?' The road would travel through Huddun.

Elders from Burao would come and say: 'the best route for the road is Huddun not Sarar.' As people were speculating and campaigning for their side, they lost the road to Garoowe and Bosaaso.

Recently when Bashe Mohamed Farah joined President Ahmed Silanyo on a trip through the eastern regions, he reminded him: *Mr. President, do you remember the ordeal of this road during Siad Barre's administration? Now that you took it through Sarar, the next one should go through Huddun.*

Osman Sayli' who knew how much Ahmed Silanyo wanted to build Erigavo road says: *When Ahmed Silanyo submitted his proposal for the Erigavo road, he stated his intention was not based on regional or clan affiliation; he was an economist and he saw building that road as a way to boost the economy of the country. He saw Sanaag as the wealthiest region with livestock, agriculture, fishery and tourism; for that purpose; he was only interested in the Erigavo road. The lack of proper roads was hampering the economy. His only intention was to boost the economy. Sanaag was rich but hindered by lack of proper roads. To take their products to Mogadishu or Hargeisa took days if not weeks and if there were roads that journey would have taken them a day. They would benefit from it and the country would benefit from it and a lot would change if they got proper roads:*

> *History would not ignore*
>
> *And Allah would reward*
>
> *As our Prophet instructs*
>
> *A little obstacle on the road*
>
> *Anyone who takes away*
>
> *Is rewarded with Allah's blessings*
>
> *Think about the reward of one*
>
> *Who supports a nation?*
>
> *And builds its roads!*

In March 2014, President Silanyo visited Erigavo to open the road from the Sanaag side where the road was to start. The people in Erigavo welcomed him warmly and they gave him an achievement award for his work well done. They expressed gratitude for a president who has realized his promise. Ahmed Silanyo expressed his pleasure to take part in starting the road which, he said, would help bring the country closer together and bring the people together and help us economically. My government is so focused on how that road would be built.

Foreign Affairs Policy

Ahmed Silanyo's first official trip was to Djibouti. It was not just a trip but a well-thought-out one. Somaliland gave special attention to two neighboring countries, Ethiopia and Djibouti. Both are friendly countries, our neighbors and both are members of IGAD. When some of his ministers asked whether it was appropriate for the president to visit Djibouti first or Ethiopia first, Ahmed Silanyo chose Djibouti. Ismail Omar Guelleh understood the reason very well and welcomed the president well.

Ismail Omar Guelleh's Speech

Mr. President, thank you and your delegation for visiting our country and thank you for making it the first country you set foot as president. Welcome to our country. Congratulations for earning the trust of your people. You have worked so hard to earn their trust and respect and I congratulate you for that. I admire your patience when you lost the election with minimum votes and I welcome you again to our country. We can collaborate. We can help each other as best we can. I welcome you again with open arms and open heart.

Ahmed Silanyo's Speech in Djibouti

The way you welcomed us is unforgettable. Djibouti is our closest neighbor to collaborate and establish a good diplomatic relationship, so we made our first trip here. Mr. President, I congratulate you for developing every aspect of your country and how your country shines in a war-torn region like ours. I also thank you for the way you tried to find a solution to the problem of Somalia and the meetings you held for them. Mr. President, today please help us with neighboring Arab countries you have a good relationship with, IGAD, and other African countries. We need your help in getting recognition for Somaliland.

We Do Not Want Mogadishu: Somaliland Did Not Want to Negotiate with Mogadishu

For 20 years, Somalilanders stuck to the statement: 'we do not want Mogadishu without any action." The idea started at the time of Abdirahman Ahmed Ali and continued to the time of Mohamed Haji Ibrahim Egal. Egal tried many times to remind his people that the Mogadishu we are talking about does not exist and asked: *the Somali seat in the United Nations is empty. Are we Somalilanders willing to fill it?'* people cried out loud against him and called him *'Somaliweyn.'* Finally, he told his story about Southern Somalia and what the government he led faced when they first went to Somalia and concluded: *'Oh you Somaliland if in the future you decide to join Hamar[colloquial name for Mogadishu], I won't be going with you.'*

President Dahir Riyale Kahin's government continued with the same statement but added, 'there *was no government to negotiate. Fifty tribal warlords exist all over the place. Somaliland cannot start a discussion until they have one united government.'*

During that period, creativity stopped, and people were afraid to express their opinions because people were so hostile to the idea of speaking with Mogadishu;

just like the way the word terrorist symbolizes anyone with a strange view, was likewise anyone with an opinion other than *"we don't want Mogadishu"* was called Somaliweyn.

Ahmed Silanyo, the fourth president of Somaliland changed the idea of "we don't want Mogadishu." The government of Dahir Riyale Kahin announced they would open a discussion when Somalia gets a legitimate government. Ahmed Silanyo took over and there was a legitimate government backed by the international community therefore there was someone to negotiate with. Since Ahmed Silanyo was the longest-reigning president of SNM, he found the courage to break the silence. He knew that to push the agenda of separation forward, Somaliland needed to negotiate with Somalia. He started discussing his idea with the opposition parties, parliament, guurti, clan elders and civil societies. Less than ten months into his administration, he submitted a proposal seeking approval to attend a meeting for Somalis that was taking place in London. It was a new government that had the confidence and trust of the people. Ahmed Silanyo's government wanted to lift the ban to negotiate with Mogadishu and that his government attends any place where they could present the issue of Somaliland recognition. He submitted his proposal to the parliament on 5th February 2012.

In a joint meeting of the Guurti and parliament they allowed the government to attend all the meetings held for Somalis in the International arena, which amends the law of 2003 that desisted individuals, groups and governments of Somaliland from attending meetings of Somalia.

Ahmed Silanyo Knocks at The Doors of Arab Countries

As we mentioned earlier in the book, it was Ahmed Silanyo's idea for Somalia to join the Arab League considering the value we share with Arabs in religion, culture and commerce and claiming that Somalia was closer in value with the Arab world than it shared with Africa in which Somalia is geographically located. Since Somaliland withdrew from the union with Somalia, the different governments before Ahmed Silanyo did not emphasize building relationships with Arab countries. When Ahmed Silanyo's government came to power, his most critical diplomatic steps were ways to collaborate with oil-rich Arab countries across the water from Berbera.

President Silanyo speaking about that, explains: *'the places I feel our interest is in relapse, and I am not saying it is easy, are Islamic and Arab countries. Although their rationale and political motivation are not to crumble the unity of Somalia and thus avoid collaboration with us, as they believe, I trust we need more effort than we have already put in. Our governments did not pay the attention needed.'*

Ahmed Silanyo's foreign policy gain is his relations with the Arab and Islamic countries. The government of Kuwait helped Somaliland build the international airports of Hargeisa and Berbera. The most significant investment recently is Somaliland's agreement with the United Arab Emirates' DP World for the Berbera port extension. DP World will spend 442 million dollars and would run the port for 30 years.

Another major investment between Somaliland and the United Arab Emirates is the military base in Berber. Somaliland and Egypt are working on how Egypt would help Somaliland with education projects. Somaliland also worked with the Kingdom of Saudi Arabia to make sure the livestock it buys from Somaliland does not stop as has happened several times before.

Since Ahmed Silanyo became president, he brought Arab and Islamic countries closer to Somaliland and encouraged them to invest in it.

Offering Ranks to Commanders: Creating Hierarchical System for The Somaliland Army

In his first speech, President Ahmed Silanyo announced that his election victory was victory for the national army who won't be rankless from now on.

Only 15 months after he took over, he fulfilled his promise. On 25 September 2012, in a presidential decree, selected a rank offering committee headed by Suleiman Omar Kujoog whose job was to evaluate and advice on the method of offering ranks to the army.

On 2nd February 2013, on the nineteenth anniversary of when the national army was created, Ahmed Silanyo distributed different ranks to twelve army officers from the police, Prisons, and the Coast Guard. The commander of the armed forces, Ismail Shaqalle, was offered the rank of Major General. In contrast, commander of the police force, Abdillahi Fadal Iman, the ommander of the prisons, Mohamed Hussein Hirane, and the commander of the coast guard, Mohamed Osman, each received the rank of brigadier General. Another eight senior officers received ranks, as well.

President Ahmed Mohamed Mohamoud Silanyo was happy that his government was the first to distribute ranks to the national army. He said that he believed the military was the strongest pillar of any nation and that they must get encouragement from their government and population.

Offering ranks to the national army was a crucial step for the nation. Somaliland created its army long ago when clan militias were incorporated into a national army in 1993, while the police force was created in 1991 and 1992. For more than twenty years, the national military worked without any ranks. Governments before Ahmed Silanyo saw the need and the importance of the national army to have ranks. Unfortunately, they did not get the courage to create a ranking system.

For the national army to have ranks was essential to maintain discipline within the armed forces. It is crucial for their morale.

Extending the Hand of Peace

Ahmed Silanyo extending a hand for peace says: *I am telling my brothers in the east who are still not happy that peace is better for the development of the people and country.*

Ahmed Silanyo's Advice to Musa Bihi:

Ahmed Silanyo's speech at the peace meeting between Khatumo and Somaliland held in Ainabo in October 2017: '*I am welcoming unity and the peace agreement with the leaders of Khatumo. It will bring the people of Somaliland development, cooperation, and harmony. We will fulfill this agreement of 13 points. Therefore, the administration after me needs to satisfy the agreement's objectives. I urge the coming president I will hand over to on 13 December 2017 to give utmost priority to the building and developing the environment of Sool region, Bohotle, Haysimo and eastern Sanaag. I also advise him to hold the delayed general meeting. Unity and cooperation in Somaliland are vital and can never be placed in the grey area.*

I believe it is rational to share the good times and the difficult times. I think whatever went wrong before can be corrected. I also believe in the equilibrium of power-sharing in our nation. I believe in the legitimacy of eliminating any complaint you have. I understand the need to look into the power-sharing of parliamentary seats in the future.'

Saeed Mohamed Elmi, a parliamentarian from Las Anod of Sool region, explains Ahmed Silanyo's achievements in Sool since he became president: '*the affairs of Sool region, South Sanaag and Bohotle, Ahmed Silanyo fulfilled two major things.*

1. Peace and reconciliation
2. Development

Regarding the issue of peace and reconciliation, Ahmed Silanyo soon after he won the election, he extended a hand for peace to Sool and Eastern Sanaag. The cost and time his government put into peace and reconciliation were the first of its kind. There is no elder in the regions of Sool, South Sanaag and Bohotle that he did not include in the meeting, debating and resolution. As soon as Khatumo started, Ahmed Silanyo extended his hand to them. Many concessions were made for Khatumo including amending the constitution for power sharing. That is why Dr. Ali Khalif Galaydh is now in Hargeisa. The other thing many people don't know is how much development Ahmed Silanyo made in the Sool region. Saeed Mohamed Elmi confirmed that the development Ahmed Silanyo did in Sool for the seven years he was in power is much more than what Siad Barre did for the 21 years he was in power. For instance, in the space of 200-kilometer, 17 water projects were completed. Water projects are the most important ones in the Sool region.

In Las Anod, while Ahmed Silanyo was in power, there was an extensive search for drinkable water. The 6th water was recently dug, and the investigation continues. In the 21 years Siad Barre was in power, it had never happened. In 18 of the 21 years, he was in power, the water agency managers were people from the Sool region. Not a single water rig was seen on the outskirts of Las Anod. He did the university of Las Anod and many other storey buildings. His government now rebuilds dilapidated government offices that were never renovated since the British colonial times. He built the boarding school in Adhi Adeeye (now to become a technical school) with a capacity of 500 students.

In Huddun, modern government services such as the police station, high school, and all the fundamental ministries like the ministry of livestock are functioning well. Police officers and government buildings are there. The government in Mogadishu did not know where Awrbogays is located let alone provide services for it.

Over 30 national army officers among them five generals are from the Dhulbahante clan. One-third of any national army in Somaliland is from the dhulbahante clan.

The governments before Ahmed Silanyo were busy with other things and did not focus more on peace, reconciliation, and development. It is not wise to complain all the time. Ahmed Silanyo has done a lot for the eastern regions.

Ahmed Silanyo's Response to The President of Turkey

Musa Bihi Abdi explains Ahmed Silanyo's response to the president of Turkey: *I know Ahmed Silanyo is patient. Allah swt granted him patience and tolerance. It is not in his old age that he became patient and tolerant but when he was a young man in the armed struggle in SNM and he had to bring victory with no money, weapons and rations, he was tolerant and patient.*

Allah also awarded him valor and eloquence. Some speak with flowery speeches but when Ahmed Silanyo finishes his speech, he always leaves with an expression that informs the truth regardless of whom he is addressing.

When we went to Turkey, Recep Tayyip Erdogan, the prime minister and foreign minister of Turkey, came to the meeting. He gave a speech thinking that he knew much about the history of Somalia and Somalis. He spoke from the time of Ahmed Gurey to Siad Barre. When he completed his speech, he asked: is there anyone to add more? Ahmed Silanyo got up and said 'my life and the life of Somaliland are so intertwined. He mentioned how as a young man during Somaliland's independence, he loved the unity of Somalis and continued from independence, how the SNM struggle came about and its long journey to freedom to the present that he is the president of Somaliland.

Then the prime minister of Turkey got up again and said: 'forgive me I did not know all this. I did not know about the genocide that happened in your country.

Ahmed Silanyo is known to advance the people's interests before his interest. That man who is the president of the country does not have land in Hargeisa nor does he have one in Burao. He has some land near the graveyard nowhere else. What can be learned from Ahmed Silanyo is training the youth under his wing. If for the past 35 years he was not guiding us many young men like me would have left politics long ago. Whenever we attempted to run away, he held us back and brought us back. He groomed us into where we are now. He is the only man who built an opposition party, became a chairman of the party, won a presidential election and then said I wanted to step down for the benefit of the young politicians after me. He is the only one who did that.

People Create Dictators:

Abdulaziz Ismail Dualeh, a member of parliament says: *'when he lost the election, I took a radio from the Nederlands called 'Hilversum'. I spoke with him the day before and told him I would bring some journalists to talk to him. When we arrived the next day and sat down to the interview, he received a call that a new Kulmiye branch was to be opened in the*

Ahmed Dhagah area and the people refused anyone but him to open it. Many influential people were there like Abdirahman Aw Ali Farah, Mohamoud Saleh Nur Fagadhe and Mohamed Kahin Ahmed. He was a bit irritated and said 'look it is people who create dictators. A small office in a neighborhood wants me and does not listen to the three vice chairmen. They push you into becoming a dictator. In that kind of mentality, there won't be a party and there won't be a country. He hangs up the phone a bit irritated and asked the journalists to continue. Toward the end of the interview, Mohamed Kahin Ahmed entered the room and told him we postponed the opening ceremony when he did not come.

Abdulaziz mentioned that Ahmed is open-minded and wants everyone in the country to become responsible.

Parliamentarian Talyanle: Ahmed Silanyo during Kulmiye Opposition

Abdirahman Mohamed Talyanle said that during the Kulmiye Opposition party, Ahmed Silanyo was like a shady tree everyone could equally rest under its shade. He treated all impartially. He did not prefer one to the other never choosing one based on status, clan, or other affiliation. He respected everyone and listened to anyone with advice. He listened and valued their opinions.

In 2003 presidential election, he lost by questionable 80 votes. He accepted the results and said: 'once the election was declared and Dahir Riyale as the winner, I am not a man to question that. He also advised others to accept the results. Dahir Riyale stayed for two more years after his five-year term was over.

Abdirahman Talyanle continues there are many things I benefitted from him. Unlimited tolerance, cool that never heats. I saw many times he was transgressed, and he was not bothered. Ahmed is not the vindictive kind who remembers those who carry around grudges against others. I can take as an example those who treated us the worst at the time of President Dahir Riyale's government. One day Ahmed Silanyo and I visited General Mohamed Saqadhi in his office. He refused to see us, and the guard told us so. I asked the officer that I was a parliamentarian and that I want to see him. He said yes, you are a parliamentarian I know, and you can see him, but Silanyo is not going to see him. I entered his office and told him: 'the chairman of the Kulmiye party Ahmed Mohamed Mohamoud Silanyo is waiting outside your office. He told me he was not going to see him. I could not believe my ears and asked. Are you kidding? He answered no. I won't see him.

Yet, he assigned positions to the men who treated him that way because he said they are suitable for the position. He nominated positions for some UDUB supporters who were very rude to him. He saw himself as the people's president and not the president of a party or some group. I know of many exemplary qualities he has.

Meles Zenawi: A Miracle Occurred in Somaliland

Awil Ali Dualeh, the minister of Finance in Dahir Riyale's government who was also one of the staunchest opposition to Ahmed Silanyo evaluates Ahmed Silanyo's character:

No politician would have accepted that he lost the election by 80 votes. Ahmed Silanyo accepted that. Even I would not have accepted it. The least he could have done was to participate in a coalition government and the international world would have welcomed a unity government of 50/50.

He is the man who cautiously refrained from putting the country into disarray. He candidly told his supporters 'I was the candidate and accepted the election results. Anyone else who was a candidate can reject the results.'

Awil also mentioned that he and Abdillahi Mohamed Dualeh visited the prime minister of Ethiopia Meles Zenawi in Addis Ababa. He told them 'what happened in Somaliland was a miracle for a candidate to concede for 80 votes only. It did not occur anywhere in the world. I won with more than a million votes, yet the opposition is still shouting after me and in your country 80 vote difference did not stir anything.

Ahmed Silanyo's Leadership Style

Ahmed Silanyo is known for sticking to what he believes is right. Many examples can clearly show that quality. When he was the minister of commerce in Siad Barre's administration, he transferred Siad Barre's brother from Kismayo and said no even to Siad Barre himself. It caused him to lose the ministerial position. When he was the chairman of the Somali National Movement many people asked him to transfer some of his executive committee and refused to change them unless they provided reasons. That has created a big conflict between him and the central committee.

Nominating Hersi to the National Election Commission

Kulmiye Parliamentary Group: We had many individuals in the Kulmiye party whom we believed were good at the post. There was a big pool of people to choose from when suddenly Ahmed Silanyo nominated Hersi who was unknown to us and we did not know his work ethic. He was not among the prominent personalities at the party. We asked chairman Silanyo who was this young man you nominated for the commission. Are you guys surprised by my decision? This young man surprised me too. There isn't a place in the world I did not get a phone call. I got calls from Europe, America and Arab countries. They were the supporters of Kulmiye and all of them asked me to nominate him for the commission. Party supporters were not only calling from overseas, but I could also not relax for a minute from his supporters inside the country. Therefore, I could not turn a deaf ear to my supporters. I, myself, don't know much about this guy but I could not find a way to ignore the request of Kulmiye supporters. When the chairman explained things to us, we too stayed quiet, so this is how Hersi became a commissioner in the National Election Commission. The next we knew he resigned from the commission without informing the party or the chairman of the party who nominated him. Amina Sheikh Mohamed Jirde who was privy to the story explains:

Ahmed was eating lunch and listening to the BBC when he heard Hersi's resignation from the National Election Commission. He was surprised and asked Amina to call him. After a while he walked into the house. Ahmed asked him: 'the position was not yours. It belonged to the party. Why didn't you inform us if you were leaving? Hersi responded, Chairman, I could not work there. I was alone; what kind of work could I do there? Ahmed Silanyo: It is your problem, but you should have told us.

Subsequent Appointment of Hersi to the Chief of Cabinet

In the beginning, Ahmed Silanyo nominated Mohamoud Hashi, his campaign manager as Chief of Cabinet, but Mohamoud Hashi requested Ahmed Silanyo appoint him as a minister. Ahmed told him that the chief of the cabinet was working *with me thus a critical position. Mohamoud Hashi answered 'yes, but it is not a ministerial position.'* Therefore, Mohamoud Hashi was nominated aviation minister. Hersi not far from where Ahmed Silanyo and Mohamoud were negotiating, saw an opportunity without expecting any ministerial position. He requested Mohamoud Hashi to take him to Ahmed Silanyo because he was interested in the position he declined.

He cleaned Ahmed Silanyo's garage, brought a computer and hired two young men whose salaries he paid. Mohmaoud Hashi took him to Silanyo. When Ahmed Silanyo took him for chief of cabinet negative propaganda spread like wildfire. They showed him with a knife, but he proved to be a young man no one could predict.

In Defense of His Cabinet Ministers

As Ms. Amina Sheikh Mohamed Jirde says: *Ahmed Silanyo nominated Hersi to the position of chief of cabinet. Hersi immediately became well known in the presidency and attracted people's attention both negative and positive. The position of chief of cabinet was translated into an indirect prime minister. Comments about him, and complaints about him abound whether they are true or not. Many Kulmiye supporters believed Hersi was going to fail the president. They thought the president should take this young hasty man away from him.*

She continues to say that some HT clan members came to him and advised him to take action against Hersi. His answer was always: why should I transfer him? You don't like him. Right? He could not fulfill what you wanted from him? I am not going to transfer him. I don't see any mistakes from his work to transfer him. I know people hate him when a person has a position even if he supervises four coolies. I would transfer him when I find him incompetent.

Four Suldaans from Ahmed's closest clan came to him and told him: this rash young man will cause you a lot. Transfer him.

He told them he was not going to transfer him instead he called Hersi and asked him to answer their allegations. They laughed and said: are you calling him a witness? They got up and left.

Hersi is an overly ambitious man. He should have waited for the man who had continuously defended him against everyone. Even when he left the job, Ahmed Silanyo still says: 'leave Hersi alone. Life will teach him lessons the hard way.

Defending Mohammad Abdullahi Omar Former Minister of Foreign Affairs

Ahmed Silanyo and a delegation he was heading went to London. They held a meeting for the Somaliland community in London. There was a debate and people were also asking the delegation questions. One of the people in the forum attacked the minister of foreign affairs. Ahmed Silanyo got upset about how the questions were presented and the naked attack on one of his cabinet ministers. He answered the question himself: *We are your leaders. When we come to you from a long way, we deserve your respect. Mohamed Harun the man holding a paper, I don't think he was reading it because there was nothing in it. I want to inform you that I have complete confidence with Mohammad Abdullahi, and I am sure he is doing a good job. We are human and can make mistakes but do not underestimate what we do for the country. It is not fair to just blame the government.*

We are willing to accept our mistakes because we know we can make mistakes because we are human but an attack on one person is an attack on all of us. If you honestly submit your complaints, we will try to fix them, but your approach should be honest. Your criticism should be something concrete that we can do something about it.

Interview With Al Jazeera Television

Nazanine Moshiri a female journalist from Al Jazeera television asked President Ahmed Silanyo about the obstacles impeding Somaliland's recognition.

Nazanine Moshiri: Mr. President, 22 years have passed since Somaliland declared its independence, you do not have international recognition. Is there any hope after 22 years?

Ahmed Silanyo: We know we are not recognized internationally yet, and getting international recognition is not easy. However, the international community works with us and we have a strong relationship with the international community. They work with us; they respect us; I just returned from a trip overseas and met with governments. Delegations from other countries come to Somaliland and work on development projects. They support us on our road to democracy.

Nazanine Moshiri: You refused to participate in the conference held in London for the Somalis. Why did you do that?

Ahmed Silanyo: We declare that we have a historical friendship with the UK. We couldn't attend a meeting held by Somalia.

The president of Somalia and his vice president were chairing the meeting. After consultation with our opposition parties and civil society we decided it was not suitable for us to attend that conference. We have heard of meetings between Somalia and Somaliland before, but this was different.

Nazanine Moshiri: Much money is earmarked for Somalia. Do you think Somaliland will get a share of that money?

Ahmed Silanyo: The international community helped us before. We received much assistance from the European Union. However, now we need to get guaranteed aid for development projects.

Nazanine Moshiri: Your trip to America recently. Did anyone promise to recognize your government?

Ahmed Silanyo: They did not tell us they would recognize our government. They promised to continue with the support they gave us.

Nazanine Moshiri: Why are things this way? Why is that? The decision of the African Union is clear. Do you think if your country is recognized, other unsettled regions will stir?

Ahmed Silanyo: Whatever the case, Somaliland and Somalia were different countries. When Somaliland became independent from the British Protectorate, many countries recognized it even before it united with Somalia. However, at the time there was a solid feeling for uniting Somali-speaking people in the Horn of Africa composed of the Somalis in Ethiopia, Kenya, and Djibouti. It was the vision of the youth generation of that time.

In any event, which had not happened because of the resistance of big powers. In the end it was agreed that the Somalis in Ethiopia remain with Ethiopia, and the Kenyan Somalis remain as part of Kenya. Djibouti declared its government.

Therefore, why does the international world ignore recognizing Somaliland that was a British Protectorate? In Somalia when the Siad regime came to power the way they dealt with the people of Somaliland was terrorism. Look at the plane in the middle of town. It is one of the planes taking off from Hargeisa airport, bombarding children, and the elderly even after fleeing from the cities. They fled to the Ethiopian border when these planes killed many of them. After that Somalilanders fought for their independence.

Nazanine Moshiri: You are participating in negotiation between Somaliland and Somalia hosted by Turkey in Istanbul. Can you tell us about its progress?

Ahmed Silanyo: We have had a discussion before. The negotiation in Turkey is part of the effort the international community wants to mediate the two Somalis. I am not against negotiations. We want the negotiations to go on fairly, and, so far, we are happy with how things are going.

Nazanine Moshiri: What have you agreed on?

Ahmed Silanyo: we have agreed to continue the negotiations, respect each other and cooperate.

Nazanine Moshiri: But Mr. President, the position of the Somali president was clear. He mentioned he wants a united Somalia.

Ahmed Silanyo: Me too. My position is clear that we keep our independence. It is not within my power or the power of my government. We were two countries as the history of Somaliland indicates. We were two separate countries, and Insha'Allah will be two countries in the future.

Silanyo: African Union Recognition of Somaliland is tardy

Twenty-three years after Somaliland regained its independence, its recognition is still stalled; that is what Ahmed Mohamed Mohamoud Silanyo says.

Honestly speaking, the African Union is as adamant as its founders wanted it to be. It is a balance of power for our continent and its power and influence are growing yearly. It provides Africans with a valuable stage where Africans can come and share their opportunities and the many obstacles facing the continent.

When we look at the AU today, the need for the African Union to respond to African crises like (the one we saw in Nigeria) and its responsibility to become an impetus for more comprehensive economic development has never been more urgent. This is challenging. For that purpose, I am resisting, as the leader of my country, to overload of an already fully booked African agenda. Nevertheless, I trust that AU does not delay the recognition of Somaliland as an independent country that our country should soon become a member of its union.

It is not the first time my young country asked the AU to move things forward. President Dahir Riyale Kahin who reigned before me submitted a request in 2005. They sent a fact-finding mission to look into what we, the people of Somaliland, have developed together since we regained our independence in 1991. They saw that our progress was remarkable when compared to other African countries. They suggested for AU come with a way to work with Somaliland's decent development.

After eight years, Somaliland is still waiting. We have just celebrated our 23rd anniversary on 18 May. Unfortunately, we are a nation whose continent is an obstacle to its recognition.

This is not good for Africa and for us. My country has achieved a lot to be celebrated. We have overcome total destruction and genocide. Knowing government is integral to peace, we built a government from the ashes, stability, Democracy in a problematic region.

Presidential transfer of power happened in a peaceful democratic manner. Government institutions such as the police force and army has been created and taken root. Terrorism finds no safe haven in our country, nor can pirates be found in our seas and coastline.

When we look at the many years of chaos, we are a poor country, but our children have free education. Our economy is one that we are building slowly. We have done much ourselves and achieved a great deal.

Nevertheless, we lack recognition from our brothers in Africa and the international community, which has been a big impediment to our progress and hope for the development of our people and our country. It won't be easy to get international aid and loan for development.

They Have Denied Us A Seat When Talking About the Future of The Horn Of Africa:

Of course, I can understand the reasons for the caution. However, twenty-three years after we regained our independence, it is time the evident truth in our country is recognized. Our population did not hesitate to take the road to their future when they overwhelmingly voted for separation from the union with Somalia in 2001 in a referendum that international observers considered free and fair.

It is worth noting that when the AU delegation came to Somaliland for fact-finding mission, they promised that if they gave a seat in the African Union they would not open Pandora's box and would not allow another country to follow us and seek recognition. The foundations of AU charters indicate they respect the colonial borders and our request for international recognition is not contrary to those charters.

Still more important is that we believe our recognition now is more appropriate than in 2006. The years after 2006, clearly our country is on solid footing. Our dark relationship with Somalia is also getting a bit better. We are pushing an agenda of cooperation, to work together against terrorism, militancy, piracy, illegal fishing, waste dumping in our seas and more. This kind of cooperation is beneficial not only to us but to the rest of the world as well. The Horn of Africa is a restless place of turmoil and Somaliland cannot play its role of extending and building peace if the international world does not view us as a partner that can work with them on peace in the region.

The idea of AU came from the hope of new countries that believed that if they cooperate and worked together, they could reach prosperity.

We are now asking for a chance to become a full member of the African Union so that we can build the strong foundation we have just put in and take a leading role in the development of the entire continent.

Ahmed Mohamed Mohamoud

The President of Somaliland

The Economist: Another Country Waiting for Recognition

The famous Economist interviewed Ahmed Mohamed Mohamoud Silanyo, the president of Somaliland, just before South Sudan separated from the rest of Sudan. The summary of that interview is as written below:

Many people don't understand why Somaliland is not recognized and why the international world is ignoring its development, democratic system, peace and stability. Ahmed Silanyo during his years as opposition and even now as president has argued why Somaliland should get international recognition. When South Sudan gained its independence quickly followed by international recognition, the people of Somaliland got a new hope that the international community would look into its recognition. Their reasoning: they felt that way because Somaliland is a fully functioning government that held several elections. In 2010 Ahmed Mohamed Mohamoud Silanyo won the election over the incumbent president. The Economist's Africa Baobab prepared this interview confirming that Ahmed Mohamed Mohamoud Silanyo informed them that Somaliland is still waiting for international recognition. He has also confirmed that African Union, the transitional government in Somalia and Somalia's terrorist groups are all against Somaliland getting international recognition. Therefore, when the referendum in South Sudan took place, Baobab prepared this interview with Ahmed Silanyo.

Baobab. Why should the world be concerned about the recognition of Somaliland?

Silanyo: Somaliland is a place of great turmoil and instability; terrorism and piracy are deeply rooted. All of these will affect the world. No country has done as much as we did in the region. We have done a lot about peace; that is not easy work, which is why we want the international world to work with us. We cooperate with countries interested in the region's stability.

Baobab. W like Ethiopia, America and UK what do you think about the referendum in South Sudan compared to Somaliland's recognition?

Silanyo: If the international community recognizes South Sudan, it will open up doors for us; the earlier statement that borders of African countries should remain the same as before the independence is changing and if that change opens up doors for South Sudan, it should also open up doors for Somaliland as well.

Baobab. How much hope do you have that the changes in South Sudan will bring focus to what Somaliland is searching for?

Silanyo. We are very hopeful, and we are working very hard on it.

Baobab. There are problems in the eastern regions where tribal governments do not recognize Somaliland and Puntland claims those regions. These problems became an obstacle to the election that could have taken place there. How are you going to deal with that?

Silanyo. We have opened up a discussion with the Guurti and clan elders. I have already sent a high-level delegation there and many of the clan leaders responded sensibly we at the same time started development projects, such as a water project and other projects for basic needs. We are also enforcing our army on that front. Our borders are not up for discussion for the country's stability. In any event there is nothing that prevents from negotiating with the elders and being very hopeful of its outcome.

EPILOGUE
VICTORY CAME TARDY

Ahmed Silanyo's feelings after his election victory

I was in Erigavo when I heard Kulmiye won the election. I remained in Erivago for the celebration. I came to Hargeisa after three weeks. I visited him at his house to congratulate him.

I said, I just came from Erigavo; Congratulations! He greeted me well but said: 'Dear Artan, I lack the jubilation I would have had for such an occasion." I was a bit perturbed because I was not expecting to hear that, but I also understood his meaning. I was saddened because victory was tardy.

As Suleiman Mohamoud Aden told me: when the president held the office for six months, he called the chairman of the Guurti Suleiman Mohamoud Aden to his office. He told him: 'Suleiman, I cannot run this office so what do you think?'

Suleiman told him: Mr. President, that statement is not appropriate today, you should have refrained before, but it is a bit too late now.

Although Ahmed Silanyo came to the presidency late in his life, he led the most effective government. He brought clear success in the economy, politics, and foreign affairs. He extended the hand of peace that ended in an agreement between Somaliland and Khatumo equally serving east and west Somaliland. He succeeded in strengthening the democratic process and International Investment. It is the only government that completed its term without a viable opposition.

Ahmed Silanyo is a nationalist, loyal to his people who did not favor one over the other. Ahmed Silanyo is the only minister who stood up to Siad Barre and told him 'No.' He was the longest-reigning chairman of the Somali National Movement. The leader of the most viable opposition party lost the election with 80 questionable votes and said several times that he would never rule from the seat gained on bloodshed. He always put the public interest over his interest and that was the reason he preferred peace to war.

TIXRAACA

- Kaydka Faylasha iyo Qoraaladda Axmed Siilaanyo (Archives).
- (Political Crisis in Somalia and Prospects for Peace in the Horn). Horn of Africa Volume 5, No.3 (1982), P 41-45)
- Somalia on the Brink of Civil Wars): the Horn of Africa, Volume VI, #3 (1983/84), p40-42
- Buugga Cabdillaahi Yuusuf.
- (**Somalia** Sources of Opposition) **Sources: The Library of Congress Country Studies; (CIA World Fact book).**
- Boobe Yusuf Ducaale.
- Ibraahim Meygaag
- Maxamed Baashe (*Waraysi, Hargeysa 2017*).
- Said Kucmudi 2016 Hargeysa.
- (Source – History of Somali National Movement ANIS Abdilahi Issa)
- Maxamed Baashe X. Xasan, Raadyaw Halgan.
- Warqadii Moorgan ee **Xalkii Kama-danbayska ahaa** (the Final Solution).
- Xigashadii walde ee Xasan Cali Mire.
- Wareysigii Siilaanyo ee 27 Mey 1988
- Wareysiga Micheal Sailham, Daily Nation Journal iyo AFP, 23kii November, 1989.
- Dhaxalreeb, Boobe Yuusuf
- Xasan Macallin
- Robin White, London *BBC World Service in English January 30, 1991, 1709 GMT [From the "Focus on Africa" program]*

- Awood Qaybsi: Soomaaliya Siyaad Barre Dabadii: Warqadii Axmed Siilaanyo, 18th March, 1991
- Gaashaamo Base Committee (Archiveska Ahmed Siilaanyo)
- Waxsansheegnews
- **Waraysigii Siilaanyo BBC** Isniintii bisha May ahayd 30 1988kii
- (Clandestine) Radio Halgan Interviews SNM's Siilaanyo in Somali 1700 GMT 3 Aug 87.
- Wareysi Siilaanyo, Robert White, London BBC World Service in English, 1515 GMT 26 Nov 1992, [From the "Focus on Africa" program].
- Akademiga Nabada iyo Horumarka Somaliland, 2003.
- C/rIsaaq M. Dubbad, Somaliland.org, Burco.
- Wargeyska Jamhuuriya
- Oodweynenews.com
- C/shakuur Xaaji Muxumed Muuse [C/heersare], Oodweynenews.com/Hargaysa/Somaliland
- (Posted 3rd July 2010 by Wargeyska Saxafi)
- (Hargeysa July 1st 2010 (TNN)-
- **(**Ballots and Bullets: The Tale of the Two Somalias)
- Ahmed's power-sharing Proposal between the SNM and the Mogadishu-based United Somali Congress (USC), March 1991.
- Aide-memoir: A memory-aid; By Ahmed Silaanyo, 1994.
- Berbera press 10kii Janweri 2011 first visit to regions
- (Somaliland.org)
- Somalilandsun.com
- (This is Africa)
- Website-ka "The National"
- Hadhwanaagnews
- Wariyaha Jamhuuriya ee London
- Maxamed Siciid Gees

- (Labada Gole 2013)
- (Shirweynihii 3aad ee Kulmiye)
- Qoraalkii Siilaanyo uu u Qoray Midowga Afrika: *AQOONSIGA SOMALILAND WAA MID DAAHSAN*
- **Nazanine Moshiri,** Al-Jazeera
- **Wareysigii Wakaaladda Wararka ee AFP**
- Wargeyska IRIN ee xafiiska Qaramada Midooobay ee Soomaaliya soo saarto oo waraystay Siilaanyo, Hargeisa, 2 July 2010 (IRIN
- **Wadan kale Oo Aqoonsi Suge ah – Axmed Siilaanyo Wargeyska** (The Economist)
- Robin White, London BBC World Service in English, 1515 GMT 26 Nov 1992, [From the "Focus on Africa" program]
- Nordem_ Somaliland_ elections Report 2005.
- Wargeyska Haatuf
- (Akademiga) Warbixin ay soo saartay Akadeemiyada Nabadda iyo Horumarintu (APD)
- Somaliland.org
- Axmed Siilaanyo Wareysi: Ka Ficiltanka Doorashada Madaxweynaha Ee USC, London BBC World Service in English, January 30, 1991, 1709 GMT, [From the "Focus on Africa" program]

www.ingramcontent.com/pod-product-compliance
Ingram Content Group UK Ltd.
Pitfield, Milton Keynes, MK11 3LW, UK
UKHW050415240426
12048UKWH00021B/1530